BACKCOUNTRY CAMPING

Other Books by Bill Riviere

THE CAMPER'S BIBLE
THE GUNNER'S BIBLE
THE FAMILY CAMPER'S COOKBOOK
THE COMPLETE GUIDE TO FAMILY CAMPING
POLE, PADDLE AND PORTAGE

BACKCOUNTRY CAMPING

By Bill Riviere

Line Drawings by Gene Filley

Doubleday & Company, Inc.
Garden City, New York

ISBN: 0-385-08779-9
Library of Congress Catalog Card Number 77-137747
Copyright © 1971 by William A. Riviere
All Rights Reserved
Printed in the United States of America
9   8   7   6   5   4

Contents

Preface

Why do men climb mountains, paddle distant rivers, tread deep forests, seek solitude? There are no pat answers, but a look at our daily lives gives us a few hints.

Wherever Man passes, his machines leave scars; he lacerates the face of the earth, despoils its waters, fouls the very air he breathes. A three-lane highway, finished yesterday, is overtaxed today, and a fourth lane will be added tomorrow. Our parks increase in numbers and expand their boundaries, but we have to wait in line for a campsite.

Big business has moved into the outdoors, but customers are no longer "campers"; they're "prime prospects" who "must be motivated" if the month's sales quota is to be met. Much of our new camping gear is collapsible, folding, expandable, contractible, easy-to-use, and generally lasts about a week, or is about as useful as its plastic wrapper. "Progress" continues.

Most thinking Americans, consciously or unconsciously, are a little sick at heart—prisoners of a job, a mortgage, pressing obligations, constant "hard-sell" harassment. These, I think, are some of the reasons men climb mountains, or seek an escape into the backcountry.

There we may recoup some control over our destiny. During fifty weeks of the year, a traffic officer tells us when to cross the street; the boss tells us when to report to work and when to leave; the bank reminds us of payments due "on or before"; airlines tell us when to rush to the airport; and the incidental demands are incessant—dental checkups, new tires for the car, shoes for the children, a donation at the office, or vacuum cleaner repairs—all of which we have no control over. The demands are *made on us*, and if we're to survive in this post-nasal drip age, we must comply.

But when we break away into the wilds, *we* make the decisions. Follow a trail or leave it; paddle upstream or down; have lunch at 11 A.M. or 2 P.M.; lie abed in the morning or rise at dawn. It's *our* wishes that direct us. Suddenly, we're exultant; happy as a mink in a henhouse!

Then there's the lack of physical achievement in modern life. Man used to build his own house, plant his garden, cut his firewood, raise his own meat, repair his own pung or carriage. Today, few of us can replace a faucet washer! A plumber finally agrees to come three weeks from Wednesday. Fuel is delivered via "watchdog" service. Housewives buy "garden-fresh" vegetables frozen a year ago. If the car acts up, a garage foreman agrees to run it through a "diagnostic" mechanical monkey. Contractors build us $18,000 "colonials" or "ranches," for which we pay the bank $31,947. If a bird gets caught in the chimney, the SPCA must handle the matter, or if a tree dies on the lawn, we hire a "tree specialist," who brings two chain saws and three helpers. We shave, open cans, sharpen knives, brush teeth, slice turkey, and reduce our paunches electrically.

Our prime function is somehow to raise enough money to pay for the machines and the specialists who perform what were, in another age, our personal chores. Worse yet, this makes us completely dependent upon others for our very survival. As a result, peace of mind comes via sedatives, which makes about as much sense as toning down the stench at the town dump by spraying it with cologne!

We can never bring back the "good old days" with their more leisurely pace and self-reliance. But we're trying. We restore eighteenth-century houses, rebuild a 1926 Essex, rehabilitate a World War I Spad. Our wives search out antique shops, eagerly shelling out sixty dollars for a decrepit chair relegated to the attic by someone's grandmother. Some of us hunt deer with a bow and arrows, or restore a flintlock rifle, or explore streams in canoes of Fiberglas-simulated birch bark. Tourist-trap gift shops are dubbed "trading posts," and they sell buckskin jackets, moosehide moccasins, and blankets like those traded to Indians 250 years ago by the Hudson's Bay Company.

At least, these are signs that we are trying, however vicariously, to regain our senses, to reclaim some of the simplicity we have brushed aside.

Why do so few of us pass up a good Western on the late show? With a snap of the dial, we can slip back 100 years. Life was simple then. The bad guys wore black hats, the good guys white ones, and the Indians wore feathers. When the palavering failed, we shot it out with one or more of the black hats, dropping him or them with a fast draw of a low-slung .44. Then we moseyed out to the spread, first driving off an Indian raid with our trusty Winchesters. With the smoking ruins of the Wells Fargo station and assorted Kiowa and Comanche bodies littering the landscape, we rode into the sunset with the girl, our troubles over. Strong, direct, uncomplicated action solved the problems.

Such easy solutions exist only on the late show, of course. But the black hats are still with us. They're not cattle rustlers, skulking redskins, or claim jumpers. Today's black hats are the poky driver who clogs traffic; the Ever-Loving Finance Company that threatens you when you're short; the politician who raises his salary one day and your taxes the next; the cop who tags you for double-parking when there isn't a parking space for nine blocks around and only five minutes remain before the bank closes, your paycheck is un-cashed, you're down to $1.20, and you're supposed to bring home an order of groceries!

Then there are defective automobiles, dope in the high schools, noxious TV commercials, stew beef priced like steak—all of these wear black hats. They irritate, they frustrate, they infuriate; but you might as well simmer down. You can't gun down *these* prob-lems with your hog-leg Colt Peacemaker.

So we head for the hills, for a weekend, for a week, or, if we're lucky, for a month, into country where the prime daily chores consist of getting three meals, catching a fish, or rigging a tent against a storm. We push no buttons, pull no levers, call in no specialists. We rise, walk, sit, squat, turn, run, jump, or pause only, if, and when, it pleases us. We are even permitted the luxury of making our own mistakes. We're back to the basics. Each simple task is a *personal* achievement, a sweet satisfaction, even at the price of a sweaty shirt!

This book is for those men and women who seek this freedom, this escape to true reality, and who yearn to view a sunrise over a marsh, to watch a campfire send its sparks star-ward, to search under the pines for Indian pipes that hang their heads shyly as man approaches.

B.R.

BACKCOUNTRY CAMPING

Chapter 1

BACKPACKING

Probably no outdoorsman attains freedom as completely as the backpacker. Within minutes you can be out of sight of the highway and, not long afterwards, beyond its rumble. Afoot there are few confinements—a pond to be circled, a steep slope to be scaled, possibly a fence to be climbed. You can walk with the wind, stand with the trees, or pause with the silence.

At one time backpacking consisted simply of slinging a pack to the shoulders and sauntering off down the trail. Basically, it's still that simple. There have been improvements in packs over the years, but glory be to little green apples!—weary muscles and wobbly knees are still a part of packing. Moving a thirty-pound burden from Point A to Point B requires physical exertion, particularly if rough country intervenes.

For too many years "experts"—who probably collapse after toting the weekly groceries from the check-out counter to the station wagon—have heralded the ease, grace, and comfort that accompany hauling a heavy load in a "properly rigged pack." The fact is, of course, that a 30-pound load still weighs 30 pounds. And if you're not conditioned to packing, it may well seem like 75 pounds before the day's end. I don't mean to imply that backpacking is necessarily unadulterated misery. It *is* heavy work but the burden can be eased by using the correct pack and loading it sensibly.

Packing literature is polka-dotted with tales of formidable loads. Asian porters have been credited with carrying 1,000-pound packs "for incredible distances"; tea porters carry 400 pounds with hardly a grunt; and voyageurs of the early fur trade trotted across portages under two, three, and even four 90-pound bales of furs and supplies. But this is the age of sedentary occupations, and, having strained under too many oversized loads, I take a jaundiced view of the all-too-freely-given suggestions that a 35- to 50-pound load is not beyond the scope of the average male in good health.

True, if you climb every weekend, you'll soon toughen muscles so that a 35-pound pack is relatively painless and a woman, similarly conditioned, can soon juggle 25 pounds, possibly more. However, few of us climb every weekend. The occasional packer should limit himself to 25 or 30 pounds; his wife to 15 or 20.

Naturally, there can be no hide-bound rules. Physical condition, terrain, type of pack, all of these govern our exploits on the trail. There is, however, one infallible rule of thumb: When you're miserable under your pack, you are overloaded! Keep loads to reasonable poundage and learn to understand the mechanics of packing.

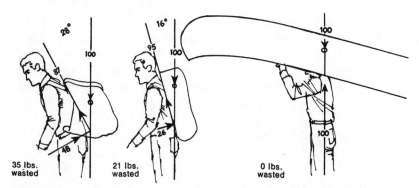

Leaning forward with a pack wastes energy. Courtesy Colorado Mountain Sports Corp.

From a technical standpoint "all packs have certain mechanical disadvantages."[1] This is clearly shown in Fig. 1. Each man is carrying a 100-pound load. The first figure has the weight slung low and protruding backwards considerably. He is working hardest of all three. The second figure has his load in a modern pack, placed close to his body with the bulk of it high and close to his shoulders. However, even he is wasting energy. The canoeman, on the other hand, has his burden placed directly over his spinal column. Not having to lean forward, he wastes no energy. African porters, before the day of the Land Rover and the mechanized safari, carried their loads atop their heads and walked erect. What

[1] How to Enjoy Backpacking, G. A. Cunningham, Colorado Outdoor Sports Corp., P. O. Box 5544, Denver, Colo. 80217.

the canoeman and the African porters are trying to tell us is that the closer the weight is to the top of a packer's spine, the easier it is to handle.

In other words, a pack should be loaded so that its weight is high and close to shoulders. This minimizes forward lean and relieves back muscles since downward pressure is applied almost directly along the spinal column to the legs, the strongest body members.

As with most rules, there are exceptions, two in this case. A rock climber, who needs his arms and shoulders unrestricted so that he can reach freely for handholds and for rope handling, generally uses a rucksack-type of pack which sits close to his body but well below his shoulders. A skier, too, whose balance must shift constantly, prefers a pack whose weight is distributed snugly along his back from shoulder to waist or he may choose one that sits at the small of his back. However, it is rare that a rock scrambler or a skier totes a weighty pack.

Certain pack characteristics can ease a packer's burden, too. A frame, for example, keeps the pack from direct contact with the back, thus providing air circulation, and reduces sweating and chafing to some degree. A back band is important also. This is a wide strap which sits atop the derriere. Much of the pack's weight rests on this and is transferred directly to the legs. A waist strap which buckles at the front holds the back band close.

The positioning of shoulder straps is critical. A pack that hangs like a Roman toga is an abomination. Straps should be attached to the frame or pack at a point level with the top of the shoulders and they should be tightened sufficiently to hold the pack close. When carrying heavy loads, the shoulder straps should be equipped with shoulder pads, usually of fabric-covered foam. If your pack is not equipped with these, they can be attached easily.

There is, of course, no such thing as an "all-purpose pack." A pack suitable for a canoe trip where heavy loads are portaged over relatively short distances will quickly evolve into the devil's own instrument of torture on a steep mountain trail. By the same token, a packframe is a nuisance on a canoe trip. Purpose and terrain must be considered, as well as weight and bulk. Don't discount the occasional possibility of compromise, however. My Border Patrol partner in northern Maine once rigged a pack for a four-day trek from a cardboard carton and a length of clothesline.

Eleanor, the author's wife, packing in the Canadian Rockies. Author's photo.

He wasn't completely happy with his "Acme Soap" pack but it served the purpose.

THE TUMPLINE

If you can stand the abuse, a tumpline surpasses all devices for toting heavy, bulky, or awkward loads. A 100-pound burden is routine among the few who understand the tumpline. During its heyday, 200-pound loads were commonplace among voyageurs in the fur trade and there are reports of 600-pound loads, at which point, of course, we are on the threshold of legend. Today's packers, possibly with a few exceptions, can handle no such loads.

It's a simple device, the tumpline, consisting of a 2½"- to 3"-wide leather or fabric headband with a 7' to 8' thong or strap attached at each end. The latter are tied to the load, which is usually wrapped in a tarpaulin, or made up of two or three duffel bags piled horizontally, one atop the other. There are no shoulder straps. The neck muscles do all the work because the headband is placed high on the forehead, the pack loosely balanced on the back. The packer must lean forward abnormally. It is not a rig for amateur packers or for occasional weekend trips. In fact, the tumpline must be approached with respect. It *will* handle tremendous loads but only after your neck muscles have been developed. No packing device depends more upon sheer bull strength, but it does the job.

A single pack of light to moderate weight can be swung into position easily by grasping the headband at each end and lifting the load into position on your back. The headband is then settled into position high on the forehead. A second and third pack may then be placed atop the first. For an unusually heavy pack, set it on a stump or in the low crotch of a tree and back into carrying position. One advantage of the tumpline is that you can jettison the load quickly with a mere twist of the neck if a fall seems imminent.

The head strap is simply a tumpline attached permanently (although some are removable by means of buckles) to a pack and here it is used in conjunction with conventional shoulder straps. By lowering the shoulders slightly, the burden can be shifted to the head strap and subsequently to the neck muscles. Inversely, by hunching the shoulders upward, you can relieve pressure on the head and neck. Thus an even division of labor between shoulder and neck muscles is possible.

THE PACK HARNESS

The pack harness, like the tumpline, is primarily for loads which will not otherwise fit into a conventional pack sack. Harnesses vary somewhat, but generally they consist of shoulder straps and two sets of straps and buckles that encircle the load. Sometimes a head strap is included. The rig is at its best when the load is formed into a cylindrical package and loaded vertically. Two or three large duffel bags, for example, can be wrapped into the harness. Unlike the tumpline, however, the pack harness can be cinched up to bring the load well up onto the shoulders and close to the body. In this sense, it is more efficient than the tumpline.

Pack harness.

When assorted gear is to be carried it is usually enclosed in a wrapper, such as a small tarpaulin or tent. In assembling the pack, be sure that "soft goods"—clothing, sleeping bags, or blankets—are packed so that they will serve as padding against your backbone. The load limit, providing the harness is of good quality (usually 2″ webbing or leather), is pretty much that of the packer. Whatever you can lift and carry, the pack harness will handle.

THE DULUTH PACK

Also known as the Northwestern, Poirier, or Woods pack, the Duluth is the favorite of Minnesota and Canadian canoemen. It is rarely used elsewhere. It violates all rules for efficient packing— it hangs loosely and hard items will gouge your backbone unless padding has been inserted—yet its popularity continues among canoe campers. While it may be an atrocity elsewhere, the Duluth is a superb pack on the canoe trails.

Equipped with shoulder straps and a head strap, the latter sometimes removable, the Duluth is simply a flat envelope of heavy canvas, usually 15-ounce, without the usual bellows sides found on most canvas packs. The cover flap is usually half as long as the bag itself. Originally it was made in three sizes:

No. 1	24″×26″
No. 2	24″×28″
No. 3	28″×30″

In recent years, however, only the No. 2 and 3 have been generally available. Better quality Duluth packs have straps of leather, although lately I've been able to find only webbing straps, adequate but not as rugged.

The Duluth has several advantages. Cost is low. Two No. 3 packs will hold a complete two-man outfit for a two-week trip. I've found, too, that you can always cram in one more piece of gear and no matter how jammed the pack may be, it can always be fitted properly into a canoe, usually without protruding above the gunwales. Making up the pack requires some care, however. Make sure there's a layer of padding against the spine!

Some pseudoexperts have attributed qualities to the Duluth which simply do not exist. "It is liked by mountaineers," says one.

The Duluth pack with head strap. Photo by Eleanor Riviere.

Another claims it "is an ideal pack for hikers." A third boasts that his Duluth can carry greater loads, more comfortably, than a pack-frame. All of which is utter nonsense. On a canoe trail, I will honor the Duluth. Elsewhere it rates an unequivocal veto. Use the Duluth for canoe trips. For climbing or long-distance packing, seek a pack adapted to the chore at hand!

THE DUFFEL BAG

There is some doubt that the duffel bag can legitimately be termed a "pack." Much like a sailor's sea bag, cylindrical in shape,

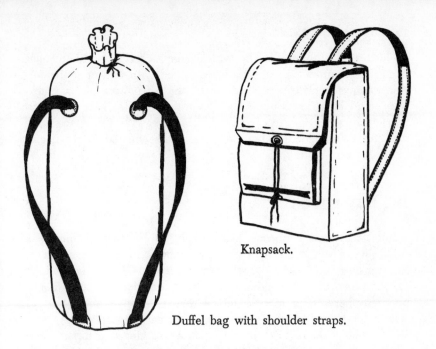

Knapsack.

Duffel bag with shoulder straps.

it is not well adapted to toting on the shoulders, except that one, two, three, or possibly four of them, piled horizontally one atop the other, can be handled efficiently with a tumpline. Size ranges from 10″×30″ to 17″×34″. My own is equipped with shoulder straps but I rarely use it. I much prefer the Duluth's greater capacity. Most of today's duffel bags have suitcase-like carrying handles, often with a zippered side opening. Others open at one end, with a drawstring closure. Loading the latter requires forethought or you may find yourself dumping the entire contents to get at an extra pair of socks tucked in at the bottom of the bag. All in all, I can generate little enthusiasm for duffel bags.

KNAPSACKS

The common knapsack is rarely used for serious packing, but as a supplementary pack or for toting odds and ends such as a picnic lunch, camera, nature guides during one-day trips, it's more than adequate. What's more, it's inexpensive. Various models are known as the Yukon, Yucca, or "boy scout knapsack," the latter certainly a misnomer since the scouts now employ much more sophisticated equipment. The typical knapsack is a boxlike canvas bag with shoulder straps, usually equipped with one or more outside bellows pockets. It affords little of the comfort of the packframe and falls far short of the Duluth's capacity. Like most all-fabric packs when partially filled, it hangs with the grace of a wet shirt. Fully loaded, however, it can be cinched up high and close. Its use is limited.

THE BELT POUCH

For small, miscellaneous loads likely to be carried during a simple day's outing, the belt pouch is difficult to improve upon. It is worn on a belt about the waist, much like a GI canteen belt. It can be worn at either side, in the back, or even in front. For a photographer it's far more practical than the conventional camera case. Rock hounds and botanists use it for carrying specimens, and cross-country skiers load it with ski waxes, map, compass, and other short-term backwoods needs. Most belt pouches are of nylon or poplin, have a zippered opening, and are reasonably waterproof.

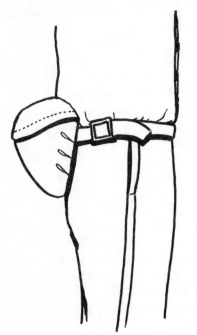

Belt pouch.

The author's Indian-made packbasket; his wife "under" it. Author's photo.

THE PACKBASKET

Most writers on the subject of packing have sluffed off the packbasket with a condescending adjective or two. They grant that the basket protects its contents and that it is easy to load or unload since it remains upright. Countering this feeble praise, they point out that the basket is inflexible, fragile, of limited capacity, hangs badly, gouges a man's back, and, unless a waterproof cover is added, exposes its contents to the weather. I'm surprised that no one has criticized it for being inflammable.

The packbasket is the favorite of woodsmen in the Northeast and in eastern Canada. Elsewhere it's looked upon as a novelty. My first was made by Joe Knockwood, a Maine Penobscot, who wove it twenty-four inches high, the largest I have ever seen. It

A Duluth pack atop a packbasket, about to go over a portage. Photo by Eleanor Riviere.

cost me seven dollars, including the harness, and, although I used it as a guide for thirteen years and for my own personal packing chores during an additional ten, it is still in excellent condition, although scarred and boasting a few burnt spots from campfire embers. It is entirely hand-woven without the use of a single nail or rivet.

I think so well of packbaskets that I have four of them, all large. However, the average basket sold today does not have the capacity of the No. 3 Duluth pack. On extended trips, I use *both*, slinging the Duluth atop the packbasket for portaging with far greater comfort than the Duluth alone affords. Snugging the shoulder straps raises the load well up on the shoulders. The "gouging" so often referred to is largely theory. Once the basket has been broken in, its woven splits of ash mold themselves to the packer's back. Waterproof covers are available but I have never bothered with them. In a heavy downpour I wear a poncho so that the back panel drapes over the basket, thus protecting both me and the load, with the added advantage of providing ample ventilation.

During recent years I've used a packbasket for toting supplies from the end of the jeep trail to our remote camp in the Maine woods. This is only a three-minute trek, I admit, but the pack easily handles a week's grub supply. Nor am I fussy about the load for such a short trip. I simply jam in two or three grocery bags, then fit miscellaneous items among them. Obviously, the basket cannot be loaded as scientifically as a packframe but it affords far greater capacity and comfort than is generally attributed to it.

Packbasket dimensions have never been standardized. Some are rated according to their height, others by the capacity in pecks. A two-peck basket stands about 15″ high; a three-peck model about 18″; and a four-peck basket about 22″, the latter generally the largest available. Baskets are invariably advertised as "Indian-made" and it's difficult to question this since some Indians, using production shortcuts, finish a basket by nailing the rim into position and by adding wooden slats to protect the bottom. A true Indian basket, one that he has made for himself, has a lashed rim and no bottom slats. This gives the basket flexibility. Another clue is the carrying handle. Mass-production baskets have handles of leather nailed between layers of the rim. Indians simply bend a half-round length of ash and lock this loosely into the woven rim. Whether your basket is Indian-made, or a mass-production model,

Packbasket at right is a mass-production model. Other two are completely hand-made. Note the lashed rims and bent-ash carrying handles. Author's photo.

it should be protected by a coat or two of spar varnish, inside and out.

WOODEN PACKBOARDS

The forerunner of modern aluminum packframes, the Alaska packboard and its commercial version, the Trapper Nelson, are still in wide use in the Northwest. Old-time packers still in the business stick by their wooden packboards, but it's only a matter of time before they disappear down the trail to oblivion, the victim of metal technology.

The Trapper Nelson is actually a two-piece rig—the packboard itself, and a removable canvas pouch. In addition there is a canvas wrapper laced to the board which cushions the load and permits some air circulation. As with other types of packframes, the Trapper Nelson is used without a pouch for bulky or awkward loads; anything, in fact, that will not fit into the pouch. An assortment of smaller packs or bundles can be lashed to the board, of course. Sometimes these are wrapped together in a tarpaulin before lashing. The Trapper Nelson has been around long enough to have carried an interesting variety of items, including small cookstoves, water pumps, roof jacks, and even wounded hunters!

With or without the pouch, the Trapper Nelson is a superb woods pack, and, as you can see from the dimensions that follow, either the board, or the board and pouch combination, is capable of toting about all the supplies a packer might want to lift and hike with!

Frame		*Pouch*
No. 1	12″×24″	17″×6″×10″
No. 2	14″×26″	18″×7″×12″
No. 3	14″×30″	23″×7″×12″

Of somewhat more advanced design is a packframe of laminated wood curved to approximate the contours of a man's back. Available in No. 2 and No. 3 sizes, this frame rides somewhat higher than the Trapper Nelson and uses the same pouches.

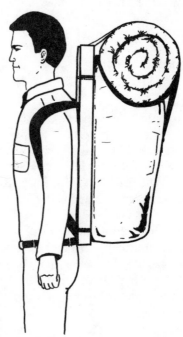

Trapper Nelson packboard.

Appalachian club members Stan Holiday and Joe Amelotte with rucksacks at summit of Mount Katahdin. Author stands in center. Photo by
Bill Riviere, Jr.

RUCKSACKS

Although the rucksack is scarcely a recent innovation, it is
certainly a sophisticated pack. Of European origin, it is the most
comfortable of all packs, except possibly the aluminum or magnesium packframes. Principal features are a tubular steel, triangular
frame and a back band which rests against the small of the back.
Characteristically, rucksacks ride low, probably because their origin
was among mountaineers and skiers. Outside pockets are numerous,
sometimes up to five—and handy. Some rucksacks are equipped
with various slots, clips, and ties for carrying skis, ice axes, rappel-
ling lines, sleeping bags, or other gear which cannot be fitted into
the pouch. Among the better models, leather is used generously,
one having a leather bottom that rises several inches up the sides.
Nearly all are made in Europe and superb craftsmanship is evident
in most of them.

Rucksack.

Loose shoulder straps
allow pack to pull away
from the shoulders.
Author's photo.

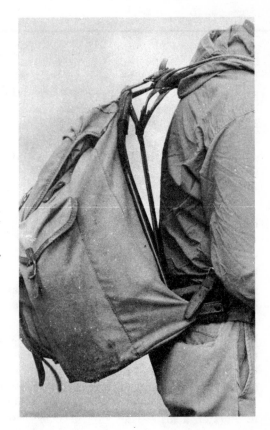

The full-size rucksack is a mountaineer's favorite. It will carry a complete, though necessarily compact, camping outfit, and because of the waist strap, it rides snugly close to the body.

A number of smaller versions are without the frame and these are used primarily for day excursions, much like our knapsacks.

My own experience with rucksacks dates back to 1936, when I bought a Bergans, made in Sweden. I've since retired the pack but the agonies to which I subjected it are a tribute to its maker. I used it for cross-country skiing, for toting supplies to my fire tower with another pack heaped on top, on several early canoe trips, on snowshoe treks in northern Maine while with the U. S. Border Patrol, for climbing in New Hampshire, and during innumerable Saturday afternoon hikes as a scoutmaster. Until the advent of my first aluminum packframe, I had never carried a more comfortable pack.

However, even in the larger sizes, the rucksack is not designed for extreme loads. Its capacity cannot compare with that of the large Trapper Nelson, for example. This is not a drawback. Bear in mind that the rucksack is a skiers' and mountaineers' pack. Only rarely do they tote really burdensome loads. It will hold as much as any climber or skier wants to carry. Like all good packs, it's at its best when the shoulder and waist straps are snug, pulling the pack in close to the body. Loose shoulder straps allow the pack to fall away from the body, creating considerable overhang and discomfort. Tighten the shoulder straps.

PACKFRAMES

From the standpoint of a comfort/capacity ratio, packframes are the ultimate in packs. I'm sentimental about my packbaskets; my rucksack is an old friend which I can't discard; my Duluth brings back memories of Minnesota and Ontario trips; even my old duffel bag, long ago a candidate for the town dump, hangs safely in my storage shed. But when appraised with an eye to capacity, comfort, ease of loading and unloading, my three recently (within ten years, that is) acquired aluminum packframes take precedence. They are supreme, superb carrying devices.

Contrary to some overenthusiastic sales literature, they will not lighten a load. They do, however, ease the chore of carrying

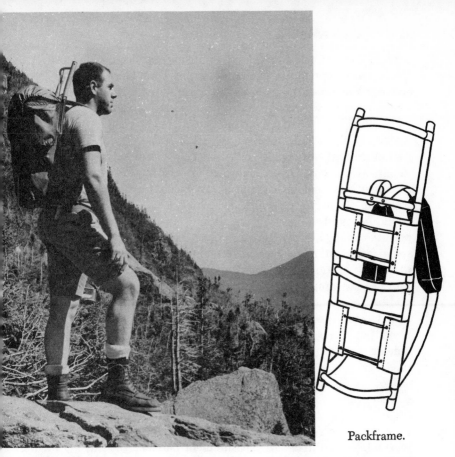

Packframe.

The author's son toting a Kelty pack in Tuckerman's Ravine. Lion's Head route to summit of Mount Washington is along steep terrain in background. Author's photo.

it, because they comply with the basic rules of packing. They place the load high, oftentimes above the head, and close to the body. And by means of the back band and a waist strap, part of the weight is applied to the hips, thence to the legs—where it belongs! No pack takes better advantage of a packer's bone structure and none eases muscle strain as well.

Like the Trapper Nelson, the packframe can be used without a pouch, in which case a "shelf" can be added on which to rest any unusually bulky or heavy item. Lashing this to the frame is still required. Then there are frame extensions which add some six inches to the height above the shoulders.

Most recreational hikers and climbers use a pouch, however. These are as varied as the frames themselves. Most are of nylon, or coated nylon—durable, waterproof, and weighing mere ounces. At somewhat lower cost, canvas pouches are available, but unless you're avoiding a budget strain, the saving in weight with nylon is worthwhile. Nylon pouches are often brilliant in color—orange, red, or yellow, not for the sake of gaiety or for sales appeal, but, rather, as a safety factor. These colors are highly visible at great distances, an asset in locating a lost or injured climber or when trying to rejoin your partner on a high trail.

Pouches and frames of the various manufacturers may often be interchanged, although minor alterations may be required. On some frames, the pouch may be mounted in a high, above-the-shoulders position, or it may be lowered for use with light loads. For general use, where a variety of gear is to be carried, compartmented pouches are favored. Thus gear can be kept neatly sorted. Most pouches, too, have numerous outside pockets, patterned after the rucksack design, so that map, canteen, snacks, or poncho can be called into service conveniently during a day's trek.

Various formulae have been developed for determining the correct frame size. One manufacturer recommends his small, medium, or large frame according to the buyer's height, with his chart ranging from 5'3" to over 6'. Another suggests that the choice be based upon the measurement between the buyer's shoulders (this determined by the cervical, or "bump" on the back of the neck) and the waist, or, more accurately, the hipbones. The vertical distance between the upper and lower attachment points for the shoulder straps should be about two inches longer than this shoulder-to-waist measurement. These guidelines, and they are reasonably accurate, have been developed for mail-order purchase of frames. They are not, however, infallible and most supply houses will exchange a frame which proves to fit poorly.

If you can visit a local outfitter, the choice of a packframe and pouch is made more easily, especially if the shop carries several brands. There's a good chance, too, that the sales clerk will have a working knowledge of packing. Most mountaineering shops are operated by experienced climbers. It's a business as well as a hobby for them. You'll get sound advice.

Even before visiting a local shop, it's a good plan to study

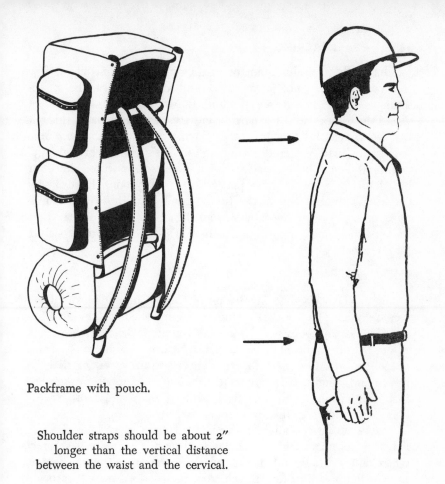

Packframe with pouch.

Shoulder straps should be about 2″
    longer than the vertical distance
between the waist and the cervical.

manufacturers' catalogs. These can be enlightening. To their credit, packframe makers rarely resort to "gobbledegook," exaggerated claims, or far-fetched boasts. They seldom acclaim "tremendous loads." Instead, they stress lightweight outfits. Studying catalogs will give you a speaking knowledge of the subject, at least.

One point to bear in mind is the natural inclination of most of us robust, outdoorsy types to buy a pack that is too large. In the comfort of your living room, with visions of manly loads being toted over distant ranges, you may decide in favor of an oversized pack that will prove a cruel taskmaster on a tough trail. Try to anticipate your needs objectively and accurately, then buy a pack that meets these needs. Leave the 100-pound rigs to the professionals.

Admittedly, the aluminum or magnesium packframe has a few shortcomings. It is not inexpensive. And at times it can be a hindrance. When my son and I climbed Mt. Katahdin last year, I was able to scramble up narrow crevices with my pack since it had no frame. Bill, on the other hand, toting an otherwise fine packframe, had difficulty wriggling its 14″ width through 13″ openings! Don't buy a packframe if your sole purpose calls for toting it over wooded trails, particularly brushy ones. Here it will catch on branches and in the brush. You'll cuss those two aluminum prongs protruding above your head. And for canoe trips, there's little need for a frame. In fact, it's difficult to pack snugly into a canoe.

THE CWD PACK

The CWD pack is an innovation of Gerry Cunningham of Denver, Colorado. The "CWD" stands for "controlled weight distribution." The pack consists of four horizontal pockets, each with a zipper closure, built into a single pouch. It can't handle bulky loads, of course. It's designed for the miscellaneous gear carried by hikers and climbers. Heavy items go into the upper pockets, so that weight rides high and close, while lighter and more fragile items ride safely in the lower pockets.

Four sizes are available, two rigged with a simple, flexible, flat-steel, A-type frame which holds the pack more or less erect when only partially filled and which serves, to a minor degree, to hold the pack just far enough from the carrier's back to provide ventilation. Frankly, and I write about *all* packframes, the "ventilation" premise is highly overrated. If the pack is well designed, fits properly, and is correctly loaded, it will not chafe or rub uncomfortably, but if the weather is warm or the climbing strenuous, you are going to perspire, no matter how beautifully the frame is contoured. Few mountaineers smell like lilacs in the spring at the end of a hard day's climb!

Two other CWD packs, in larger sizes, are designed to be attached to regular aluminum or magnesium frames. My own CWD pack is one of the smaller units but it's more than adequate for a weekend outfit—sleeping bag, tent, food, and cooking gear. It's a spartan weekend, sure as beaver make chips. Nonetheless, I've used the pack on two strenuous mountain trips and I wouldn't trade it for a farm down East!

The CWD pack holds the author's complete weekend as he contemplates The Headwall in Tuckerman's Ravine, Mount Washington. Photo by Bill Riviere, Jr.

PAPOOSE PACKS

The gift of the American Indian to the white man, the papoose carrier is now in wide use among young couples with children too young for hiking but old enough to go along for the ride. Two general types are available: one in which the child rides facing forward; the other faces the child backwards. The latter pack tends to overhang abnormally and I suspect that there must be some psychological disadvantage to having a child see where it's been rather than where it is going.

These packs are made for youngsters from about four months of age up to those weighing about thirty pounds. Frames are generally of tubular aluminum with a fabric seat. The frame usually has a back band.

During the four summers when I conducted a family-camping school, we found that while youngsters emitted loud wails of displeasure when first placed aboard, they settled down to enjoy the ride once Mom or Dad got underway. Some even cried when finally removed!

Parents who use these packs should check the child frequently or investigate immediately should he start to cry. It may be that the seat or sling is uncomfortable or that fabric edges are chafing tender legs. Be cautious, too, in walking along wooded trails where overhanging branches may snap back against the child's head or face. The constant jostling, no matter how gentle, may be upsetting to the child's stomach. Know your child's capacity for riding piggyback before trying a lengthy walk.

Such packs are hardly designed for extended trips and certainly not for rough terrain or steep mountain trails. This is a matter of parental judgment and decision, of course, but bear in mind that overexposure to strong sun and wind might be harmful to a youngster too young to hike.

Pack Recommendations

For general packing, such as supplying an outlying camp:
    Trapper Nelson with large pouch; or 20″ to 22″ packbasket.
For hiking or climbing trips, not involving technical climbing:
    Packframe with compartmented pouch.
For weekend or overnight trips:
    Packframe with compartmented pouch, large rucksack, or CWD pack.
For technical climbing or cross-country skiing:
    Rucksack. For skiers, CWD pack also good.
For day trips:
    Small rucksack, knapsack, belt pouch, small packbasket.
For canoe trips:
    Large Duluth and/or packbasket.

Chapter 2

POLING, PADDLING,
AND PORTAGING

The canoe is more than a mode of transportation into the wilderness. It's really the key to your acceptance, to your becoming a part of the wilds. Paddle a canoe along a backwoods river or lakeshore and you'll become one with a hawk swooping overhead, unafraid; a grouse budding on a birch branch, unconcerned. Deer stand alert and at a distance, but at ease. Not even the silence is disturbed. You become a wild thing, too, not a noisy, dangerous intruder. You are accepted.

Such acceptance doesn't come cheap, however. There's more to a canoe trip than idling along a quiet shore in the forest shade. There'll be long portages, black flies, windswept lakes, stew instead of steak, and at times you'll wonder if you shouldn't have vacationed at Cal's Cozy Creek Cabins, where outboard motors whisk you about and bring you back to camp to a hot shower, an elaborate menu, and cushioned armchairs. But, then, when you've rounded that last bend in the river and you sit by the glow of your campfire, full and deep contentment will reach into the very marrow of your soul.

Canoe travel *is* arduous. Anyone who portrays it otherwise has probably never made an extended trip. But the rewards are limitless. And the discomforts can be eased. The secret lies in choosing the proper craft and gear, and in having a knowledge of their use.

The ideal cruising canoe for a two-man outfit is 17′ to 18′ long, with a midship depth of 12″ to 13″ and a beam of about 36″. Beware of specifications which include "depths" up to 16″. These are measured at the bow and stern, not amidship. When shopping for a canoe, observe its fullness fore and aft. If it tapers sharply from amidship to either end, giving it a narrow appearance, you'll have a fast canoe but one that will knife into oncoming waves instead of riding over them. However, if the midship width

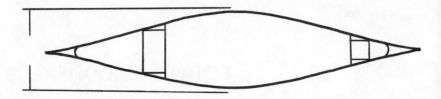

These canoes are the same length and beam. Above) is faster, easier to paddle; below) is more seaworthy, can handle a heavier load.

is carried well forward and aft, the canoe will handle heavier loads and ride over waves gracefully. In rough water this is more important than speed. Such a canoe will also afford you at least 6″ of freeboard when laden, the minimum for wilderness travel on large waters. Freeboard, incidentally, is the vertical distance between the waterline and the gunwale, measured *amidship*. A relatively flat bottom is an asset, too. This means shallower draft, a greater payload, and increased ease of handling. Sharply rounded bottoms mean more speed, but such a canoe sits lower in the water and is more difficult to maneuver.

Small canoes, although easier to portage, are not well adapted to long-distance trips. Anything under 17′ long will prove hard to handle and sloppy in rough water when loaded with two persons and their gear. Choose a canoe for what it can do *on the water*, not on a portage. In fact, choose the largest canoe you can handle gracefully.

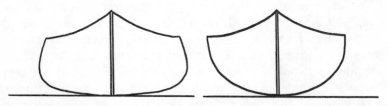

Left: A "flat" bottom canoe; right: round bottom.

One exception is the Canadian Prospector (not a brand name, but a type) known as the Workhorse of the North. The 16-footer, for example, is 2″ deeper and 2″ wider than conventional 16-foot canoes. In fact, the 16-foot Prospector's capacity is equal to that of the 18-foot Guide's Model. In longer lengths it is proportionally wider and deeper. Unfortunately, it's available only in wood-and-canvas construction, the 16-footer weighing 75 pounds. Makers of aluminum canoes should investigate its superb lines.

The waters on which you'll travel should govern keel design. For stream and river work, the canoe is best without a keel, so that you can "set over" broadside with ease, or make quick changes in your course through rapids. A keel hinders these maneuvers. For lake travel, however, a keel minimizes side drift caused by wind. Few cruising canoes are used exclusively on lakes or on rivers, so a compromise is necessary. This calls for a shoe keel, 2″ to 4″ wide and about ½″ deep on wood-and-canvas canoes. On aluminum canoes, the shoe keel is somewhat narrower. Such a keel permits a side thrust or a quick turn yet serves to cut down wind drift on an exposed course.

End view of a shoe keel.

WOOD-AND-CANVAS CANOES

Many a premature dirge has been sung to mark the "passing" of the wood-and-canvas canoe. It has been a hasty requiem. The canvas canoe is still very much with us although, admittedly, in annually decreasing numbers. And I suppose the day will come when it will take its place as a museum piece.

Yet it persists, available in several sizes and models, to supply the needs of canoemen who appreciate its quietness on a wild shore at evening and for those with a romantic penchant who associate it, justly, with the birch-bark canoe of yesterday. Having owned five of them, I've satisfied myself that they maintain better headway against the wind than aluminum; while being poled in fast water, the raised bow of a wooden canoe is less susceptible to wind; they are naturally buoyant, requiring no flotation chambers; and—contrary to popular opinion—they are no heavier than standard-grade aluminum canoes. Only the so-called "lightweight" grade of aluminum (made of .032" metal, as opposed to the standard grade's .051") canoe is lighter than the wood-and-canvas. As for Fiberglas, most canoes made of this material outweigh all other types.

The wood-and-canvas craft is tougher than aluminum or Fiberglas advocates would have you think. I used one for ten years while guiding fishermen, hunters, and canoe trips, finally selling it for only three dollars less than I paid for it! It had one cracked rib, several patches on the canvas, and a few interior scars but was otherwise sound.

However, it must be granted that a sharp rock *will* cut the canvas, and you may easily split a rib or section of planking if you strike a boulder while running a swift sluice. It needs frequent refinishing to prevent its absorbing moisture and thereby adding weight.

If you're the type of canoeman who enjoys stealing stealthily along quiet streams, if you're the romantic type who conjures up visions of voyageurs when you step into a canoe, and if you're willing to devote care and attention to your craft, you'll find the wood-and-canvas canoe far superior to any other type.

ALUMINUM CANOES

Few knowledgeable canoemen buy an aluminum craft solely because of its reputed lighter weight. They buy it for its durability, its toughness, and because it requires no upkeep. Not that it's akin to a Sherman tank, but it does glance off rocks without damage, and it can be dragged over gravel bars. You can leave it in deep snow through the winter or in the hot sun during the summer. It absorbs no weight with age. Painting is never required. Its weight, in standard grades, compares with that of wood-and-canvas canoes.

Aluminum canoes, however, are not completely without short-comings. When lightly laden, their extreme buoyancy makes them difficult to handle in a high wind. Leave one overturned in the sun and you'll need asbestos gloves with which to pick it up, or use one in a springtime flood in a kneeling position and you'll quickly acquire chilblained kneecaps. Tiny riplets slapping against the sides imitate a snare drum, and to duplicate the sound of a bass drum, simply tap the gunwale with your paddle. Aluminum is noisy! Stealing silently along the shore is virtually impossible. Another quirk is its "self-righting" feature when capsized. It will right itself in a flash, which can be an asset, but on a windy lake, make a quick grab for it or it will be quickly blown out of your reach.

However, recounting the shortcomings of aluminum canoes involves "pretty small potatoes." Balance out the drawbacks and the advantages and the aluminum canoe evolves into a superior all-round craft, well adapted to wilderness trips.

FIBERGLAS CANOES

Very few Fiberglas canoes qualify as wilderness craft. On the whole they are smaller than either wood or aluminum, usually narrower in beam and shallower in depth in a given length. This is probably an attempt by their makers to produce Fiberglas canoes within the weight limits set by aluminum or canvas. The length will be there, but depth and beam are often skimpy.

Exceptions include an 18-footer by Old Town with a 37" beam and a 12" midship depth, weighing 92 pounds; an 18-foot model by Rivers and Gilman, with a 38" beam, 12" depth, weighing 85 pounds; and the Canadian, 18½ feet long with a 36" beam, 13" depth, weighing 85 pounds. All three of these are superb craft, with their weights not unreasonable considering their size. These are large canoes, suitable for wilderness cruising.

DO-IT-YOURSELF KITS

With canoe prices at an all-time high, it's not surprising that a number of do-it-yourself canoe-building kits have appeared. With these you can build a canoe inexpensively and produce a craft suitable for relatively quiet waters, but I would not want to trust my outfit aboard one of them, 200 miles out in the puckerbrush! Such canoes are generally small, and in order to make their construction possible in home workshops, framing and planking are often inadequate for a rough-water canoe.

PADDLES

It has become increasingly difficult to buy good canoe paddles. Mass production has stepped in with "pudding sticks,"[1] heavy, stiff, thick-edged blades, as graceful to wield as a peavey handle! Their principal crime is lack of flexibility.

With the start of each paddle stroke an almost imperceptible tug is transmitted to the arms and shoulders, a trifling matter early in the day, but by three in the afternoon, the cumulative effect can be devastating to muscles and shoulder sockets. Flexible paddles absorb much of this shock. Too, many canoemen add a final flip, or surge of power, at the end of each stroke. A resilient paddle adds to this terminal thrust of power.

Maple and ash paddles combine sturdiness with resiliency. Maple, while heavier, is sturdier; ash, the more flexible. Some canoemen thin down the shaft where it joins the blade and at the grip, further enhancing limberness. As a rule, women prefer spruce paddles, not as limber as maple or ash, but much lighter in weight.

The wide *vs.* narrow blade controversy has outlasted 10,000 campfires and is still not settled. Theoretically, a narrow blade— 5″ to 6″—is easier to draw through the water but it affords less purchase. A wide blade—7″ to 8″—will give you a substantial "bite" but requires more energy to wield. The choice must be yours. I prefer a wide blade, particularly in the stern, since the canoe answers more readily. Whatever type of blade you choose, make sure it has a thin edge. This slips quietly into the water

---

[1] "Pudding stick" is also a short paddle, usually about two feet long, carried for emergencies. *Woodcraft,* by "Nessmuk" (New York: Dover Publications, Inc., 1963), p. 93.

and can be feathered for a soundless "Indian stroke." A thick-edge blade "plops" noisily.

The standard formula for determining paddle length specifies that a bow man's paddle should reach from his toes to his chin; a stern paddle, from toes to eyes. If we must have a formula, this is as good as any, but my preference is for slightly longer paddles, especially in the stern. Here I use six-footers (I'm 5' 11"). With a longer paddle I can occasionally paddle while standing, and when sitting or kneeling I like a blade long enough so that it can be fully immersed in the water without my having to reach awkwardly. A short paddle makes this difficult; it's noisy, too.

The grip and the lower section of the shaft should be free of blister-creating varnish. The blade and the shaft may be varnished to protect them but I've never known a professional guide to bother. Nevertheless, the blade especially should be cared for. Don't use it for a pole, pushing against the bottom, or you'll develop a fuzzy edge and possibly initiate a split. Ed Holloway, of the Shenango Valley Canoe Club at Sharon, Pennsylvania, sands the tips of his blades, then molds a ¼" bead of epoxy putty around it. He then shapes this with a sander and applies varnish. The hardened epoxy may nick in time, but it affords far better protection than the frequently applied strip of copper. What's more, it keeps a knifelike edge.

PADDLE TECHNIQUES

There is only one proper station for a solo canoeman paddling an unladen craft, and that is amidship, kneeling. Kneel just aft of the center thwart, slightly off-center so that the canoe lists to the paddling side. This may seem precarious. It isn't. In time, you'll learn to handle your canoe with the gunwale nearly awash, at speeds impossible from any other station. If your knees cry out in pain, pad them with foam or a sweater.

The most common mistake is to perch on the stern seat of an otherwise empty canoe. This raises the bow dangerously. In the case of an 18-foot canoe, for example, you'll find yourself paddling a 10-foot canoe with an 8-foot overhang! Placing a counterbalancing weight up forward isn't sound canoemanship. You'll need weight at least equal to your own! Why carry 150 pounds of rocks,

Proper one-man position in a canoe. Photo by Eleanor Riviere.

A ten-foot canoe with a six-foot overhang results from sitting astern in an empty craft. Photo by Eleanor Riviere.

then paddle these around as cargo? Other beginners use the bow seat, facing astern. This is more stable but due to the wide beam at this point, paddling is awkward.

Some safety experts suggest that canoe seats be removed but I consider this the utter height of nonsense. Removal of the seats, they claim, forces canoeists to kneel, thus lowering the center of gravity. Kneeling *does* accomplish this, and on a wave-tossed lake, it affords better control and greater power to your strokes. In such water, by all means, kneel. But *don't remove the seats*. When you slip into placid waters, edge up onto the seat and relax. Your center of gravity will have been raised negligibly and your aching knees and ankles will be grateful!

Tandem paddling calls for co-ordination. The bow man sets the pace with a rhythmic beat and the stern man matches this. The two should dip, draw, and retrieve simultaneously, co-ordinating the degree of effort. If the bow man pulls too hard, for example, his stern partner will have to counter the canoe's tendency to turn off course. This becomes a matter of experience between partners.

Some canoemen can paddle all day on one side of the canoe. They become skilled on the port side, for example, but are awkward and uncomfortable when stroking on the starboard side. Learn to paddle equally well on both sides so that when one partner calls "Switch!" the change can be made gracefully without missing a beat. Periodic switchovers, during a long day's trek, break the monotony and distribute the work load more evenly among body muscles.

The *Cruising Stroke*, simplest and easiest to learn, serves solely to propel the canoe. Both paddlers reach forward with their blades, dip, and draw back *parallel to the keel*. The bow paddler draws *toward* the gunwale; the stern man, *away from it*. Beginners are prone to follow the gunwale line with their strokes, thus setting one paddle to working against the other.

The *J Stroke* is the most common stern maneuver but is inefficient. The paddler duplicates the Cruising Stroke until the blade is about to be withdrawn, then he turns the blade to form a rudder and thrusts outwardly with it, away from the canoe. Unskilled paddlers end up on a zigzag course. The J Stroke is tiring and slows momentum, too.

The *Canadian Stroke* is more efficient. It is similar to the J

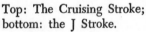
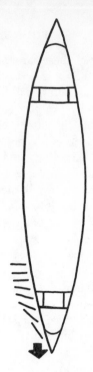

Top: The Cruising Stroke;
bottom: the J Stroke.

Pitch Stroke.

Stroke except that, instead of sweeping the blade sideways away from the canoe, the paddler feathers it and brings it forward *underwater* to a point opposite his own position. He then flips it forward for the next stroke. The advantages are threefold: the stroke is less tiring than the J Stroke, it keeps the canoe on course, and it does not perceptibly slow its progress.

The *Pitch Stroke* is marvelously effective. It starts in the conventional manner, but as the blade passes the hips, it is feathered *underwater,* close to the canoe, back of the paddler, to form a rudder. It is held at this point but a moment, then withdrawn in feathered position for the next stroke. Feathering, and turning for the stroke, is done by the upper hand, of course.

In the *Underwater Stroke*—some call it the Indian Stroke because of its stealthiness—the blade is never removed from the water. This eliminates dripping and "plopping" noises. Following the backward draw, the blade is feathered and returned to its forward

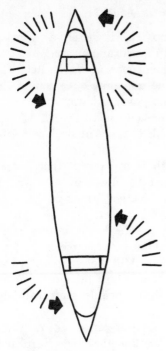 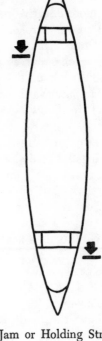

The Sweep Strokes.　　　　　Jam or Holding Stroke.

position underwater. It can be combined with the J, Canadian, or Pitch strokes.

The J, Canadian, Pitch, and Underwater strokes are all stern maneuvers. Strokes which are commonly used in either bow or stern stations include the various *Sweep Strokes,* serving to turn the canoe. Both paddlers may reach forward with their blades fully extended and immersed, *but on edge,* as with an oar. The blade is then swept back in a wide arc. With both sweeps on one side, the craft will turn in a wide circle. A *Reverse Sweep* is the same maneuver executed in reverse. For instance, if the bow paddler performs a Reverse Sweep on one side, and the stern man executes a *Forward Sweep* on the other, the canoe will turn almost within its own length.

The *Jam* or *Holding Stroke* is not actually a stroke. It is simply "applying the brakes," by jamming the blades vertically into the water, at right angles to the canoe. The *Backwater Stroke* is even more effective for a quick stop. This is merely a reversing of the Cruising Stroke. The blade is dipped and *pushed forward*.

The *Draw Stroke* is a common maneuver in fast water. The paddler reaches out as far as possible and draws the flat of the blade toward him. This sets the canoe over sideways. The *Push Stroke*, an awkward and difficult maneuver, is the direct opposite of the Draw. The flat of the blade is inserted close to the canoe and pushed away.

The *Pry Stroke* resembles the Push Stroke except that instead of pushing the blade away, the paddler uses the shaft as a pry, or lever, against the gunwale. It's an emergency move, hard on paddle shafts but effective for a quick set-over.

The *Bow Rudder* is initiated much like the Forward Sweep, the blade being thrust into the water at about a 30 degree angle from the canoe. It is then held in this position. With the canoe underway, this requires strong arm muscles but it will turn the craft sharply. The secret is to have a firm grasp of the paddle shaft with the lower hand in *back* of the shaft.

The *Throw* or *Lift Stroke* is for the master canoeman. Executed at the bow, the blade is thrust quickly into the water vertically, close to the gunwale in feathered position. The upper hand then turns the blade, as if it were a rudder, either toward the canoe or away from it. Even at moderate speeds, this calls for great strength and paddle prowess. Practice it in shallow water at slow speeds. Badly executed, the move can pull the bow man into the water, snap his paddle, or wash it back under the canoe!

Few experts consciously choose one stroke over another. They react automatically, often combining strokes, improvising their own variations. There is no fine line between one stroke and another. One blends into another, as the situation warrants. With a little practice, any canoeman can develop a sixth sense and an automatic reaction which produces the correct stroke. It simply takes practice.

POLING

Poling a canoe is not a stunt. With paddles you'll make little upstream headway in shallow but swift water, and in rapids, paddles are useless against the current. In such cases, poling is necessary. And, quite frankly, poling is also fun. Not many canoe-men learn to use a pole, possibly because it violates the oft-repeated but absurd directive: "Never stand up in a canoe." In order to pole effectively, you must stand. This is safe when confined to shallow waters.

The pole may be anywhere from 10' to 14' long, of ash, maple, or hickory. It should be equipped with a soft-iron "shoe," which keeps the pole from fraying and which grips rocks and ledges to prevent slipping. Such a pole, or the shoe alone, can be obtained from logging equipment suppliers.

For your first try, seek a lakeshore with a gently sloping beach, sheltered from the wind. A single passenger, seated on the floor aft of the bow seat, will stabilize your canoe until you acquire a sense of balance in this new world. You won't have to poise gingerly over the keel. Take a position that raises the bow slightly, your right foot forward and to the right; your left offset and to the rear, straddling the keel line at about a 45 degree angle.

Grasping the pole loosely, thrust it into the water gently just back of your left foot and as close to the gunwale as possible. As the shoe strikes bottom, apply a light thrust to the pole. As the canoe moves forward, "climb the pole" with a hand-over-hand motion until you reach the top, always maintaining a backthrust pressure. Then crouch slightly, flexing the knees, and give a final, but not sudden, push. Be prepared for a burst of speed you've never experienced with a paddle! A canoe, thus propelled, is a lively craft. Before the momentum is lost, lift the pole smartly from the water, never dragging it, and take another purchase. Repeat the "climb-the-pole" thrust. You are now poling. It's that simple. If your canoe swerves off course, alter the thrust of the pole to compensate.

Next try snubbing. This slows or stops the canoe and is used for downstream running. While underway (still along the lake-shore!), reach forward, driving the pole to the bottom close to the gunwale. Brace yourself, knees flexed, leaning into the pole, and apply *forward* pressure. At slow speeds this will halt your craft abruptly. At greater speeds, or in a fast current, you may have to snub repeatedly.

You can then "graduate" to a slow-running stream, relatively free of obstructions. Push your canoe upstream and you'll notice that the current tends to steady it, providing you keep the bow headed directly into it. Veer from this course and the water will set you over toward shore. This is actually a useful maneuver known as "ferrying" or "setting over" but save it until you've acquired a little more experience. For now, practice poling directly into the current. Don't try to make impressive headway at first. Concentrate on control. As your skill and confidence increase, move to faster running water, possibly with a few boulders or other obstructions to challenge you. When scouting a course, thrust the pole to the bottom and hold your canoe stationary while you plot a route. When you've chosen one, move upstream, but not until you're sure the way is open. A dead end is awkward! To get around a rock, don't cut diagonally across the current at first. Use a side thrust, pushing your canoe broadside. As your skill increases, you can then ferry, using the current to help you.

How swift a current can a poler negotiate? When you find yourself making no headway, or only slight progress at the expense of extreme effort, you've met your match. This happens to experts.

Poling downstream is a delightful experience, with little effort required except when snubbing. The current does most of the work. Forward thrust with the pole is minimal. Snub frequently to retain control. And if a clear channel lies ahead, use the pole for all its worth! You'll get an exhilarating ride!

THE OUTBOARD MOTOR

East to West, North to South, long before the invention of the outboard motor, the North American continent was traversed by canoe. And, ideally, this is still the most rewarding method of water travel—without a motor. True, the new outboards are relatively quiet and their smoke belchings have been reduced to mere puffs; yet they are foreign to a canoe's natural environment. Buzzing along a waterway, you'll see only a blurred wall of trees —not birches, pines, spruces, or poplars; you'll overlook the cardinal flower at the water's edge; and the beaver's feed bed will be nothing more than a vague bit of greenery. Your sense of achievement, too, will be just about equal to that of a motorist who drives from Milwaukee to Chicago. The outboard motor, in fact, is a thief. It will rob you of your wilderness citizenship; you can be nothing more than an intruder, an interloper. The rich joys of the

Proper stance for poling upstream in shallow rips. Photo by Eleanor Riviere.

Snubbing on a downstream run. Photo by Eleanor Riviere.

canoe country come most surely to those who leave the outboard motor at home.

However, as in so many other instances within our mechanized society, this isn't always possible. Sometimes, in order to cover great distances during available vacation time, a motor must be used. And for moving weighty loads, supplying an outpost camp, or for commercial use, the outboard's advantages cannot be denied.

Square-stern canoes are well adapted to their use, especially the aluminum 19-footers and the larger Canadian freighters, some of which can handle a two-ton payload. For most wilderness travel, the aluminum 19-footer with its 40" beam and 14" midship depth is a good choice. It will provide about 6" of freeboard with 1,000 pounds aboard. Its one drawback is its weight—115 pounds, permissible if portages are short, and few. Otherwise, look into a 17-footer weighing about 85 pounds with close to a half-ton maximum capacity. Horsepower on a 19-foot square-stern should be limited to about 7½, while smaller craft can usually handle up to 5½ horsepower.

Don't overlook a tool kit. Minimum equipment should include pliers, screwdriver(s), crescent wrench, spare sparkplug(s), plug wrench, spark gap gauge, cotter pins, spare propeller and nut, wiping cloth, friction tape, and a tube of lower-housing grease. And, of course, ample fuel.

A standard double-ended paddling canoe can be converted to outboard use by means of a bracket mounted on the port side, immediately back of the stern seat. In fact, I prefer this type of mount over the square-stern model. With the latter, the motor is rigged directly back of the helmsman. Guiding and throttling calls for an awkward and tiring arm position. With a side mount, the motor's steering lever is conveniently at the helmsman's side.

TRIM FOR TRAVEL

Loading a canoe with camping gear starts long before the craft is launched. It starts, in fact, at the trip's planning stage, when the equipment and supply list is made up. Weed out all non-essentials, especially those items which "might come in handy." They rarely do. Whether you use Duluths or packbaskets, or a combination, try to cram the entire outfit into two packs, three at the most. Generally, the kitchen department goes into one—

grub, cook kit, match supply; into the second go the tent, sleeping bags, and clothing. Miscellaneous items can be added to either pack, of course. At any rate, keep the kitchen pack sacred. Don't mix in too much other gear not related to cooking or eating. Here's why: upon arrival at a campsite, one partner unloads the kitchen pack, starts a fire, and gets supper underway. His chores should be simplified as much as possible. He shouldn't have to probe among binoculars, extra underwear, or fishing tackle to reach a bag of onions! While he's getting supper, his partner unlimbers the other pack (or two), erects the tent, unrolls the sleeping bags, and generally gets the camp ready for the night.

With such organization, actual loading of the canoe is easy. The packs can be placed amidship over the keel so that the craft does not list. The cargo should be distributed, also, so that when both of you are aboard, the bow rides slightly high for lake or upstream travel. If you're headed downriver, load with the bow a trifle heavy or an even keel.

Canoemen disagree regarding tying in gear. One faction contends that this makes a capsized canoe difficult to right and this is true. They prefer packs to float freely away, to be retrieved later. A small float is sometimes attached to each pack. On smaller rivers, or where the rapids are of a gentle nature, this trick works well. However, when a pack gets away on a brawling river, it may take a day or two to recover it—*if* it's found at all! On a canoe trip, I begrudge time spent on this nonsense. Actually, capsizing a well-laden and properly trimmed canoe verges on the impossible if the canoemen are at all adept with paddles. Just in case, however, I prefer to tie in gear.

In rainy weather the packs can be wrapped in a waterproof tarpaulin (or the tent). This is protection against spray during rough going, too. Government-surplus waterproof bags are sometimes available and these are used by white-water canoeists to protect extra clothing. However, over the years, I've found the Duluth pack and the packbasket adequate protection against wetness, especially when the tent is used as a cover.

LAKE TRAVEL

It's a rare day when big lakes lie flat as a ballroom floor. Even a light breeze can kick up a healthy chop. With a robust wind, waves may range up to three feet high. I've seen six-footers, thirty feet between crests! On such waters you have three alternatives: (1) stay ashore; (2) seek a sheltered route along a lee shore even if travel distance is increased substantially; (3) buck the waves. The first two alternatives make sense. The third doesn't, except in an emergency. The first few minutes in wild water may be exhilarating and you'll "whoop it up" like a Comanche who has just scalped a cavalry colonel, but the excitement will be short-lived, turning to weariness. With weariness comes loss of control and possibly disaster. Deliberately tackling such water is foolhardy. There *are* canoemen whom the wind cannot blow off the lake but these are experts.

Every canoeman, however, is caught out in rough water at some time or other. If no lee shore is at hand and you *must* travel to reach shelter, don't simply point the bow into the blow and "put the ash to 'er." Finesse is called for.

Slip into a kneeling position and quarter into the waves. This will allow your bow to rise gracefully over each oncoming comber. Heading straight into the waves, your canoe will cut into them and the bow man will get a lapfull of water, which will eventually find its way into the bilge. If quartering puts you off-course, plot a zigzag route, altering the tack every few minutes, but always in the general direction of your destination. Paddle only hard enough to keep a steady headway. Driving the canoe too hard will cause it to plow into the waves rather than ride over them.

Running downwind can be deceptive. Off a lee shore the waves may be small, and sailing along with the wind, you'll exult at the great speed attained with so little effort. Remember, however, that waves increase in size as you progress downwind. You may soon find yourself among six-foot rollers to whom a 1,000-pound canoe load is a mere feather.

Survival here requires that you ease up on the paddles. You'll discover that as your canoe climbs to the crest of a wave, it is carried forward with a tremendous rush, like a surfboard. This is fun and good technique if properly executed. The trick here is for the stern man to use his paddle as a rudder. Try to hold the canoe on the crest as long as possible, riding the wave until it outruns your craft. The canoe will then drop into the following trough, until the next wave picks it up—first the stern, then the midsection, then the bow for the next "surfboard ride." The bow man's primary chore is to keep the bow downwind matching his partner's rudder action at the stern. As with running into the wind, keep the craft on a quartering course, but not enough so that the danger of broaching is imminent.

You'll be tempted to paddle vigorously to increase your speed. Don't. Let the wind and the waves carry you. Concentrate on control. Accelerate too fast and you may find yourself shooting down the forward slope of a giant comber. When you strike the trough, you will either plow into the next wave or broach and swamp.

If you have a choice, night travel is far safer. Winds usually drop with the sun and you can use a compass or the North Star as a guide. If you know the country, you can probably see well enough to use the surrounding hills as landmarks. However, on a cloudy night, or on waters that are rock-strewn, or littered with logs or other obstructions, stay ashore.

WHITE WATER

Standard advice regarding white water is: "Don't run it. Portage." At the risk of calling down upon myself the wrath of safety "experts," I suggest that you portage only if you have to! Once you've acquired some degree of skill with a paddle and pole, run some of the lesser rips, those which are obviously not dangerous. How else are you going to learn? However, appraise the rapids beforehand, honestly and objectively. If the water "sings" or "burbles" gently over and among the rocks, and you can locate a passable channel, by all means try it. A heavy rumble, though, is another matter. The deeper the voice of the rapids, the wilder they are. Rapids have either a friendly laughter or a foreboding bellow. Learn to differentiate between the two.

Reading white water is not difficult. You'll need no red warning signs on rocks and dead ends which you can see, obviously. Underwater obstructions, those lying just below the surface, bear close examination. Basic "trail" signs are quickly interpreted.

A V pointed upstream, for example, indicates a single underwater obstruction a few inches or a few feet *upstream* of the V, depending upon the force of the current. A V pointed *downstream* is simply the current squeezing between *two* obstructions. Water circling in a leisurely manner so that part of it flows upstream comprises an eddy. In a slow current, this is no problem. In turbulent rapids, however, crossing an "eddy line"— from a downstream current into an upstream one—may slue your canoe about violently.

Obviously, learning to run white water must come through experience. No book, let alone a single chapter, can make you a white-water man. Try the gentler rips. Then move up into the heavier stuff as your skill improves.

REPAIRS

With access to a tool shop almost anything can be repaired, including a battered canoe. On the trail, however, you may have to resort to native ingenuity, or to a limited repair kit. Unless there is major structural damage, the wood-and-canvas canoe is the easiest to repair. A canvas cut, for instance, needs only to be dried. Then daub an oval patch of canvas—or even a piece of your shirttail—with Duco or Ambroid cement. With a knife, slip this *under* the cut. Allow it to dry a few minutes, then place a second patch *over* the cut. If the cut is a long one, you may have to sew the edges together, just as a surgeon sutures a gash. Lacking cement, use pitch from a spruce, fir, pine, or other resinous softwood. If hard, this will melt quickly in a can or even—in small quantities—on the tip of your knife! And it is fully as effective as commercial cements.

A repair kit expedites matters and can be conveniently carried lashed to a thwart, or seat, or jammed into the forepeak. Basic contents should include: a 12″×18″ piece of fabric—canvas, muslin, heavy sheeting—cement, a sturdy needle or awl, a few copper tacks, some heavy thread, a small roll of No. 28 copper wire.

Splintered ribs or planking pose more serious problems. Your best bet is to press them back into position and reinforce them on the inside with a batten tacked to nearby undamaged ribs. The greater the damage, the more ingenuity is required. Sometimes, though, repairs in the field are impossible. I once brought in a 16-foot canvas canoe whose entire bow had been sheared off by a falling tree. By perching myself at the stern, the open bow rose above the waterline and no more than a little spray reached the bilge!

Damage to an aluminum canoe usually consists of minor dents, rarely worth bothering with. A larger dent—one that hampers the canoe's handling qualities—should be pushed back into shape. The canoe will never again be the same, but you can attain some semblance of its original form. Such "repairs" should be made *in the water*. Have your partner hold the canoe in the shallows while you pound the dent back into shape, using a block of soft-wood, 3″ to 4″ in diameter, as a mallet. The water will cushion the blows, yet allow them to re-form the aluminum. If the dent resists this treatment, have your partner take a firm grip on the craft to steady it. Then walk gently on the dent. Chances are your weight will spring it back to approximately its original contours. Attempting such repairs to aluminum on dry land may result in greater damage, a split or crack.

An actual split or crack is unusual in aluminum but if it does occur, a cloth patch can be applied, one inside and one out, with cement or pitch.

Repairing a Fiberglas canoe, in the case of minor leaks or breaks, can be effected the same way, but a Fiberglas swatch daubed with resin is preferable. Carry these in a repair kit. Severe structural damage is not easily repaired. A seasoned wilderness traveler will, nevertheless, improvise ribs of split green maple or ash to reshape the craft. With these, a length of rawhide lashing, a swatch of canvas or glass cloth, and he'll be afloat before long, lame but navigable!

Paddle blades may start to split, usually starting along the bottom edge. Before this progesses upward, lace the split with fine copper wire. A broken shaft can be splinted and wound with wire or even a boot lacing. It won't stand much abuse but it may get you back to civilization. In a real emergency, it's not impossible to whittle a new paddle from a 6″ diameter log of birch or ash, providing you're adept with an axe and a knife—and determined! The best precaution, though, is a spare paddle.

PORTAGING

Portage trails are not always clearly evident. At one time, many were marked by a "lob tree," a tall pine whose upper branches had been trimmed, but these have largely disappeared. Portages in some national forest canoe routes are marked by signs. On the whole, though, finding a portage may require careful map reading and a thorough search of the shoreline.

The blackened rocks of a fireplace, possibly a tea stick (used for holding a kettle over the fire) propped against a tree, and, in this day of callous littering, a rusty can or two may mark the landing. A river portage, if there is a bend in the rapids, will likely be on the *inside* of that bend, providing the terrain is suitable. To locate a portage between two lakes, seek a low place in the intervening hills. Early canoemen didn't tote their craft over hills if they could avoid them; they sought valley routes.

Various types of carrying yokes are available commercially, usually consisting of a removable center thwart with shoulder pads. These are generally quite comfortable although some I've tried proved flimsy. The criticism that they raise the canoe too high on the shoulders is hardly valid. An inch or two makes little difference.

I've always preferred lashing two paddles to the thwarts so that the flats of the blades rest on my shoulders. This takes care of toting the paddles, and with a sweater or shirt for padding, the rig is fully as comfortable as a commercial yoke. Lash the paddles securely, however, so that they cannot slide sideways. For a short carry I rarely bother even with these, simply resting the center thwart of my 16-foot Prospector on the back of my neck. This isn't to be recommended for more than a few hundred feet, though.

Portage labors can be organized to advantage. One partner hefts the lighter of the two packs *and* the canoe. His partner heists the heavier pack, plus the spare paddle *and the axe*. With the latter he crosses the portage first, clearing any blowdowns which may hamper the passage of the canoe.

During early summer in the North, black flies, "no-see-ums," midges, or mosquitoes like to ambush canoe voyageurs, so daub your face and hands with repellent *before* picking up your load. Smoking is quite effective but a stray spark may start a forest fire. Insect dope is safer. Enjoy a smoke *at the end of the portage*.

All sorts of "tricks" have been proposed for lifting a canoe—assistance from your partner, propping one end in the crotch of a tree, even "scootching" under it—all amateurish nonsense suggested by those who have never learned the proper technique. For a craft of up to 85 or 90 pounds, there is only one method and this

Lashing the paddles to form a portage yoke. Photo by Eleanor Riviere.

can be accomplished by any male in reasonably good physical condition. It requires no great strength.

Draw the canoe out of water until its midsection is on dry land. Roll it on its side, its interior facing away from you. Reach down with one hand, grasping the center thwart as low as possible, with your other hand on the upper gunwale. Give a forward shove with your knees against the bottom. This is important. It is the start of the actual lift. At the same time, pull the canoe upward, *tossing* it in a rolling motion to your shoulders. Don't attempt a slow, deliberate lift. Literally *toss* the canoe upward. When it reaches shoulder height, it will be nearly upside down. Duck your head into the carrying yoke and allow the craft to settle on your shoulders.

Picking up the canoe
for a portage,

reaching across to
far end of thwart,

ready for the portage!
Photos by Eleanor Riviere.

rolling the craft
to the shoulders,

Once in position, the canoe should be slightly tail-heavy. This raises the bow so that you can see where you're going. For a comfortable balance, reach forward and place one hand on each gunwale, pulling down slightly. The canoe should balance perfectly.

If yours is a "bouncy" stride, you'll find that the canoe bobs annoyingly on your shoulders. Try to walk with a "swivel-hip" motion, a sort of slinking stride.

Two-man carries are often suggested. Frankly, unless the canoe weighs more than 85 pounds, a one-man carry is easier. It is virtually impossible for two men to synchronize their steps, with the result that the canoe bobs erratically, gouging the shoulders of one or the other of the two carriers. This can fray tempers. Better that one man do the canoe toting, swapping loads when he wearies.

Lowering the canoe at the end of the portage is an exact reverse of the pickup. Push upward on the gunwale with one hand, duck your head out from under the yoke, and roll the craft downward, maintaining a firm grip on the center thwart. As the canoe turns upright, then faces away from you, lower it gently to the ground.

CAR-TOP TOTING

With increasing alarm, highway officials are casting baleful glares at the haphazard manner in which so many canoes are lashed to car-top carriers. It's easy to envision the mayhem that could result when one of these badly secured craft flies from its carrier and plunges into the windshield of a following car, especially at today's expressway speeds. Yet I've seen canoes tied down atop speeding cars with a single strand of cotton clothesline!

At seventy-five miles per hour, the pressure against a canoe is equal to that of a hurricane! This is to say nothing of the suction or lifting effect of winds compressed between the top of the car and the canoe.

The car-top carrier itself, providing it is firmly attached to the vehicle's rain gutters, is less important than the manner in which the canoe is lashed to the car. Firstly, the craft should be tied to the carrier so that it cannot slide from side to side. Next, the

The author and his son brought their canoes over a woods road in this manner for a fast run on a Maine river. For highway travel the craft would have been more securely lashed! Author's photo.

back end is tied down, using ¼″ manila rope or nylon line. The secret to a secure lashing is to cross the lines so that they pull *diagonally*. A single line from the canoe to the center of the bumper is of little value. Secure the diagonal lines on the canoe at least two feet ahead of the bumper so that they not only pull *downward* but also *backward*.

Then, from the front end, pull the canoe forward as far as possible, increasing the tension on the rear lines. The front lashings, too, should be crisscrossed so that they pull diagonally. And they too should be attached to the canoe well back from the bumper, so that the front and back lashings actually pull against each other. This locks the canoe into position. It cannot slide forward or backward, or sideways. If you're apprehensive about the lashings rubbing the finish from the car's hood, pad these spots with foam rubber or cloth.

For a lengthy trip, or during periods of high winds, or when part of my route is over high-speed interstate highways, I attach a second line to the front end, completely separate from the main lashings.

Remember that manila lines attached when wet or damp will stretch as they dry. Check them every hour or so during travel. I seldom experience actual fear in a canoe, even in the roughest water (I have that much confidence in the craft)—but I suffer a gnawing terror that my canoe may fly off my car and plunge through someone's windshield. I lash my craft to minimize that worry.

Chapter 3

UNDER CANVAS—AND NYLON

No tent camper ever completely outgrows the excitement, the sense of adventure, the secure feeling of snug protection against the elements and some unknown danger, which he experienced as a youngster during his first night under canvas. After thousands of nights in them, tents still have that effect on me. A night in a tent, even close to home, becomes a stopover on the Canadian Barrens, a pause during a far-off expedition, a base camp from which to assault an unclimbed mountain. A tent is never anything so prosaic as a mere shelter. Canvas conjures up far places.

The backwoods camper, in a tent, knows real freedom. He can perch his camp on a mountainside, miles from the road and 3,000 feet above it; by a wild river, overlooking a marsh, by a rarely visited pond. The thick forest isn't a barrier; it supplies him with shelter, fuel, even food. The world about him is his, and his alone, a nice feeling in this day of jammed elevators, waiting lines, bumper-to-bumper freeways, and crowded campgrounds.

It's true, of course, that specialized gear is not an absolute necessity for a wilderness trip. You can make do with a canvas knapsack, a castoff blanket or two, household cooking pots, even an ancient axe borrowed from Grandfather's woodpile; but, carried to extremes, this can often lead to misery. It's like paddling a canoe with a five-foot pine board, or skiing with toe straps.

Trudging wearily down the trail from Chimney Pond to Roaring Brook after a climb up Katahdin, I once met a picture of disorganization, bad judgment, and ill-chosen equipment in the form of a half-dozen boy scouts and their scoutmaster. It was nearly dark, the trail ahead of them was no boulevard and they had at least two and a half uphill miles to go.

The scoutmaster, stepping gingerly in street shoes, carried two loosely rolled sleeping bags, one under each arm; the packbasket carried by one boy resounded with rattling pots and pans; one husky youngster had a huge duffel bag atop one shoulder and a sheathed Hudson's Bay axe in one hand; another carried his sleeping bag in his arms, like a peck of groceries; still another panted under an overloaded packbasket, walking like Father Time at 11:58 P.M. on December 31! This outfit, badly rigged, improperly equipped, couldn't possibly have reached Chimney Pond before dark. It was a catastrophe trudging up the mountain to happen!

Such situations can, and should, be avoided. And this is best done by acquiring a working knowledge of the technical aspects of outdoor gear, particularly with respect to sleeping bags, stoves, clothing, and tents. The wrong tent, for example, can ruin a trip.

Fabrics are puzzling in view of the many brand names applied to them—semi-deceptions such as "Wildcat Cloth," "Mountaintop Fabric," or "Dew-Tite." Such terminology is meaningless. There are basically only four tent fabrics to be considered: duck, poplin, drill or twill (they're similar), and nylon. Few other materials are used.

The most durable of the cottons is army duck. It has little to do with the military. Both the fill and warp are doubled and twisted before weaving, and the weave is a tight one, so tight, in fact, that starches and sizing are not added for bulk. The most popular weight in use among tentmakers is 10.10 ounces per square yard.

Drill is the most commonly used fabric, however, with durability depending upon tightness of weave and the quality of the yarns used. Drill is tricky to buy. It is found in $39 "bargains" as well as in sturdy shelters costing $100. It can be identified by its characteristic diagonal weave pattern and its quality determined by any woman who is accustomed to buying yard goods. If she finds a high sizing or starch content, steer clear of the tent. Lacking someone who knows fabrics, depend on a dealer who wants you to return to buy other equipment!

Poplin combines light weight with durability. Not as rugged as army duck, it is nonetheless durable. Weight is usually 6 ounces per square yard. Poplin is a tightly woven fabric, with a thread count of 160 per inch, and it repels wind and rain well.

Nylon is used primarily in mountain climbers' and hikers' tents. Two types are used. One, known as "Rip-Stop," is a closely woven, untreated fabric. The other is coated nylon, treated with a layer of urethane or vinyl to make it absolutely waterproof.

Rip-Stop weighs as little as 1½ ounces per square yard; coated nylon, slightly more. "Rip-Stop" will shed wind and light rain but a heavy downpour will force a mist through it, whereas the coated nylon will turn back the heaviest shower. At a glance, the coated variety seems the best choice for tents. This isn't necessarily so.

The reason has to do with the human body's function of giving off moisture, a form of "insensitive perspiration" of which we are unaware. This escapes into the air, and within an enclosed tent that is fully waterproof, it condenses upon striking the cool surface of the fabric and falls back as perceptible moisture. Small puddles may actually form on the tent floor. Coated nylon, because it is fully waterproof, prevents the passage of this moisture into the atmosphere and is, therefore, unsuited for use in enclosed tents. Uncoated cottons and Rip-Stop nylon *do* permit the passage. They are "breathable," and better suited for tent use.

Army duck, drill, and poplin *are* treated, but not with a true waterproofing. They are made water-repellent, so that they will turn the heaviest shower, yet allow the passage of interior moisture to the outside. Two types of treatment are applied, one "dry," the other "wet." The dry finish is usually applied to army duck, poplin, and the better grades of drill. It does not result in tackiness, it won't rub off, has no odor, and generally lasts the life of the fabric. Material treated in this manner will not stiffen in cold weather, or soften under a hot sun. Nor does this finish add weight.

This is not true of certain drills which are treated with a paraffin-type finish. In this case, weight may be 40 per cent greater than specified. Catalog weight stated as "7.68 ounces before treatment," for example, may actually be closer to 10 ounces. Such fabric can be identified by its slightly tacky finish and characteristic "tent smell." It will soften or stiffen according to temperature and sometimes color may rub off. Given reasonable care, though, this fabric may last for years.

All finishes are advertised as "mildew-resistant," which is tantamount to touting a car as having "crumple-resistant fenders." A cotton fabric tent is truly mildew-resistant only so long as it remains dry. Wet it, and it becomes susceptible to mildew.

There is no "best, all-round" tent fabric. Purpose dictates the material. For a tent to be used roughly, in the woods, or to be toted aboard a packhorse or in a jeep, army duck is the most durable. For a canoe trip tent, where weight becomes a factor, poplin is an excellent choice. Any tent to be backpacked should be of nylon. In the latter case, choose a tent of Rip-Stop or other untreated nylon and add a fly of coated nylon. The tent itself will allow the outward passage of moisture and the coated tarp will prevent heavy rains from striking the tent.

Certain tents have tops of light-colored fabric on the theory that this turns the sun's rays and provides a cooler shelter. In Wisconsin's Chequamegon National Forest, I put such a tent to tests and found it no cooler than a similar model of all-dark fabric. A tent can be cooled by adding a fly or double roof and by raising the sides to allow the passage of breezes. Color is largely hypothetical, or a matter of taste, except for mountain tents, where high visibility is desirable.

Sewed-in floors are now common and this helps in setting up. Stake out the four corners and your tent is automatically squared. While in use to a great extent among family campers, such floors have a place in wilderness tents, too. A mountain tent, for example, may have to be pitched on snow, and here a sewed-in floor of coated nylon serves to keep out moisture. On canoe trips during the insect season such a floor helps keep out crawling and flying pests.

Many tents sold to the family-camping trade have sewed-in floors which have not been waterproofed. These soak up water, mud, and grime, and soon become permanently soiled. Better quality tents have floors of coated nylon which not only resist soiling but are washable. Some American makers now copy the European innovation of the "tub floor," simply a coated fabric which extends up the sides of the tent a few inches, hence the "tub." This eliminates the need for ditching and protects the lower edges of the tent walls from ground moisture.

In a floorless tent, the sod cloth takes on importance. This is an apron, usually about nine inches wide, sewed to the bottom edge of the tent walls. It is usually tucked into the tent so that a separate ground cloth overlaps it, but in winter it may be spread outside and snow heaped upon it for a tight closure against the cold.

Nearly all modern tents require a special framework, almost invariably of interlocking tubular aluminum sections. Such frames are a must for mountain tents used above timberline, where natural poles can't be obtained. Umbrella tents, because of their design, also require special frames. Interior frames are difficult to set up since you must work inside the collapsed tent in semi-darkness, and probably near suffocation if a hot sun is beating down. Exterior frames are easier to erect and sturdier. Backwoods campers, however, generally frown on toting a bundle of aluminum poles, and justly so. Fortunately, there are several excellent tent models which can be suspended on poles cut at the campsite.

In choosing a tent there are several seemingly minor, but important, points to examine. Where seams are lengthy, more than 5' to 6', these should be reinforced with webbing or cotton tape. Stress points, too—peaks, ridges, corners—should have doubled fabric. If there are zippers, these should be rugged, at least No. 7s. And if your tent comes equipped with jute guy lines, rather than the sturdier manila or nylon lines, its maker has taken shortcuts. Beware.

MOUNTAIN TENTS

Specifications for a true mountain tent are strict. Maximum weight for a two-man model is generally set at about six pounds; a three- or four-man version, at nine pounds. Every ounce is critical on a mountain slope. Then, because such a shelter is often used at high altitude, frequently above tree line, it must withstand winds that would flatten most woods-type tents. Also, it must be easily and quickly erected; no complicated suspension systems or complex guy lines are acceptable. And it must shed rain, snow, sleet, and ground moisture while allowing interior moisture to escape. That such a tent was ever achieved is one of the wonders of the outdoor world. Yet several versions are available.

They are expensive and usually obtainable only from shops specializing in mountaineering equipment, or through mail order. They are hardly luxurious summer lodges. A typical two-man model is barely 5'×7' with a 4' height, resembling a pup tent. This grants each occupant a bare 17 square feet, some of which must be taken up by his pack. A 3-man tent may be as small as 6'×8'; a 4-man model, a mere 8'×9'. Some are slightly more spacious but none affords more than basic protection.

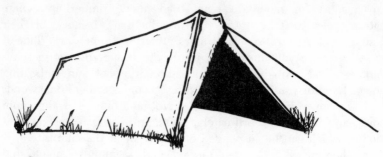

One-man mountain tent.

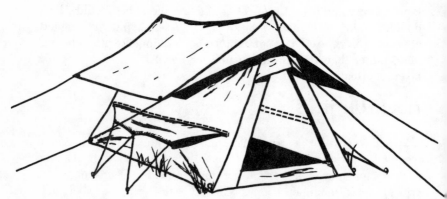

Two-man mountain tent of coated nylon; ventilators along side.

Three- or four-man mountain tent.

Most of them are made of untreated nylon, sometimes as light as 2 ounces per square yard, with a supplementary fly, or double roof, of coated nylon, for reasons already explained. One or two versions are made entirely of coated nylon and require no fly. Ventilation, to eliminate interior sweating, is provided by protected openings and these are probably adequate during the summer, but during winter encampments escape of heat through these ventilators casts some doubt on their value as year-round tents. Also, the effectiveness of the ventilators for passing off interior moisture is questioned by some mountaineers.

The lightest of all tents is one of coated nylon, weighing a mere 1 pound, 9 ounces, consisting of a flat sheet of fabric which can be erected to house one man comfortably, two if they are friendly. I've found this tent adequate only in reasonably good weather, but in high winds or extreme cold it falls far short of being a snug shelter.

Capitalizing on the growing interest in mountaineering, several manufacturers have produced ersatz "mountain tents" of unsuitable fabric, some weighing up to fifteen pounds. These are little more than glorified pup tents, much too heavy and not well enough enclosed for high-altitude camping. Nylon is a basic requisite for a true mountain tent and such a shelter will cost you from $60 up to $160. This is a hefty price tag but on a gale-swept slope, every penny will seem a good investment.

CANOE TENTS

If you're a map eater aiming at a fifty-mile-per-day stint in a canoe, you'll pare weight to the barest minimum. For this type of a canoe cruise, a mountain tent will prove a blessing, but don't expect the luxury of headroom or the reflected warmth of your campfire to be cast into the tent. These are strictly highly portable, minimal bedrooms.

The standard canoe tent is the Explorer, with slight variations known as the Cruiser and the Canoe. Except for size they are pretty much alike with walls sloping from a short ridge, usually about 18". Poplin is the common fabric. A sewed-in floor, insect-proof netting, and a canopy are generally standard. The Canoe model is the smallest, about 4'9"×5'6"; the Cruiser, 5'9"×6'6";

Explorer tent on shear-pole rig.

the Explorer comes in a variety of sizes, ranging up to $7' \times 8'$, with $5'$ to $6'$ of headroom. The heaviest will run up to 12 pounds, not unreasonable for a fully enclosed tent and not too heavy for canoe cruising.

Included with most Explorer-type tents is a single, sectional aluminum pole, atop which is set a short tubular ridge pole, forming a T. In a wilderness setting, however, most canoe travelers will suspend the shelter on shear poles cut at the campsite. This saves toting aluminum hardware, and frankly I enjoy such a "woodsy" rig far more than the soulless mechanics of fitting one metal section into another. Guy lines vary in number, up to six on some models, but the fewer the guy lines the better I like it. This eliminates carrying or cutting stakes.

For spring and autumn trips, when insects are absent, there is a "tropical" Explorer. This lacks a floor and netting, and there is no canopy. In place of the latter, a hood extends over the wide door, from which the warmth of a campfire can be enjoyed.

Eleanor prepares to break camp. The Explorer tent is used as a wrapper to protect packs in the canoe. Author's photo.

The tent requires only four stakes (more can be added if high winds arise) and two guy lines.

Another superb tent for canoe trips is the Miner's, a pyramidal shelter not unlike a "square teepee." It is probably the easiest of all tents to erect, requiring only a center pole and four stakes. The peak may also be suspended from an overhanging limb or on a pair of shear poles. The original Miner's was little more than a wrap-around of duck, without floor or netting, its shape chosen because the winds of western prairies and mountain slopes couldn't topple it. Modern versions with sewed-in floor run about 7′×7′, with a 6′ peak, weighing about 13 pounds. Several imaginative variations of the Miner's were produced for many years by Walter Stern, noted New York tentmaker, but with his passing in 1969, there is some doubt that these will be continued.

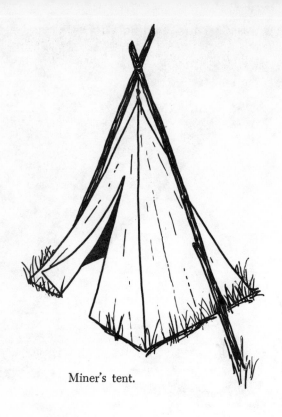

Miner's tent.

The Baker tent, a canvas version of the open-front Adirondack lean-to, is sometimes seen on canoe trails. Bakers are available in poplin and in drill, some with sewed-in floor and insect netting. A 7′×9′ version in poplin, with a 6′ ridge height, weighs 10 to 11 pounds. These are roomy shelters from which a campfire can be enjoyed even during a rainy evening. A large canopy is standard and this can be dropped to enclose the tent fully. The Baker is not an easy tent to erect and it is susceptible to winds, especially from the front. It is really a better woods tent than a canoe-trip shelter.

It is not unusual to see a pup tent at a canoe campsite, and somehow my heart always goes out to any camper who must suffer through a trip housed in a canvas dog house. Pup tents are usually about 5′×7′, which in itself is not unbearable. What I dislike is the lack of headroom—barely 4′ under the ridge. It's true that some mountain tents are no larger than this, but since

Rigging a Baker tent with poles cut at the site. Maine Forest Service photo.

these must be packed afoot, their skimpy size is justified. On a canoe trail, a larger tent is not a burden. However, the pup tent, even when equipped with a sewed-in floor and netting, is inexpensive, and if it makes possible a canoe trip for a budget-limited couple, more power to it!

Where economy is a factor, rigging a tarpaulin over an over-turned canoe will provide adequate shelter, but you'll need netting over your sleeping bag during the black fly season! No poles are required, only stakes. Headroom, of course, is negligible and you'll have to dress and undress while lying down, should it rain. A tarpaulin can also be rigged as a lean-to, as a teepee, or as a pup tent without end walls.

Tarpaulins carried on a canoe trip can be quite large, up to 12′×12′ providing they are of coated nylon. These will roll into a bundle about the size of a football and weigh no more. Cotton tarpaulins, usually treated with paraffin, are bulky and quite heavy.

A shear pole rig put to good use. Note wood-burning stove with pipe run through canvas wall. N. Y. State Conservation Dept. photo.

WOODS TENTS

Considerable latitude is permitted in choosing a tent for a semi-permanent camp accessible by boat, jeep, or packhorse and established for a week or two of fishing, hunting, prospecting, or simply to enjoy a "stay-put" vacation. Weight is not a serious consideration. Durability is. Family-camping tents can be used, of course, if you're willing to contend with half a bushel of aluminum poles. But many of these tents simply won't stand the gaff. Wilderness or backwoods usage is rough on tents.

One that will stand up well, figuratively as well as literally, is the old stand-by, the Wall tent. These range from $7' \times 9'$ up to $9' \times 12'$ or $10' \times 14'$, with a minimum of 6' headroom in these sizes. As a woods shelter, little can be said about the Wall tent that isn't complimentary. It sheds rain and snow well; properly anchored it will resist a severe blow. In hot weather, or for desert camping, a fly stretched over its ridge will repel much of the sun's heat. In cold weather it can be heated easily with a portable wood stove, the smokestack running through an asbestos or metal ring in the top or side. With bedding deployed along each wall, ample space is left in the center for "traffic" and equipment storage. For use in insect country, some models come equipped with a sewed-in floor and netting; for cold-weather use, with a sod cloth.

Suspension systems are varied, each manufacturer touting his as the easiest to set up, the lightest, the most stable, ad nauseam. None has yet matched the shear pole rig which can be cut at the campsite. Granted, cutting these may be somewhat of a chore, but I prefer doing this to lugging a bagful of aluminum sections, then struggling to fit "Section A into Opening Z"! Once cut and set up, the shear pole rig is far sturdier than the best aluminum frame and it is much easier to erect and adjust. The best type of Wall tent for a woods camp is one with an exterior tape ridge through which are strung rope loops. These are the secret of easy set-up and stability. The ridge pole is run through the loops; then the end shears, lashed together at the top, are positioned under the ridge pole and raised. Staking follows, then tying eave guy lines to a side rail. Slackening of tension is done by spreading the shear poles slightly; to tighten the fabric, push the poles closer together, scissorlike.

Obviously, the shear pole rig is not for campers making a series of "one-night stands." It's for a semi-permanent camp. For campground hopping, the conventional interior ridge pole and end uprights are a better choice.

Several up-dated versions of the Wall tent have evolved into "cottage" tents with four-foot, or higher, walls. These are designed primarily for family campers who want to use double-decker aluminum bunks for added capacity. Various frames are included and catalog illustrations often show them minus guy lines, without which a ten-knot breeze will flatten the tent!

One valid adaptation is the tropical Wall tent. This is the conventional model except that the sides can be rolled up to reveal an inner tent of insect netting. This permits full ventilation by the slightest breeze. In addition, the tent is equipped with a large fly with considerable overhang, thus keeping the sun from striking the tent during most of the day. A considerable number of guy lines are required, but the comfort afforded makes these worthwhile.

Nearly all of the better quality Wall tents are made of army duck. So-called "popularly priced" versions are usually of drill.

Probably the finest woods tent for fall and spring camping is the Whelen lean-to, an open-front shelter whose back panel slopes directly to the ground and whose sides splay outwardly so that there is not a single square inch of fabric in a vertical position. Because of this, a campfire's warmth is "bounced" from all three walls onto the occupants, much like a reflector oven bakes a batch of biscuits! Coupled with the fire's direct heat, this makes an easily heated shelter even in the coolest weather. In addition to the sloping walls, a three-foot hood overhangs the front to ward off rain. When you purchase a Whelen, you get only the tent—no poles, no framework. Suspension is by means of a ridge pole set into a pair of six-foot forked saplings. The tent may also be suspended on a rope strung between two trees.

The Whelen is a tent for the deep woods, where privacy matters little and where winds can't reach you with great force. It goes up in five minutes, once the poles are cut. I know of no tent which so well fits into a woods campsite, becomes so much a part of the forest, is so much in keeping with the real spirit of

The author's favorite tent, the Whelen lean-to. Photo by Eleanor Riviere.

backwoods camping. Using a Whelen, I'm out in the open, yet comfortable; I'm sheltered, yet unhampered. If I seem enthusiastic about this tent, it's simply because I am!

Locating a Whelen may prove difficult. Only one or two makers produce it and they're keeping rather quiet about it. However, its design is simple and it can readily be reproduced at home on a household sewing machine. Hence, I've included a diagram for a two-man model.

The easiest fabric to work with, and the least expensive, is 6-ounce poplin, available from many tentmakers and some outfitters. Width varies from 40″ to 45″, and with judicious cutting you'll need about 12 yards, producing a tent weighing under 7 pounds. First make a full-size pattern (using newspaper or wide wrapping Kraft paper) of three panels—the back, the hood, and one side. The latter can be flopped to fit both ends. Allow

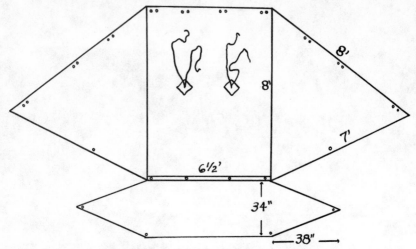

Pattern for making Whelen lean-to tent.

an extra inch for seams and reinforce these with ¾″ webbing or cotton tape. Also allow 2″ for hems. Place on fabric, trace, and cut material.

Sew the four panels separately, then assemble them, double stitching through the webbing or cotton tape, with a ¾″ overlap. Where the hood attaches to the center panel, add a 5″ strip, doubled to 2½″ to form a tape ridge. This must be sturdy since grommets will be inserted. Bottom hems should be about 1″ wide so that they too can accommodate grommets. In the center of the back panel, sew two 5″ squares of fabric about 18″ apart. To each of these attach a D-ring with a short length of webbing or tape. These will serve to hold tie-back lines to keep the back wall from sagging.

For grommets, you'll need 2 dozen No. 0, ¼″ inside diameter, preferably of brass or other rustproof metal. Seven pairs are attached to the bottom hem, the grommets in each pair about 3″ apart. Stake loops are then made of ¼″ rope, one end run through each grommet and knotted firmly. Four grommets are required in the tape ridge, through which 16″ lengths of rope are run, then tied to form loops. The ridge pole will be run through these when setting up. Grommets are also inserted into the hood where indicated in the diagram. All in all, the Whelen

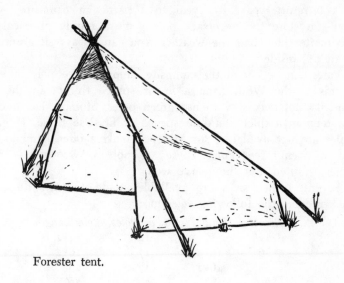

Forester tent.

is an easy shelter to make at home at about a third of the "store-bought" price.

Another little-known but excellent open-front tent is the Forester, an ideal two-man shelter for use in the spring and fall. Like the Whelen, every square inch of its fabric works to gather heat from the campfire. Dimensions vary slightly, but generally a good Forester is 7½' deep, 7' wide at the front, and about 6' high at the peak. Its back wall is triangular, 4' wide at the base, 2' at its peak. Also, like the Whelen, it is without a floor. Its general shape can be likened to half a cone, its open side on the ground.

Few tents are so easily set up. Four stakes hold the sides (six may be required in a strong wind), and three poles suspend the tent. Two of these serve as shear poles at the front, the third as a sloping ridge pole. Guying is rarely required. If you enjoy sleeping where you can watch the stars and feel the warmth of your campfire, you'll enjoy a Forester. Set it up facing away from the direction of the wind for best protection during a rain.

The Indian teepee is generally considered a crude shelter, a plaything at summer camps for children. Not so! It's not an easy shelter to move, or to set up, but once it is rigged there isn't a finer tent for a semi-permanent camp, even during the winter.

If you return year after year to a particular campsite (where you can store the necessary poles) it's a highly practical tent. No matter how bad the weather, you can always sit around the campfire, inside!

Poles can be cut at the campsite, among lodge pole or spruce stands in the West, from a fir or spruce thicket in the East. And it's not necessary to use green poles. Stump-dried trees are common in a thick stand of spruce or fir. Use these. If natural poles are not available, some teepee makers offer bamboo poles up to twenty feet long. These are not as "woodsy" as native poles, granted, but they serve well.

Several teepee sizes are available, made of army duck. One maker offers the following selection:

Diameter	Height	No. of Poles	Pole Length
12′	11′	14	14½′
16′	15′	17	18½′
18′	16½′	17	20′
20′	18′	20	23′

The 12′ (diameter) model is suitable for two campers and their gear; the 16′ size accommodates three to four plus equipment. The larger sizes may prove somewhat cumbersome to set up but they're marvelously spacious. Setting up a teepee calls for raising the tent on a tripod formed with three of the poles. Additional poles are then positioned, spreading the canvas until it is slightly taut. Two poles are used to regulate the smoke flap in the peak.

The bottom rim of the fabric should not fit snugly against the ground since an opening here must provide the draft for the fire. If this draft becomes objectionable, drape a "dew cloth" around the inside of the teepee, leaving an opening away from the occupants. During the insect season, drape netting about the inside perimeter.

The fireplace should be small, no more than two feet in diameter, and in the precise center under the smoke flap. Try to use woods that will not shoot sparks (see Chapter 6); otherwise these may burn holes in sleeping gear ranged along the wall.

There are not many teepee users today. Even Indians have given them up, just as they have traded their canoes for outboard motor boats and their snowshoes for snowmobiles. In using a teepee perhaps you will have found something they have lost!

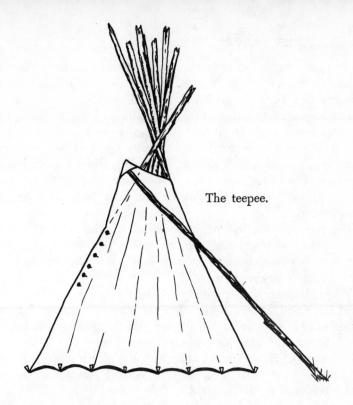

The teepee.

TENT CARE AND REPAIR

Since army duck, poplin, and drill are susceptible to mildew, never store a wet cotton tent for more than a few hours. Dry it thoroughly first. If you have to break camp in the rain and are homeward bound, dry the tent at home before storage. Check the seams. These remain damp long after the panels have dried. When breaking camp in the morning with the intention of setting up again that night, there's little to fear from mildew, except possibly in the extreme humidity of the tropics.

Synthetics, such as nylon, are impervious to mildew but storage when wet may result in stains. One problem with uncoated nylon can be eliminated in camp. This is its tendency to stretch under stress, so that puddles that are allowed to remain on relatively flat surfaces—such as on a canopy—cause the fabric to sag slightly at that point, creating a "baggy" effect. This is a permanent condition once it occurs. Spill such puddles frequently during a rainstorm, or the first thing in the morning following a night's rain.

In time, cotton tent fabrics may develop leaks, either tiny rivulets occurring along the seams, or as a mist seeping through a larger area. In the case of dry-finish fabrics, this can be remedied (after drying) by spraying the seams thoroughly, as well as any misting areas, with an aerosol-type waterproofing. Then roll the tent loosely and store it for a few days in a plastic bag or securely wrapped in a sheet of plastic. This will allow the solution to permeate the fabric completely. Afterwards, hang the tent loosely in a dry, warm room for a day or two. Your leaks have probably disappeared.

For wet or paraffin-type finishes, set up the tent in the sun, then apply a waterproofing solution with a paintbrush. One gallon will usually cover about 100 square feet. Allow the tent to remain upright for a day or two.

When buying waterproofing solutions—they're available from most large tent dealers or outfitters—be sure to specify the type of finish on which it is to be applied. Waterproofing solutions are not satisfactorily interchangeable. Several homemade solutions are possible, too. These involve the melting of paraffin in gasoline or kerosene, but in view of the low cost of commercial preparations, they are hardly worth the risk of fire.

Small leaks in wet-finish tents can also be eliminated by rubbing the area, inside and out, with a candle or with a commercial "wax stick."

Small tears in nylon tents can be repaired with "stick-um" type patches obtainable from mountaineering supply houses. These can also be used on cotton tents, as can Ripair tape, designed for use on sails. Patches of like material can be applied to cotton fabric tents by sewing with a heavy needle or awl. A sewing machine stitch is preferable, however. Seams and stitches on the patch should then be waterproofed.

Bird droppings and tree drippings annoy some campers who find their tents stained. Rather than tamper with the fabric's waterproofing simply brush the spots. However, if you insist upon absolute neatness, wash the areas lightly with a mild soap and lukewarm water. This will minimize stains, not necessarily remove them, and re-waterproofing may be called for.

Air mattress repair kits may also be used for patching most tent fabrics, especially the coated types.

Chapter 4

SLEEPING OUT

There is a popular fallacy that backwoods camping means "roughing it"—going unshaven, eating out of a skillet, washing only every other Saturday night, and, most important, sleeping on the ground. Those who seek this image are welcome to it. I prefer to "smooth it!" Comfort in camp isn't a felony. However, I didn't always think so.

During the late 1930s, on our early canoe trips, my wife, Eleanor, and I used inexpensive kapok-filled sleeping bags. Air mattresses were financially out of reach, so we slept directly on our little tent's canvas floor. We seemed to get ample rest, but I think the excitement of being out in the wilds blotted out the fact that we slept miserably! During one of my early climbs in New Hampshire's White Mountain foothills, I recall contracting bronchitis, probably brought on by having slept through a heavy downpour with no shelter other than my flimsy sleeping bag. Then, during my years with the U. S. Border Patrol in northern Maine, I often slept in abandoned trappers' and log-drive shacks, some of them askew and providing scanty shelter in cold weather. Eventually I concluded that there must be better techniques. Sleeping out, I decided, shouldn't be nocturnal misery. I began to study the subject.

I learned, for example, that blankets and sleeping bags do not *make* you warm. The wool in a blanket and the insulation in a sleeping bag trap dead air space and *this* prevents the escape—or reduces it—of natural body warmth. What's more, as much insulation is required *under* the body as over it, for warm air can escape in any direction. The thicker the insulation, the better.

BLANKETS

Wool blankets wrapped around you provide insulation. But they are relatively heavy, bulky to pack, and unless well tucked in, they may be "chilly around the edges." And since thickness of insulation is what counts, you may need three or four blankets to equal the thickness provided by a sleeping bag. Obviously their weight and bulk would become a burden if backpacked. For use in a wilderness cabin or during summer nights, blankets may be adequate. For cold weather, a good sleeping bag is called for.

DOWN SLEEPING BAGS

Most sleeping bags used by mountaineers, hikers, and professional outdoorsmen who must pack their sleeping gear are insulated with goose down. This is not an immature feather but, rather, a fuzzy pod from which grow many fine filaments. These are located *under* a goose's feathers, next to the skin. Some sleeping bag makers insist that white goose down is best; others claim gray is equally efficient. Frankly, I can't see how its color can affect my nighttime comfort! It is universally accepted, though, that no man-made insulation can match down for its light weight and its loft or "fluffiness."

And loft is what counts in a sleeping bag. One ounce of goose down can be compressed to under twenty cubic inches without damage to its fibers. This means that down sleeping bags can be rolled or jammed into a relatively small space for carrying. Yet, when the bag is unfurled, this same ounce of down expands to about 500 cubic inches, all of which trap dead air to provide insulation. Nature should be complimented on an amazing product!

In addition, down "breathes," permitting the outward passage of body moisture; it is resilient—you can compress and "fluff" it repeatedly; and it can be washed. It has one disadvantage. It is costly.

Quality of down varies. Better sleeping bags are invariably filled with virgin goose down; cheaper ones may be insulated with used or reprocessed down; still others may contain a mixture of down and feathers, or a combination of down and synthetic fibers. When buying a down bag, read the label carefully or buy a well-known brand. Avoid "bargains" sold by cut-rate department stores and similar outlets. A good down sleeping bag

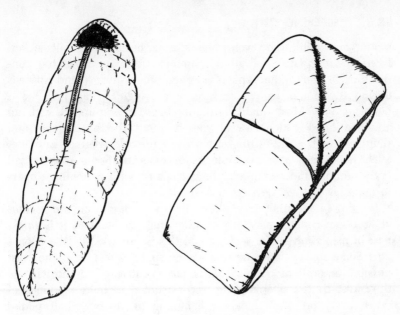

Hooded sleeping bag.   Down-filled rectangular sleeping bag.

Down-filled mummy bag.

is a substantial investment. Make that investment where you can be assured of the best possible quality.

Mummy-type bags, roughly shaped to conform to the body, are preferred by backpackers since they are less bulky, are lighter than the rectangular type, and actually require less down to provide a given comfort range. Be sure to buy a mummy bag amply large enough so that you can enjoy some freedom of movement. If you are unusually tall or portly, choose an oversize model or you'll spend your nights in a horizontal strait jacket! Even an adequate, well-fitted mummy bag may prove too constricting if you're the type of sleeper who squirms and sprawls during the night. In which case, a rectangular bag may be a better choice. Most quality mummy bags are equipped with an attached hood which can be closed about the head, face, and shoulders with a drawstring, a necessity for cold-weather camping. Such hoods are also available as accessories. Some makers sell both mummy and rectangular bags in pairs, with matching zippers to serve as double sleepers for couples.

Judging a sleeping bag solely by the *amount* or the *weight* of its down content may prove misleading. Remember, it is *thickness* of insulation you're seeking and this is provided by the down's loft. Some makers seek to attain a given thickness with the least possible amount of down. This is not an attempt to shortchange the buyer. If the sleeping bag is constructed to hold 2 pounds of down to attain a 2″ thickness, jamming in an extra half pound merely raises the cost of the bag without increasing its thickness. Too, this is why a high-quality, virgin down is the best choice. A thickness of 1″ of this may well be more effective than 2″ of reprocessed down or a combination of down and feathers.

Down bags consist of a number of parallel tubes into which the down is blown. If these tubes are formed by stitching through two flat layers of fabric, the insulation value between the tubes will be little. Somewhat better design is known as "box construc-

Tubular construction for sleeping bag. Seams between tubes are sewn through.

"Box construction"
tubes in sleeping bag.

Overlapping tubes.

tion," in which all of the tubes are of equal thickness through their breadth, being formed by vertical walls of fabric. However, heat loss will occur to some degree through these tube walls. Overlapping tube construction is a further improvement. At no point within the sleeping bag does the tube thickness vary and at no point does any fabric or stitching go directly from the inner shell to the outer covering. The tube partitions, being angled, keep a relatively even layer of down between the sleeper's body and the outer air.

Some sort of tube construction is necessary. Otherwise the down would shift, overfilling one section, robbing another. This was a major problem with the now out-dated kapok-filled sleeping bags. In some mummy-type bags, a "differential cut" is incorporated. The inner circumference of the bag is markedly smaller than the outer circumference, thus providing equal thickness throughout.

Catalogs are replete with charts and statistics indicating "warmth ratings" of various sleeping bags. These are but guidelines, despite reported "tests" and implied guarantees. No two campers have the same rate of metabolism—the body's ability to generate heat— at a given moment. In fact, this may vary with the same person according to how well he has eaten, what he has eaten, and how tired he may be. And it's doubly difficult to appraise these guide-lines since some are conservative, others obviously overenthusiastic. Other factors affect warmth, too. Sleeping out on a clear, cool night will subject you to radiational cooling. Sleeping in a tent cuts this down. A strong wind will draw warmth from your sleeping bag.

There is no precise formula for prescribing the thickness of insulation your sleeping bag should provide. Perhaps the nearest approach to such a rule might be to buy a bag that is rated about 25 per cent warmer than your anticipated needs. Nor am I fence-straddling or dodging the issue. One rule is infallible: Buy thicker rather than thinner! You may be slightly overwarm during an occasional night but this is better than being chilled frequently. Don't go overboard, though. Buying an arctic-type down sleeping bag "just to be sure"—some of these will keep you comfortable at 40 below—will result in stewing in your own juices at 15 degrees! Some models take this problem into consideration, pro-viding a separate foot opening to allow cooling ventilation without exposing the more sensitive neck and shoulder areas.

Following is a chart of typical specifications for down-filled sleeping bags as supplied by manufacturers:

Down Content lb.	oz.	Loft	Weight of Bag	Shell Fabric	Type	Rating
1		*	2½ lbs.	Nylon	Mummy	25 degrees
1	3	1¼″	3¼	″	″	35
1	8	2¼	3¼	″	″	20
1	12	2¼	3½	″	Rec.	25
2		3¼	3¾	″	Mummy	5
2		*	4	″	Rec.	10
2	3	2½	4¼	″	Mummy	20
2	3	3¼	4¼	″	Rec.	10
2	8	*	4½	″	″	0
2	9	3	4¼	″	″	0
2	10	4	4¾	″	Mummy	−20
3		*	5	″	Rec.	−10
3	8	*	5½	″	″	−20
4		*	13	Poplin/Nylon	″	−15
5		*	18	Sateen/Cotton	″	−50
6		*	**	Cotton	″	−60

Rec.=Rectangular
* Maker did not stipulate loft
** Maker did not stipulate weight of entire bag

A far greater variety of down sleeping bags is available. I have included only a representative cross section of catalog specifications for comparison purposes. While some of the temperature ratings are conservative and others somewhat overenthusiastic, the overall ratio between the "Loft" and the "Rating" columns seems consistent. The variations in bag weight are accounted for by the difference in cut of the fabric, the fabric itself, size of the bag, and its construction.

The efficiency of any sleeping bag can be increased somewhat by sleeping with your feet pointed *into* the wind when bedded down in an exposed area. If possible, however, sleep in a tent or other shelter on extremely cold nights; the smaller the shelter the warmer it will be, even without a fire or heater. Immediately upon setting up camp, unpack your sleeping bag (but leave the zipper closed) and "fluff" it, even though you may not be ready to turn in. Fluff it again just before retiring. This will produce maximum loft.

The mass of today's down sleeping bags have inner and outer shells of nylon so closely woven that it is "downproof" but don't worry if an occasional bit of fluff escapes. If you find down leaking from the bag in quantity, look for a tear in the fabric or a seam that has started to part. Some bags are made of cotton or cotton-synthetic combinations. All of these "breathe."

Traditionally sleeping bags have been rolled, many catalogs showing neat, usually undersized, compact rolls. Down bags, however, should *not* be rolled. Better that you stuff them—literally—into a waterproof "stuff bag," handful by handful. Strange as it may seem, this is less harmful to the down filler than rolling.

When a down bag becomes soiled, dry cleaning is not necessary. If the shell and liner are washable, so is the down. When storing the bag during the off-season, remove it from the stuff bag and lay it out flat, or hang it in a dry room. This should also be done between trips, if the latter are infrequent.

POLYESTER SLEEPING BAGS

Polyester fiberfill, commercially known as "Dacron 88," "Kodel," or "Fortrel," is the best of the man-made sleeping bag fillers. In sleeping bags, polyester is used in pre-formed layers, not loose or in bulk. Making these layers to match the thickness of a given amount of lofted down is an easy matter. To compress it into as small a bundle is impossible. In other words, a sleeping bag insulated with two inches of polyester fiber will be as warm as one filled with two inches of down, but when rolled it will form a much larger pack. Too, the weight of polyester is considerably greater than that of down. Hence a polyester bag of a given thickness will weigh much more than a similarly insulated down bag. For these reasons, few polyester bags are used by backpackers. Weight, and especially bulk, rule them out.

Few makers of polyester bags rate them according to the thickness of the filler. Instead, they indicate its weight. To assist buyers, and sometimes as an advertising gimmick, some manufacturers apply "ratings." Like those for down bags, these ratings are generally consistent and reasonably accurate. The actual comfort range of a polyester bag, however, is more susceptible to variation because of the sleeper's metabolism rate, weather conditions, exposure of the campsite, and the bag's construction.

Some critics claim that polyester does not have the porosity of down, that it retards the outward passage of body moisture. Having used both types of bags extensively, I have never noticed such a shortcoming in either. Within the temperature ranges for which my polyester bags are designed, I have always found them dry and comfortable. And lest I be accused of hasty conclusions, we have nine polyester-filled and two down-filled bags in the family!

Certain other synthetics and natural materials are used as sleeping bag fillers, including acetate, cellulose, and wool. None is as effective as polyester. Still less efficient are vaguely labeled fillers which, upon examination, you will find are reprocessed, reconstituted, restored, reconstructed, reactivated, or rehabilitated! Give them all a wide berth. A frequent ruse is a picturesque label, usually on the plastic wrapper. Don't be deceived by a snow-capped mountain or a lovely alpine meadow. These won't assure comfort. Look for the words "new" or "virgin" polyester.

Following is a representative selection of polyester-filled sleeping bags with specifications supplied by their makers:

Polyester Content	Weight of Bag	Shell Fabric	Type	Temperature Rating
2 lbs.	4¾ lbs.	Poplin	Rec.	40 degrees
2	5¼	"	"	35
2	7¼	"	"	30
2½	5	Nylon	Mummy	30
2½	5	Cotton	"	25
3	8¼	Poplin	Rec.	30
3	4½	Nylon	Mummy	20
3	5¾	Poplin	Rec.	30
3	6¼	"	"	25
3	8	"	"	25
4	11	Cotton/Nylon	"	35
4	7¼	Poplin	"	15
4	8½	"	"	15
4½	12	"	"	15
5	13	Duck	"	0
5	12	"	"	25
5	10	Poplin	"	−10
6	13	Duck	"	15

Some of these temperature ratings appear to be inconsistent. One 5-pound bag is rated at 10 below zero, a second at 0, and a third at 25 above. Probably none of these is accurate. Except under the most favorable conditions, sleeping in a 5-pound polyester bag at 10 below could prove a chilly experience!

Despite the discrepancies among the 5-pound bags, the chart generally agrees with most experts that a 2- to 2½-pound polyester bag is suitable down to about 30 degrees at best; a 3- or 4-pounder down to 15 or 20. For colder temperatures a 5-pound bag *might* be suitable. I would prefer down.

Detachable hoods, also polyester-filled, and closing about the shoulders and head help keep in body warmth. A wool liner will add insulation and, of course, a canvas tarpaulin wrapped loosely about the bag will also help.

On several occasions I inserted a badly worn war-surplus down mummy bag into an inexpensive kapok-filled rectangular bag. Sleeping in an abandoned trapper's shack, at below zero, I found the makeshift combination reasonably comfortable. Inserting a good down bag into a modern polyester unit should produce a fairly good sleeping combination even in extreme temperatures. The combination will be bulky to tote, however.

While polyester bags are unsuited to backpacking, they can be used to advantage on canoe trips, or when a packhorse or jeep is doing the toting. If your budget puts a down bag out of reach, a polyester sleeper will do for such trips. Its cost is only about a third to a fifth the price of a goose down bag!

Among the fabrics used for making shells of polyester bags are poplin, nylon, duck, Pima cotton, and various combinations of natural and synthetic weaves. Nylon is the lightest and durable; duck, the toughest—and heaviest; poplin, the most popular, because of its low cost. One of my poplin bags has been used close to 500 nights, and although the flannel liner is now worn dangerously thin, the outer shell is still adequate.

Avoid any sleeping bag with a bottom panel of rubber, plastic, or coated fabric of any kind. Being waterproof, such a panel is often touted as a "built-in ground cloth." Such bags can neither be washed nor dry cleaned; what's more, they retard evaporation of body moisture. You'll awaken in the morning in a damp, clammy bag.

Among inner liners there is some choice. Outing flannel is most common but it can be a nuisance if you're wearing flannel pajamas. One material clings to the other. Come morning, you'll find yourself twisted like a cruller and probably choking on your pajama string! Nylon and sateen liners are "slippery" and eliminate this nuisance. They're cold to the touch at first but warm quickly. Removable liners attached with tie tapes or snaps are advantageous. Women, who like to sleep between sheets, can insert a sheet liner. And a wool liner, already suggested, will add warmth and may be used with a sheet liner by those to whom wool against the skin is "itchy." Best of all, the liner can be removed for washing without having to wash the entire bag.

When buying man-and-wife bags, buy two alike, with matching zippers to form a double bag. With similar zippers, a 3-pounder can be matched to a 4-pound bag. Examine the zipper when shopping. Seek a No. 7 of die-cast metal or molded nylon with inner tab so that the bag can be opened or closed from the inside. Should your zipper become balky, rub its teeth with wax or Zip-Eaze. An insulating baffle at least 2″ wide and running the full length of the zipper will prevent the escape of warmth through the latter.

Unless the sleeping bag has bellows sides, an air mattress inserted into the pocket provided for it will crowd the sleeping compartment. For a slender sleeper this is no problem. If you tend to overweight, you will be uncomfortably restricted. In this case, it is better to lay the sleeping bag atop the air mattress.

Perhaps the most ludicrous accessory on polyester sleeping bags is the "head tent," that woodsy little canopy set up on forked sticks in most of the catalogs. No one has ever devised a graceful means of getting into or out of the bag without collapsing the silly rig! Also, such a "shelter" implies that the bag can be used in the rain without additional cover, which, of course, it cannot. The outer shell is *not* waterproof. True, a mosquito netting can be rigged over such a canopy but this is better done with a pair of arched green saplings. The only authentic purpose of the canopy is to serve as wrapper for the sleeping bag.

As with a down sleeping bag, the polyester type should be opened and allowed to loft some time before use. For obvious reasons, all sleeping bags should be aired frequently, every morning if possible.

FOAM PADS

Because down compresses so readily, the bottom panel loses much of its insulation value under the weight of a sleeper. Some sort of padding must be used as a bed upon which to rest the sleeping bag, not only as protection against the hard ground but as supplementary insulation. Otherwise, even the finest down bag will provide cold sleeping. Polyester compresses to a much lesser degree but also should be padded.

Among backpackers foam pads have come into wide use. I have one which is 20″ wide, 36″ long, and 1½″ thick, covered with waterproofed nylon, certainly a midget mattress but it's about all I can carry in my pack without crowding out other necessities. The pad is a compromise. It's more comfortable than a rocky ledge, but it's far from being an innerspring mattress! And if the ground slopes even slightly, it's difficult to remain on the pad through the night. But it does fit in my pack. I roll it and insert it vertically into a stuff bag, then allow it to unroll until it pushes the sides of the bag out to form a hollow cylinder. Into this hollow I stuff my two-pound down bag.

Larger foam pads are available, up to 24″ wide and 72″ long but still only 1½″ thick. Despite the latter, they are rather bulky when rolled. Thicker pads, up to 2½″, are even bulkier and are out of the question for backpacking or canoe trips. When rolled they are about the size of a two-pound polyester bag! Such pads, however, provide ample cushioning on the roughest ground and superb insulation. But they're for semi-permanent camps accessible by jeep or boat.

AIR MATTRESSES

The air mattress still finds favor despite the coming of the foam pad. When deflated it occupies little space in a pack and its resiliency can be adjusted by varying air pressure. Some campers claim it is more comfortable than foam, certainly true in the case of 1½″ pads. Inflating and deflating are slow processes though, unless some sort of pump is used. Also its insulation value is less than that of foam.

The variety of air mattresses is wide. They range all the way from those of rubberized nylon, 22″×48″ and weighing 1¾ pounds for backpackers, up to rubberized cotton models 32″×75″, weighing 8 pounds. The backpacking types are little larger than the midget foam pads but they take up no more room than a folded T-shirt. The larger sizes make up a relatively small package when deflated. One style among the larger air mattresses is tubular in design, sometimes with outside tubes considerably enlarged to keep the sleeper from rolling off. The tufted variety is generally more comfortable, and more expensive. All can be inflated by mouth, by hand or foot pump, and there is even an electric pump which operates from a car's cigarette lighter outlet. It brings howls of derision from true wilderness campers, but *it works!*

Overinflating an air mattress makes for an uncomfortable bed. After all, compressed air has no more "give" than a pine plank. Don't test pressure by probing with the weight of one knee. This

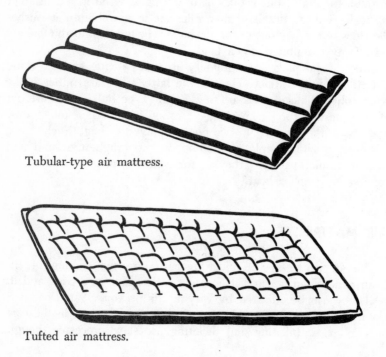

Tubular-type air mattress.

Tufted air mattress.

concentrates weight at one point and the mattress offers no support. Test it by lying on it. Inflate it so that you lie *in,* not *on* it.

Compact repair kits are available.

COTS

I can't recall the number of siwash camps I've enjoyed, bedding on the ground, and cooking meals in a No. 10 can. Nevertheless, despite the scorn of hairy-chested outdoorsmen for "lace curtain trimmings," I like to use a cot at a stationary camp. The ground gets harder with age, my age, that is! During the summers of 1961 and 1962 my family camped out from June 15 to September 15, sleeping in tents, cooking meals out of doors. No Indian ever spent more time under the sky during any three months of his life. Yet we bedded down on cots. For lengthy camp-outs, full comfort at night is mandatory. Our cots were lightweight, compact, sturdy, two of them with aluminum frames, two of steel. Ten years later, we are still using the aluminum ones! Eleanor's is insulated with polyester fiber for added warmth, the insulation attached to the *underside* so that it is not compressed when in use. Such cots are also available with down insulation.

BOUGH BEDS

One of the most comfortable of all camp couches, the bough bed, is fast disappearing. Few campers know how to build one. Judging from some of the remains I've seen in various parts of the North, their makers must have spent miserable nights. Invariably these were no more than 2″ to 3″ thick. A bough bed should be at least 18″ deep. Such bunks are frowned upon nowadays, but back in the deep woods, boughs from blown-down or broken softwoods are plentiful. Making a bough bed need not arouse the ire of a conservationist.

The suggestion that you build a log enclosure to contain the bough bed makes about as much sense as erecting a fence around your overturned canoe. Neither is going anywhere! Omit the logs. For the first 12″ of depth, use spruce boughs, well curved and up to 1½″ in diameter at the butt. Lay these windrow style, arching upward over an area about 3'×7', making sure that each butt is overlapped by several thinner branches or tips. Next overlay 6" or more of fir tips and small boughs, up to ½" in diameter at the butt. A tarpaulin over these will protect your sleeping gear from pitch. Try out the bed during the day, since you may have to adjust a bough or two to prevent gouging during the night. With use the boughs will lose some of their springiness and they will compress somewhat, but by rearranging them every two or three days you will restore initial comfort. Such a bed will last two weeks or more.

If spruce or fir boughs are not at hand, use those of other short-needled softwoods for the top, long-leafed varieties for the base. When you break camp, don't leave the boughs piled at your campsite to become a fire hazard. Distribute them in the nearby woods, away from trails or woods roads, where they will rot and soon become forest duff. Nature wastes nothing!

Chapter 5

WOODS CLOTHING

CLOTHING

Coming in from a woods patrol some years ago, I arrived at Rockwood, near the outlet of Moosehead Lake, to find the thermometer at the Canadian Pacific Railway station registering 46 below zero. By way of contrast, Eleanor and I, deep in Georgia's Okefenokee Swamp, once had to cut short our explorations because the heat made us feel "woozy." The temperature hit 110 that day!

Such extremes are not unusual in various parts of North America. Man has withstood much hotter, and colder, weather. These are my personal records: 46 below and 110 above, and I've no desire to break either record. In wilderness camping temperature isn't the only vagary you'll encounter. Mother Nature throws other types of tantrums, too—humidity, winds, snow, sleet, drizzle, rain, and thunderstorms, to say nothing of an occasional hurricane, cyclone, and waterspout! How the human body adjusts to these variables is for better minds than mine to explain. But you don't have to be a physiologist to grasp the importance of suitable clothing.

Proper fit is vital. Clothing that is too small binds, restricts circulation, hampers free movement of arms and legs, even the torso. In cold weather, body warmth escapes readily through tight clothes; during the heat of summer, they may cause chafing. Outdoor clothing shouldn't hang like a hound dog's ears, but, generally, better loose than tight. Appropriate fabrics are important. Some are virtually windproof, necessary in the winter. For summer wear, light cottons and synthetics ventilate the skin for a cooling effect. Some fabrics insulate against cold; others shed rain and snow. For backwoods camping, you'll probably use all of these at some time of the year.

The wilderness is hard on clothing. I once took a new wool shirt on a canoe trip. When I returned two weeks later, it was literally in shreds. The backwoods is not a fashion palace. It's not the place for "mod togs," more colorful than practical. This does not necessarily mean an expensive wardrobe. In fact, the most practical outdoors clothes can be bought most reasonably, except for specialized garments used by winter climbers. In choosing clothes for the wilderness, buy those which can be put on or removed in layers, and plan it so that you require as few garments as possible and will still be comfortable.

SUMMER WEAR

Conventional everyday underwear is suitable for men and women during summertime backwoods trips. However, some feminine newcomers to outdoor life perhaps need a word of advice. During my years as a guide, I accompanied fishing, hunting, and canoeing parties which often included women. Normal activities of these trips were obviously difficult, apparently even painful, to some of the women because of overrestrictive undergarments. Frankly, guides soon grow rather blasé about such matters, but I would rather have observed graceful, easy movements than a well-trimmed figure that had trouble getting in or out of a canoe, or clambering over a blowdown along a hunting trail. Unless such garments are essential to health or comfort, leave the girdles at home!

Glamour is out of place in the puckerbrush, too. Women who are experienced in the outdoors forgo high fashions and time-consuming hairdos. You need not look like a state-aid case, of course, but any woman who insists upon primping an hour or two every day is doomed to failure. Wind and rain will raise hob with your glamour in a matter of minutes, to say nothing of the irritation you will create among those who must wait for you.

For men and women, cotton and synthetic shirts, blouses, slacks, and trousers are ideal. They're easily washed, even in a galvanized bucket. Blue jeans are a favorite, even for women, but not the western type. These fit too tightly for freedom of movement. Shorts, especially for hiking, afford leg freedom. However, when biting and stinging insects are about, avoid short sleeves and shorts. Cover as much of the body as possible.

In the North particularly, warm days often are followed by cool nights. Even an evening campfire can be a chilly occasion. A cotton flannel shirt will be welcome, possibly even a wool shirt, sweater, or jacket. Wool slacks or trousers may be necessary. Don't underestimate these temperature variables. On the Mexican border I've seen frozen car radiators blow off steam at 6 A.M., but by noon we were in shirt sleeves!

Headgear isn't always necessary, but take along a hat or a visored cap, not only as protection against the sun and rain but to ward off insect pests that attach themselves to woods hikers. During a patrol along the Quebec boundary on a warm August day, my partner failed to wear a hat. A swarm of deer flies adopted him, following for miles, buzzing about his head. Strong men have been driven berserk by such persistent pests and, at one point, they seemed to be getting the best of my partner. Finally, he wrapped a sweater about his head. This foiled the deer flies but his "turban" was hardly appropriate for the 80 degree temperature. A hat or cap is not a luxury.

RAIN GEAR

Greenhorns usually go to one of two extremes when it comes to rain wear. They will wear an inadequate "city-type" raincoat, or they will cover themselves from head to foot with rubber. Obviously, the conventional raincoat designed for fashion and token protection is unsuited in the backwoods. The full covering afforded by so-called "navy rain suits" of rubberized fabric, or by their waterproof-nylon counterparts, is an abomination if you're active. Since these usually consist of a parka and trousers, snugged at the neck and waist, excess body warmth cannot escape, nor can perspiration. These rigs are walking Turkish baths!

The rain shirt, not unlike an old-fashioned nightshirt with the addition of a hood, is an improvement, but not much. As a fishing guide I wore one of these aboard my open boat because I could drape it to cover my entire body, including my feet. Only my hands and nose were exposed. As long as I was inactive, seated at the helm, this was perfect protection. Ashore, however, I quickly peeled it off since it, too, had the makings of a strolling sauna bath. It allows only slightly more ventilation than the rain suit.

The poncho is far superior to both. Little more than a flat sheet

Poncho provides rain
protection and ventilation.

of waterproof fabric—coated cotton or nylon—it has a hole at the
center through which the wearer pokes his head. Some models
include a hood and nearly all have snaps down the side so that
they can be closed. Hanging loosely, it provides ample ventilation
even during fairly strenuous activity, yet sheds a heavy downpour.
It does not, however, protect the lower legs and, in fact, drippings
from the poncho will soon soak your trousers from the calves down.

Lightweight nylon rain pants or chaps can be worn if travel or work in a heavy rain is essential. With or without this leg protection, though, the poncho is a good choice.

Most caps are poor protection, even those of so-called "treated" fabrics. Unless coated with plastic or rubber, they saturate easily. A hat with a brim drips water onto your shoulders instead of down your neck. Such hats are available in coated cotton. I suppose it's because of my woods background but I have as yet to find better rain headgear than a battered old felt hat. With the crown pushed up domelike, and brim turned down, it sheds rain like a beaver hide. Too, in a moderate rain, I often forgo my poncho in favor of a heavy wool shirt. It sheds moisture surprisingly well.

SPRING AND FALL

Spring and fall are the seasons during which it is most difficult to "suit up." With regard to the weather, anything can happen. Summer may stride in during April, or it may snow in June. During the hunting season, it may be a matter of only a few hours between a heat wave and snow flurries. At these times of the year you have to cover all bets. Carry summer-weight underwear, one set at least, but be sure to pack more substantial "skivvies," too.

The oft-told yarn that lumberjacks sew themselves into "hand-hammered, double-barrel, all-wool long johns" in October and wear them until May isn't completely true. Some choppers peel theirs off in April. You'll want to change more frequently, of course, but during moderate cold spells with limited exposure to winds, long woolen underwear is a wise choice. If you're allergic to wool, there are cotton-lined types for both men and women.

This is the time of year for wool outer garments, too, at least in the North or at high altitudes in the South. Wonder fabrics are common nowadays but none has ever excelled wool for general cold-weather wear. A wool shirt, worn under a wool mackinaw, is about as comfortable a combination as there is except, naturally, under arctic or sub-arctic conditions. A fierce wind will penetrate wool. Over it, wear a parka or jacket of tightly woven fabric such as nylon or poplin. This is usually necessary in an exposed position. In the thick forest, high winds will bother you little. During the years that I guided hunters in the Maine woods, where winter sets in during October but the deer season continues to December first, I found the wool shirt and mackinaw combination excellent. If the weather turned warm during the day, I cached the mackinaw, picking it up on the way back to camp.

The worst atrocity ever perpetrated upon sportsmen are the bright red or red plaid, heavy wool "hunting breeches," which fit like a clown suit—which is just what northern guides call clothing often worn by city hunters. Most of us could spot a greenhorn by his britches and tired expression, the latter the result of toting his pants around! Such breeches are too heavy as a rule and badly tailored for walking.

The most comfortable "woods pants" are copies of the river driver's "stagged britches"—actually not breeches but, rather, conventional wool trousers of medium to heavy weight (depending upon the season) with the cuffs trimmed off just above the ankles, usually with a knife! The river driver was a combination beaver and antelope and he was wet from dawn until dark. The wool kept him warm and "stagging" his trousers gave him leg freedom. Both qualities are still desirable. What's more, he had no cuffs to load up with snow, slush or mud. By way of further freedom, the log driver wore suspenders instead of a belt. This gave his torso the same freedom his legs enjoyed, so that, if he was lucky, he could dance among the logs nimbly enough to avoid being "sluiced."[1]

I'm not implying that if you don't wear stagged pants, you, too, will be sluiced, but the fact remains that the traditional woodsman's garb has never been improved upon notably; at least, not for use in the woods and on the rivers. Better woolens are woven, stitching is sturdier, but the basic concept of warmth, freedom of movement, and durability has not been surpassed.

WINTER

Dressing for winter camping could mean simply adding to the spring and fall layers of clothing; except that, as the wind pene-

---

[1] On a river drive, being "sluiced" meant falling in among the logs either to be drowned or crushed. This meant a quick burial by the river's side with the only monument being the unlucky driver's calked boots hung on a branch over the grave. A few miles below my camp in Maine, a pair of boots marked such a grave on Deadman's Island until a few years ago.

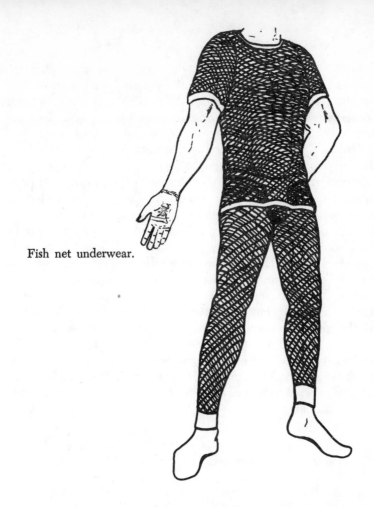

Fish net underwear.

trates deeper and the cold takes a sharper bite, an element of danger is added.[2] Here, special fabrics may be necessary.

For winter underwear, two materials are effective. One of these is used in so-called "thermal" underwear, a coarse "waffle-weave" cotton which quite effectively traps and holds body warmth. However, activity is this fabric's downfall. Excess heat does not pass off

[2] For excellent reports, in laymen's terminology, on the physiological effects of cold, heat, altitude, and exertion under these conditions, see: Dr. Marlin B. Kreider, "Clothing, Shelter and Cold Hardiness," *Appalachia*, June 1969, p. 375, published by the Appalachian Mountain Club, 5 Joy St., Boston, Mass. 02108; and Gerry Cunningham, *How to Keep Warm*, Colorado Outdoor Sports Corp. P. O. Box 5544, Denver, Colo. 80217.

sufficiently and perspiration may be trapped, soon soaking the underwear. Moisture on the body at extremely cold temperatures can be dangerous. A better fabric is "fish net," a recent newcomer to America although in use among Scandinavian fishermen for many years. It's easy to recognize by its large, open mesh, ⅜" to ½" square. This permits body warmth to flow freely about the body carrying away excess perspiration.

Except during very sedentary winter occupations, down- or polyester-insulated underwear, worn next to the skin, is wasted. It fails to provide sufficient ventilation for perspiration. Once it is wet—both down and polyester garments absorb moisture—insulation value becomes negligible, sometimes even freezing to outer layers of clothing. This can be extremely dangerous! Down and polyester can, of course, be worn *over* fish net underwear but they are poor substitutes for the latter.

As with a sleeping bag, the preservation of body warmth depends upon the insulation about your body. Sleeping or active, the principle is the same except that, because the more active you are the more heat your body gives off, thickness of insulation should vary. The U. S. Army Quartermaster Corps developed the following chart, which is not to be considered a hard-and-fast rule, but rather a set of guidelines:

| | | Insulation Required | |
| | | Light | Heavy |
Temperature	Sleeping	Work	Work
40 F	1.5"	.08"	.20"
20	2.0	1.0	.27
0	2.5	1.3	.35
−20	3.0	1.6	.40
−40	3.5	1.9	.48
−60	4.0	2.1	.52

Sleeping conditions are generally fairly stable through the night although the temperature usually drops gradually. This can be anticipated. However, daytime activity varies, sometimes arduous, sometimes leisurely, so that the body's output of heat and perspiration fluctuates. Clothing has to conform to these changes.

Wool adapts itself well to the "layer" format—up to a point. For example, if you're wearing a wool shirt and a heavy mackinaw, and you still feel cold, what do you do for an encore? More wool is *not* the answer. You may have reached the point where the protection of wool is offset by the burden of having to carry a heavy and rather bulky load of woolen garments. The solution may lie in a windproof parka of lightweight but tightly woven fabric such as nylon.

As a basic layer over underwear, wool is almost infallible. Shirt and trousers, worn over fish net underwear, can be ample at well below freezing temperatures. As the thermometer drops and winds rise, down-insulated outer clothing comes into its own. This may be a jacket or in extreme cold an arctic-type parka. With a filler loft of 2½" such a parka may be sufficient protection at 60 below if you're moderately active. Best of all, the combined weight of the fish net underwear, the wool shirt, and the parka is not tiring. All-wool garb for such temperatures, if it were possible, would be burdensomely heavy.

Arctic-type down-filled parka.

Heavy wool trousers are ample protection at far lower temperatures than is generally credited to them. During a fourteen-mile trek for grub along Maine's St. John River at 36 below, all I wore on my legs were conventional wool underwear and a pair of heavy, stagged wool pants. Admittedly, I was active, slogging along under a pack. In an exposed area, such as above timberline, it would have been folly to rely solely on this garb. On the St. John, my body produced warmth for my legs as fast as a gentle breeze sucked it through my trousers. But on a mountain slope, my pace would have been much slower; I would have generated less warmth and the wind would have been far stronger. Under such conditions, down-filled trousers are necessary. These can be worn over wool trousers but the bulk may make walking difficult. Mountaineers' down pants, worn over fish net underwear, are a better choice.

Where arctic conditions prevail—and these are not confined to Alaska and northern Canada but also at high altitudes from Maine to Washington—even down-insulated clothing may be insufficient in the face of fierce winds. Windproof parkas are then worn, too.

Even with the best of arctic-type garments there is danger if excessive sweating occurs. Despite all advice to the contrary, this is difficult to avoid. After all, climbing, packing, snowshoeing are not parlor games. However, perspiration can be minimized. Keep your pace down to the point where you are warm but not excessively so. Should you "work up a sweat," open your collar to allow some of the warm air to escape; unbutton your jacket; even remove headgear for short periods—ever careful about frost-nipping your ears! Some mountaineers' clothing has auxiliary zippers for ventilating the lower legs and wrists.

Headgear presents problems. The body process of vasoconstriction sees to it that the bulk of the warmth is reserved for the vital organs in your torso, and for your head. However, surface areas like your cheeks, ears, and eyebrows are susceptible despite the best efforts of your body's heat factory. Keeping these safe from frost without overheating the head is no mean feat! Years ago I acquired a muskrat fur hat with ear flaps, which I still wear occasionally, probably for nostalgic reasons and because it's woodsy. But certainly not because it is ideal headgear! For inactive wear, it's ideal. But if I'm snowshoeing or otherwise exerting myself, my head becomes wet with perspiration within minutes. The hat is simply *too* efficient with no provisions for cooling, short of removing it. Fur hats are romantic, that's all that can be said for them, and it's beyond me to understand how TV's Dan'l Boone can wear his all summer!

Far better headwear is a combination of a wool toque and a down-filled hood. Toques can be rolled down to cover the ears and some can be converted to face masks covering all but the eyes. Depending upon activity and the weather, a down-filled parka can

Wool toque which converts to face mask.

be worn with or without such a toque, too. This is the "layer format" applied to the head.

Probably the most useless item of wear in extremely cold weather is a pair of gloves. Even when made of wool, their insulation value is minimal simply because the fingers cannot be padded sufficiently without bulk that would hamper the wearer. The felony is compounded by the fact that the hands are usually shortchanged by the body when heat is distributed. The hands are the last to receive body warmth and they get the least.

Mittens are the answer. Your four fingers combined can hold body warmth more efficiently than each finger can separately. What's more, within a mitten, your thumb can be slipped into the finger compartment. Lumberjacks' "choppers" are excellent for active wear. These are simply a pair of wool mittens worn within a pair of buckskin shells. They fit rather loosely but not so much so that they slip off easily. Polyester-filled mittens are made for snowmobilers but mountaineers prefer a down-filled type. With either type, see that they fit snugly about the wrists or overlap your sleeve cuff generously. Attaching mittens to the sleeves with a sturdy twine is not a childish precaution. Mountaineers do it. They know the outcome of a lost mitten in arctic weather. Mislaying a mitten isn't the only danger. High winds may blow it out of reach if it's removed even for just a moment. Anchor your mittens down!

FOOTWEAR

Napoleon may have believed that "an army marches on its stomach," but frankly a hearty meal does little to comfort or protect my feet. Good footwear does.

Sneakers or tennis shoes may make you feel as fleet of foot as an Indian runner, but fifteen minutes on a rough trail may have your feet begging for mercy. They lend no arch support; their thin fabric uppers don't protect against abrasion; they wet through almost instantly in wet weather; and they're about as sturdy as birch-bark moccasins!

So-called "camp moccasins" of leather, particularly the low-cut, gift shop variety are not much better than sneakers, although both may be comfortable for lounging in camp or walking on a well-trodden trail. However, if you're tempted to buy the soleless type because they're more Indian-like, think twice. Small pebbles will soon have you known among your friends as Chief Pain-in-the-Foot!

Camp moccasin.

One concession should be made to moccasins and sneakers, though. They are marvelously comfortable in a canoe, something that can't be said of sturdier leather shoes and boots. If portage trails are reasonably smooth and short, you won't have to change footgear, but if the carry trails are anything like some of the obstacle courses over which I've had to tote canoes, switch to more rugged footwear.

"Larrigans"—ideal canoe shoes or footwear for snowshoeing. Photo by Eleanor Riviere.

Another style of moccasin well suited to canoe use is 6″ "larrigans." You won't find them in most sporting goods or shoe stores, although they are slowly regaining their lost popularity. Their only maker, so far as I know, is the Palmer Shoe Co., of Fredericton, New Brunswick. They fit more snugly than the low-cut moccasin; they can't flop off yet they are flexible. I refuse to launch my canoe until I've had time to put mine on. However, except for the added protection to the ankles, they are hard on the feet if worn over a rough trail. Originally, they were made for snowshoe wear, since their soft soles won't harm snowshoe filling. Worn with two pairs of wool socks, they're ideal footgear for snowshoeing.

A favorite woods boot—when it's dry underfoot or even in rainy weather—is the 6″ or 9″ all-leather-soled boot with a moccasin vamp. Generally, the 6″ model, sometimes known as the "guide's shoe" is ample for most woods travel, even some climbing. For woods work I prefer the 9″ height. Mine run the gamut from muddy beaver bogs, blueberry barrens, cedar swamps, to rocky hillsides. And for cutting the annual wood supply with a chain saw, they are steady and protective underpinnings. And I like them for hunting, at least until the snow becomes more than a couple inches deep. Anything higher than 9″ belongs in a Hollywood script, unless, of course, you're planning to prowl among rattlesnake nests! For a good fit, wear wool socks, a light pair next to the skin, a heavier pair over these.

Some leather boots are insulated and these *are* efficient, but I find their bulk and added weight awkward. But then I suppose this is true of *any* insulated boot. Insulation requires thickness; this means bulk.

The pioneer "insulated" boot was a 9″ to 10″ felt shoe over which was worn an ordinary street rubber. These were favorites among French Canadian woodsmen when I first worked in northern Maine thirty years ago. And I never met one of these woodsmen who suffered from cold feet! The felts were inexpensive, then, but their price has skyrocketed since they became popular as liners for snowmobilers' boots.

With snow underfoot or when woods trails are muddy, "gum rubbers" are used extensively. These are rubber-bottom, leather-top boots made famous as the "Maine hunting shoe" by the noted outfitter, L. L. Bean of Freeport, Maine. The bottoms protect against moisture while the more flexible tops, with full lacing, afford comfort and support for the ankle and lower calf. The L. L. Bean Company will attach new bottoms when these wear out, thus perpetrating the old woodsman's joke that he "wore the same pair for seventeen years, including three new bottoms and two new tops." Most woodsmen insert felt innersoles, which absorb perspiration, changing these daily—one pair afoot, the other drying. I've never been able to get a good fit with this type of footgear—and I've tried a number of brands—so that, for use on bare ground, I much prefer all-leather boots.

When travel calls for slogging through snow, slush, or mud, the all-rubber boot, usually about 11″ high and sometimes insulated, has become a favorite. These are rather heavy and well qualified as awkward "clodhoppers," but their efficiency in sloppy going cannot be questioned. Felt innersoles must be worn in them to absorb moisture and to pad the foot. Some ventilation—frankly, this is only token—can be attained by leaving the lacing partly open. If worn too loosely, though, the upper edges may chafe the calf.

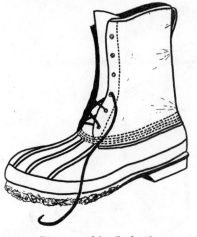

Leather boot with rugged sole.

"Gum rubber" leather top and rubber bottom.

All-rubber woods boot.

Snowmobile boots, sometimes all-rubber, sometimes copied after Bean's Maine hunting shoe, are badly designed for walking. Usually insulated with felt liners up to ¼″ thick, they are very bulky. However, their purpose is to keep inactive feet warm aboard a snowmobile and at this they succeed well.

When arctic conditions prevail footwear becomes even more specialized. The original "mukluk," a sealskin boot with knee-high

Mukluk.   Mountaineer's boot.

uppers, has never been improved upon, despite the introduction of leather, canvas, and even crepe soles! True mukluks are loose-fitting boots, with leg windings that tie just below the knee. They are worn with a liner or with an appropriate number of heavy wool socks. Unless made in the Far North, modern mukluks lack height and are designed primarily for "outdoorsy" glamour. Some even have zippers! And they are outlandishly expensive.

Another specialized boot is the snakeproof type with loose-fitting, thick-leather uppers, reaching to the knees. The Gokey Company of St. Paul, Minnesota, has made a specialty of these, including field tests wherein rattlers were prompted to strike the boots but were unable to pierce them. In country where poisonous snakes abound, I'd rather have a pair of these boots than a six-foot club!

Mountaineers' boots, too, are specialized. These must be sturdy enough to protect the feet yet flexible enough to permit "rock scrambling" and comfortable walking during approaches to actual climbing. It's not unusual for them to have built-in steel shanks. The ankle and tongue are padded to prevent chafing and to provide a firm but gentle grasp of the foot. Thick soles with heavy lugs are common, often of Vibram. The lugs tend to stick to smooth rock surfaces and prevent accidental sliding when a climber encounters "scree"—loose pebbles not unlike a hillside of marbles! Some mountain boots are insulated with Fiberglas and for extremes of winter climbing double boots are available, the inner pair of light leather lined with wool felt.

"Kletterschuhs," boots used for technical climbing often involving rope work, are quite light with a reinforced toe and a narrow welt, the latter so that the edge of the sole cannot turn over or curl when gripping a steeply pitched ledge. The toe is also designed so that it can be wedged into a narrow crevice for a foothold.

Hiking shoes, according to laymen, are any type of leather "high top" boots, but only until they've worn a conventional pair of "leathers" on an extensive trek. Too often, the uppers are excessively soft and lacking in support; and they frequently allow the foot to slip within the boot. During a climb on Mt. Washington in New Hampshire I discovered this form of torture. My boots had been superb footwear in the woods, but during the descent from the summit, my weight drove my feet forward into the toe of the boots with each step. At the Appalachian Mountain Club base camp, I discovered that I had lost several toenails! Along the trail, I overtook a young woman having the same problem. I overtook her because she was walking backwards, relieving the pressure on her toes! We commiserated a while, then she removed her boots and descended the rest of the way in her stocking feet!

Hiking boots require *perfect* fit. "Good enough" isn't good enough! Suitable boots for extensive walking, and especially for climbing, should almost be molded to the foot. For this reason, mail-order purchases are rarely satisfactory. It's better to try on hiking boots for a snug fit. True hiking shoes somewhat resemble mountaineers' boots, including lug soles, but generally they are lighter in weight.

In an arid climate, engineer's boots, or Wellingtons, may be suitable. Their rather loose uppers provide excellent ventilation. Riding boots belong in the stirrups, not on foot trails, where for obvious reasons they are foot killers.

BOOT CARE

All leather boots require a preservative to eliminate drying and stiffening and to make the leather water-repellent. With sufficient application of dressing, leather boots can be made *waterproof* for a short time. However, if you want truly waterproof boots, buy the all-rubber type. Leather boots should be treated to preserve the leather, not to keep out water.

Neat's-foot oil is superior to any other dressing for woods boots. First, warm the boots, at least to comfortable room temperature, then dampen them slightly with a wet cloth. The oil, too, should be warmed. Apply this liberally with a discarded toothbrush, the best instrument with which to work the oil into the seams and along the welt. Don't be alarmed when the pretty tan color of a new pair of boots turns to a grimy brown or dingy black. No properly treated pair of woods boots ever won a beauty prize at a shoe fair. Allow the first application to stand overnight. In the morning, you'll find that all of the oil has soaked in. Repeat the application several times, until the leather is soft and supple. Your boots will then fit like a second skin. Don't overdo the dressing, however. Excess oil will allow the leather to stretch as you wear the boots, thus developing a sloppy fit.

Various "waterproofings" are on the market, some including silicones and other "special formulas." Frankly, I have found that silicone dressings do not last as well as neat's-foot oil. The latter isn't permanent—it should be renewed when the boots show signs of drying out or stiffening—but it outlasts silicone. Neither silicone liquids nor neat's-foot dressings should be used on boots which should retain stiffness—mountaineers' boots, for example. Use a wax paste on these. It will waterproof—to a degree—and protect the leather without softening it.

Placing leather shoes too close to a fire will cause excessive drying. The leather becomes stiff, brittle, and prone to cracking. Dry boots and shoes gradually. Even if they are still damp in the morning, fresh wool socks will keep this dampness from your feet. Frequent wetting and drying are harmful, too, since this rapidly dissipates the dressing. At the first sign of stiffening, apply dressing.

Shoelaces may seem a trivial matter, until one breaks while you're reaching for a precarious toehold. Always start a trip with a fresh pair of sturdy laces. For woods boots, rawhide is excellent. In fact, I equip my woods boots with 40″ rawhide laces, far longer than I need. If a break occurs—this is rare—retying them is easy with ample length left for lacing. I wind the excess around the boot tops so that I always have an emergency cord with me. Once, when

I unexpectedly ran into a superb trout pool, I used both laces as an anchor line for my canoe. The trout I caught justified the many times I had wound excess lacing around my boot tops!

SOCKS

Despite all of the wonder synthetics that go into the making of our clothing, nothing has equaled a good pair of wool socks! Wear them year-round for comfort in the woods, light in the summer, heavy in the winter; one of each in extremely cold weather. Wool cushions the feet, absorbs moisture, insulates, and does not mat as readily as cotton or some of the synthetics.

There are combinations of wool and synthetic fibers. Here you get the advantages of wool, plus the durability of the man-made fibers. Hand-knit socks are usually superior to factory or mass-production versions, since the yarns are heavier and coarser, often more durable.

When hiking or climbing, change socks even during the day if they become excessively moist from perspiration. In cold weather, change them whenever wet or damp. At any rate, no matter what the weather or travel conditions, change them at least daily, not necessarily as a concession to aesthetics, but for comfort and foot protection. If they wear thin at the heels or toes, discard them, because their cushioning and insulation values have depreciated beyond salvage. If wool next to the skin causes excessive itching, wear a pair of light cotton or synthetic socks, with wool over these.

Chapter 6

CAMPFIRES AND FIREWOODS

Firebuilding is still a practiced art among backwoodsmen and a few of the more skilled summer visitors to the wilds. They know (1) that it's possible to build a fire in any kind of weather at any time of the year in a forested area; (2) that a cookfire will produce a greater variety of meals—and in less time—than any propane or gasoline stove ever invented.

Safety with fire is not so much a matter of obeying rules or regulations. Common sense is a more practical guideline. For instance, we have been educated to "build fires only in fireplaces," but where the backwoods camper travels there may be no such facilities. Whether he builds one or not depends on the type of fire and its location. *A fireplace is not always imperative.* A "noonin' fire," for example, which burns only a matter of minutes to heat a pot of tea or soup with which to wash down sandwiches, needs no encirclement of stones. On a gravel bar or beach, build the fire at the water's edge and kick it into the water when you're finished with it. This is a small fire, of course—seldom consuming more than a half-dozen sticks of softwood. Such a fire is safe, too, on hardpan or wet ground, even away from water, providing that the site is clear of brush, grass, or weeds which might dry out and ignite. Here the fire can be buried in mineral soil when you're finished with it. But be sure that it *is* mineral soil (gravel, sand) and not forest duff.

For an evening campfire, or for cooking more extensive meals, a fireplace is virtually a necessity. It confines the blaze and provides a platform on which to rest a grate or utensils. Where a fireplace exists, use it rather than build a new one. Fires leave ugly scars and a campsite with several of these is rarely an attractive spot. If the fireplace needs repair, rebuild it on the original site. If a new one is required, set it on mineral soil or on a ledge from which the fire can't escape or creep underground. Where bare soil isn't evident, rake away the forest debris—leaves, grass, needles, or twigs—for several feet around. If this does not reveal mineral soil, clay, or ledge, move on; you've chosen a poor place for a fire. Forest humus is nothing more than rotting leaves, needles, twigs, and branches and this is sometimes up to two feet deep, dark and damp, seemingly fireproof. It isn't. Once warmed, it dries quickly and becomes inflammable. This is the material through which under-ground fires creep unnoticed, sometimes not surfacing for a day or two.

Whether it's for cooking or evening companionship, keep the fire only as large as is absolutely necessary. A noonin' fire needs only to lick the bottom of your tea pail; for frying, a handful of red coals will do. A full-course meal requires more, but remember that the bigger the fire, the more wood you'll have to "manufacture," the sooner your grub will scorch, to say nothing of the discomfort that comes with working close to an oversized blaze. If the evening is chilly, huddle near a small fire. This is more practical than a minor conflagration, which will roast your knees while your posterior acquires chilblains.

When finished, *literally* drown your fire, until the ashes float! Turn over charred sticks; they may be smoldering underneath. Douse them individually. Stir the ashes, then add more water until they are cold to the touch. Every pail of water you carry to the fire will increase your peace of mind after you've left. Nothing will ruin a day so completely as the nagging thought that perhaps your fire wasn't really dead when you left it.

If you've camped in a remote area, not likely to be visited by others, replace the forest debris as well as possible, thus restoring the ground cover. Along established routes, though, it's just as well to leave the fireplace as you built it. It may encourage others to be careful with *their* fires.

FIREPLACES

Located on a non-inflammable base, your fireplace may consist simply of four rocks on which to rest a grate. Two green logs, 6" to 8" in diameter and 2' long can be substituted, but I'd rather carry rocks a reasonable distance than cut down a tree unnecessarily.

At a semi-permanent camp a more substantial fireplace is desir-able. Two or three types are worth building. One of these is the U-shaped, open-front style, about 2' wide and 18" deep, with rock

U-shaped stone fireplace permits all types of cooking—boiling, frying, broiling, and baking. Note steak in broiler propped vertically. Photo by Eleanor Riviere.

walls no more than 8″ to 10″ high. Use rocks found on dry soil, not picked from streams or lakeshores. Such rocks may contain pockets of moisture, which have been known to explode when heated. The U-shaped fireplace has several advantages. With the opening faced into the prevailing wind, you'll get ample draft; it permits the use of a reflector oven; makes the planking of fish or meat easier, as well as baking bannock in a skillet; and hot coals can be raked from it for flameless cooking. The three walls provide a solid base for a grate and serve as shelves on which to keep pots warm.

The most common backwoods fireplace is a circular enclosure of large stones but this limits cooking techniques to boiling or frying. Baking with a reflector oven is difficult, although a skillet can be propped for pan baking. A variation is the "keyhole" fireplace. One side of the circle is extended narrowly. Coals can be raked into this extension and a small grate placed over it.

Few camping books fail to illustrate or describe the so-called "Hunter's Fire," built between two logs set a few inches apart and hewn flat on the top. Horace Kephart,[1] in fact, recommended logs a foot thick and six feet long, hewn on top and inside, but then he lived during an era when skill with an axe was common. Despite its persistence in literature, I have never seen such a rig in actual use. During the time required to fell a tree and hew the log, a skilled camp cook will have fed a party of six and done the dishes!

The pit or trench fireplace is a delusion, too. It is dug supposedly to guard against excessive draft on windy days and to keep sparks from flying. It fails miserably. The less digging we do in our remaining wilderness, the better. Moreover, the wind will still fan the flames violently and scatter sparks. If conditions are so dangerous as to warrant such far-fetched precautions, *no* fire should be built.

Snow eliminates fire danger but creates problems of its own. During a two-day snowshoe trek my partner and I built cookfires on log platforms. Otherwise the fires would have melted the snow and sunk out of sight! The logs were easy to come by: we merely knocked down a rotted fir about 6" through at the butt, and broke it into 4' sections. The wood, which had been damp until freeze-up, was now frozen and virtually fireproof. After one meal, my partner heaped snow on the fire. "You figure it'll spread?" I asked him. He glanced about sheepishly at the six-foot snow cover. "Habit, I guess," he grinned.

A fireplace grate, described as "essential" in outfitters' catalogs, is not really necessary. It's a convenience. Commercial varieties have folding legs but some of these are rather flimsy. A shelf from a discarded refrigerator makes a sturdy grate when set on rocks and provides a larger cooking surface. Even this can be omitted when traveling light. Use, instead, two or three green saplings, 2" thick, laid across the fireplace. Trig them so that they won't roll. If used only while actually cooking, they'll last two or three days before burning through.

[1] Horace Kephart, *Camping and Woodcraft* (New York: The Macmillan Co., 1917).

FIREPLACE RIGS

When it comes to hanging pots over a fire, the simpler the rig the better, but it should be *sturdy*. Following a four-day jaunt some years ago, I made camp and rummaged through my pack to find that I had only two potatoes, a small chunk of bacon, a can of corn, and a tin of evaporated milk. This added up to a corn chowder naturally, although I'd go hungry the next day until I reached the "outside" some time late in the afternoon. I hung the makings on a pole over the fire. When the chowder steamed a come-and-get-it aroma, I reached for it. The stick broke. The pail fell. The chowder put out the fire. It was a long, hungry night and all the next day I was gaunt in the middle! Since then, my fireplace rigs have been rugged enough to tether a wild bronco.

The simplest of these is the dingle stick, also know as a gin pole, tea stick, wangan stick, waumbec, or, among the Micmacs, as a "chip-lok-wagan." It's nothing more than a sapling, 2″ at the butt and some 6′ to 8′ long, propped so that it overhangs the fire and on which is hung a kettle. It can be set in a vertical crotch with the bottom end weighted by a rock; the lower end can be driven into the ground to anchor it; or an inverted forked stick can

Dingle stick.

be staked over the butt end. (Figure opposite.) Indians believed that to leave a chip-lok-wagan standing over the ashes of a dead campfire invited the wrath of the Red Gods. I've never found one left standing on an Indian campsite, nor do I leave one! Lean it against a tree, a nice gesture toward campers to follow.

A tripod can be used for an extra-heavy kettle, but otherwise, why cut three poles when one will do?

At a semi-permanent camp where extensive cooking may be called for, the fireplace crane is versatile. This is simply a lug pole set into a pair of forked saplings staked one on each side of the fire. The uprights should be of hardwood, 2″ in diameter at least, and driven firmly into the ground. The lug pole should be equally rugged. Kettles are not hung directly from this, however. You'd have to slip the pole through the kettle bails, a dangerous nuisance. Hangers for the kettles can be made from wire coat hangers bent into an S shape or short sections of light chain whose lengths can be adjusted by means of small S-hooks. Nature provides sturdy pot hooks, however, free for the cutting. Find a maple or alder crotch, 2″ in diameter. Cut off one limb of the crotch about 5″ long, leave the other 12″ to 15″ long. Notch the latter as below, right. I usually cut three or four of different lengths to vary the height of the kettles over the fire.

Fireplace crane; note pothook detail.

FIREWOODS

Most organized campgrounds supply campers with firewood. Otherwise, state and national parks would look like wildcat logging jobs, with trees felled indiscriminately. In some campgrounds, "firewood" takes on the form of old bridge timbers, barn boards, sawmill slabs, or old guardrail posts. The camper has little choice; he burns what is supplied, which probably helps to account for the popularity of the gasoline camp stove! The backwoods camper is more fortunate. He can often pick the correct type of wood for various purposes. He doesn't have to use an old railroad tie for tinder, kindling, *and* fuel!

Without doubt the best of the natural tinders is the bark of the white birch. Even when soaking wet it remains highly inflammable. But don't peel it from a live tree, since this leaves a permanent scar, ugly evidence that a callous camper has passed that way! In birch country, curlicues of bark are often stripped from trees by the wind, or you can peel it from a fallen tree. It's not unusual to find hollow cylinders of bark from which the wood has rotted. In the rain, build your fire *within* one of these cylinders. The infant flame will be protected until the fire gets underway enough to ignite the bark, by which time you'll have a healthy blaze going. The bark of the silver birch is also good tinder, along with that of gray birch.

The shredded bark of a cedar or cypress is also excellent. Scrape the trunk firmly with the edge of your knife, using an up-and-down motion, catching the shreds as they drop. Even during a rain, one side of a cedar is usually dry since this tree tends to lean. Scrape only the outer surface, and gently. Gouging too deeply may injure the tree.

Other natural tinders include dried leaves or grass, softwood needles (softwood *cones* ignite slowly unless placed in a brisk fire), and small twigs known as "squaw wood," the latter suitable only if they are brittle enough to break easily. Twigs that bend or twist are either wet or green. Don't discard or burn paper wrappers or small cartons. You can avoid littering by saving them for tinder.

A quick fire is produced by shavings, too, whittled from seasoned softwood such as pine, fir, or spruce. Shavings should be thin enough to curl. A variation of these is the "prayer stick," whittled

The prayer stick, surest and quickest way to a campfire. Photo by
Eleanor Riviere.

Splitting open a dry stub for kindling. Photo by Eleanor Riviere.

so that long, curly shavings protrude from the stick in all directions. Two or three prayer sticks, heaped one atop the other, will almost guarantee a brisk fire.

Homemade fire starters eliminate the need for tinder. Sheets of newspapers soaked in molten paraffin, then cut into small sections, work very well. Candle stubs are helpful, too. Avoid using kerosene-saturated fire starters. Kerosene, being an oil, has a permeating odor which is difficult to dispel.

Commercial fire starters are inexpensive and effective. Probably the best is a 1½″ cube of urea-formaldehyde, which sounds foreboding but is actually clean and safe to handle. I tested such cubes during the winter. They burned an average of nine minutes, even while sinking into the snow.

Pouring kerosene or gasoline on a reluctant campfire is utter folly. I once helped haul a young camper twenty miles to a hospital after he'd attempted this. He'd used outboard motor gasoline on a smoldering breakfast fire and the flare-up burned him from chest to knees! These fuels are simply *too* flammable.

Besides tinder, you'll need kindling, a sort of "Stage II" in fire-building. The best is seasoned softwood split no thicker than ½″ to ¾″. Failure to split this thin enough is the common source of fire-building troubles. Cedar is the best of all, with spruce, pine, and fir also good.

The best source for any of these is a "dry stub," a dead tree left standing. Even following a week's rain, the interior will be as dry as a Vermont joke. During a rain the exterior surface swells and keeps out further moisture. With an axe, pry off the outer shell, then dig out the dry "innards."

"Fat pine" isn't a species. The term applies to any resinous soft-wood, even a badly rotted one. Punky stumps, knots, and crotches of most spruces and pines contain pitch pockets which are highly flammable. These can be chopped out, but beware of hemlock—its knots are hard enough to break the bit of an axe!

Other possibilities are dry brush—alders or laurel; the lower limbs of softwoods which have shed their needles; and, in a pinch, even dry grass can be rolled tightly to serve as kindling. In prairie country, seek the bottomlands where cottonwoods grow, using dead branches. In the desert, mesquite is more than adequate.

Now that you have tinder and kindling, you'll need more sub-stantial wood for a continuing fire. When there is a choice, remember that evergreens are classified as "softwoods" and that they are as a rule fast burning, leave no coals, and will snap sparks all over a half-acre lot! The hardwoods are those which shed their leaves annually—they're known as "deciduous" species—and they generally burn slowly. Some create coals that glow for hours.

Recognizing a hardwood as opposed to a softwood is, of course, easy. One has leaves, the other needles. But even this classification is misleading. For example, poplar and aspen are deciduous and qualify for a "hardwood" rating. However, their wood is much softer than that of the Red or Norway pine, which, since it is an evergreen, rates as a "softwood." If you're completely puzzled at this point, you are not alone. You have probably concluded that a camp cook needs a degree in forestry.

Actually, identifying the various species isn't *that* difficult. A few days afield with an experienced woodsman will soon have you differentiating between fir and spruce, pine and hemlock, maple and hickory. Most forestry and conservation agencies issue pamphlets describing tree growth in their respective regions, and with the help of one of these, you'll soon learn to recognize major species. An acquaintanceship with six or eight fuel woods will elevate you to the rank of expert, especially among the millions who think that *all* evergreens are "pine trees!"

Trees, like people, have individual characteristics. Some, too, bear watching when used as fuel, because they "snap, crackle, and pop," tossing sparks about freely. These can burn holes in tents, sleeping bags, packs, and clothing, to say nothing of igniting the woods! They are box elder, cedar, chestnut (now rare), balsam fir, hemlock, the pines, sassafras, the spruces, and tulip.

A few species toss sparks when first ignited but soon settle down to steady burning. These include rock maple, beech, white oak, and hickory.

Some green woods burn reluctantly, so much so that they are almost "fireproof!" Even in their obstinacy they are useful since they can be used for fire dogs, andirons, fireplace walls, and cranes. They burn eventually, of course, but it's a slow process. They are:

Aspen	Box elder	Hemlock	Spruces
Balsam fir	Buckeye	Persimmon	Tamarack
Basswood	Butternut	Pin oak	Tulip
Black ash	Cottonwood	Pines	Willow
Black haw	Elm	Poplar	

It is by no means an infallible premise, but the wood of trees growing in low, wet areas such as swamps or streamsides, is generally a "slow burner." Those found on dry hillsides usually burn well.

The ideal fuel wood burns with a minimum of smoke, creates intense heat without sparks, leaves a bed of long-lasting coals. The ultimate wood ignites easily and burns well, green or seasoned. I've never met a woodsman who didn't agree that hickory qualifies on all counts! It is our finest firewood. After hickory comes an area of disagreement even among experts. Most of us are inclined to favor woods with which we are familiar. My own experience has been primarily with northern species, and on the basis of this, I've listed the following in the order of *my* preference. There's probably just cause for disagreement but there's little doubt that all of these are *excellent* firewoods!

White ash	Rock maple	Pecan	White birch
Hickory	Black birch	Post oak	Mulberry
White oak	Chestnut oak	Apple	Osage orange
Yellow birch	Overcup oak	Locust	Hornbeam
Beech	Black oak	Holly	

Burning firewood is one thing; cutting it is another. Hardwood, as a rule, is tougher than softwood and requires greater effort with an axe and saw. Some woods are difficult to split, the grain often twisted and gnarled. Northerners have an advantage over Southerners; *all* woods split more easily when frozen. If you maintain a permanent campsite to which you return year after year, cut your wood during the winter and stack it loosely to season.

A few firewoods are the devil's own chore to split when they are seasoned but can be "manufactured" quite easily when green. These are: hickory, beech, dogwood, rock maple, white birch, and young-growth yellow birch. Some are obstinate, green *or* seasoned, including box elder, buckeye, cherry, hemlock, sweet gum, honey locust, sycamore, tupelo, and old-growth yellow birch.

No neat, orderly chart can be devised to pinpoint the virtues or shortcomings of various woods. Whether or not a species is useful depends upon the use to which it will be put. Many a woodsman has a favorite firewood, sometimes unorthodox. Alders, for example, are a nuisance to most people, especially stream fishermen, but the wood produces a quick, hot fire with negligible smoke. White ash burns readily, green or seasoned, the most easily ignited of all hardwoods. Cedar, when seasoned—and it dries quickly—is the most flammable, a delight to split, and its smoke has an aroma that must rank with that of sweet grass! Even the lowly poplar has its uses. When well seasoned, it gives quick heat but creates no soot to soil pots.

"Dry-ki" is driftwood left high and dry along lakeshores by receding waters. Small pieces are often good cookfire fuel, while heavier chunks produce varicolored flames for an evening camp-fire. Useful firewood, then, is where you find it.

If I seem to have dwelt rather heavily upon the importance of knowing one tree from another, there is good reason. Firstly, it's fun to know and understand your environment; secondly, a knowl-edge of woods eases camp chores, makes for greater comfort, adds depth to your forest experience; and, finally, from the forest can come all you need for survival—shelter, warmth, and even food.

BUILDING A FIRE

This is the era of specialization, even on campsites! We even have "special" fires—the Teepee, the Log Cabin, the Lazy Man's, the Self-Feeding, the Hunter's, and, for all I know, someone will come up with a Leaky-Canoe Fire!

When conditions are right, a child can ignite almost any com-bination of tinder and kindling, but when the chips are down—and wet—this romantic gibberish has a hollow ring and a penchant for failure. The Teepee Fire topples, scattering its flames; the Log Cabin Fire burns out in the center, leaving the "walls" barely scorched; the Lazy Man's Fire is no such thing—the butts will not burn without heaps of added fuel; and, as for the Self-Feeding Fire, it's about as reliable as a seven-dollar shotgun. I need not repeat my earlier critique of the Hunter's Fire.

Firebuilding should be a simple procedure. Cut your entire supply of tinder, kindling, and fuelwood in advance so that you won't have to chop and saw when you should be tending your fire or cooking. Split kindling fine, especially if damp or slightly green. In building the fire, remember that it needs air *underneath*. If you pile kindling on top of the tinder, the latter will be crushed to the ground, cutting off its air supply. Instead, lay a single stick of wood—2″ to 3″ in diameter, in the fireplace. Pile tinder loosely next to this, on the *windward* side. Now rest two or three sticks of kindling over the tinder. Add five or six more, in a helter-skelter fashion. Light the tinder as close to the ground as possible on the *windward* side. This will blow the infant flame *into* the fire. With kindling resting on the base stick, it cannot fall further and crush the tinder. Air circulates underneath and you get a full draft. Firebuilding is *that* simple.

When adding wood, *place* it; don't toss it. Set it on the fire crisscross fashion, not closely paralleling, which cuts off updraft. Anticipate your needs. Hardwood takes a little time to reach its full heat potential, so don't overload your fire. When it "takes off" you'll have a conflagration! A skilled woodsman gets as much heat from as little firewood as possible.

A cookfire is converted to an evening campfire simply by removing the fireplace grate and adding wood. However, don't burn choice, well-seasoned hardwood the cook can put to better use. Burn odds and ends of dubious value—partially rotted logs, pieces of stump, knotty or gnarled chunks, or heavy forks you've been unable to split.

NIGHT FIRES

Many experts frown on a night fire. It's dangerous, they say. It may burn down your tent or spread into the woods while you sleep. You can be sure that such proclamations come from "authorities" who have done little camping! When the night is cool, I like a fire, especially if I'm using my Whelen tent. With proper hardwood, no sparks fly. And as a fire warden who has had his shirt and shoes burned beyond salvage in forest fires, I learned long ago that night brings humidity except on rare occasions. I have seen forest fires that raged uncontrollably during the day—we ran for our lives once—die down at night, creeping at a pace that would irritate a patient snail. Skillfully arranged, a night fire is 99 and $44/100$ per cent safe. I'm willing to risk the remaining $56/100$ per cent, even while I sleep.

Judgment is called for, of course. When a high wind persists into the night, forgo a fire after you retire. When the forest floor is unusually dry (if it's dusty when you kick it, it's *much* too dry!), skip the fire.

But when the dew is heavy, the night still, and the air bone-chilling, the all-night fire is a woodsman's companion. It's for use with an open-front tent or when you're sleeping under the stars. There's no point to a fire if you bed down in a fully enclosed shelter. A night fire requires a deep bed of glowing coals, possibly left over from the evening campfire. Pile five or six logs on these, three directly on the coals, two atop these, mixed with a few sticks of smaller hardwood. Knot and limb stubs will keep the logs from nesting together too close, so pile them pyramid style. You won't get a roaring blaze at any time during the night, just a slow, steady fire that casts a warm glow. Such a fire, however, casts little warmth beyond five or six feet.

Few night fires will last until daylight. But I count among some of the richest moments of my life those that I have spent at about 4 A.M., replenishing the fire. Slip on a heavy shirt, light up a pipeful. Listen to the river whispering nearby, or to an owl's predawn challenging hoot. Life is full at such a moment. Then, back to bed until daylight.

When it comes to using fire in the forest, keep your life simple, uncomplicated, uncluttered with impractical nonsense, ever mindful of the responsibility that rests on your shoulders when you strike a match.

WOOD STOVES

For cold-weather camping, a portable wood stove is a marvel of efficiency both for heating and cooking. These are sheet-metal burners, some folding, some solid, which can be set up in a tent with a smokestack running through a fireproof "smoke hole" sewed into the tent top or side. No heat is quicker, not even modern thermostatically controlled systems, and even on a cold day, a small fire will keep most tents warm.

Such stoves can be set directly on the ground on short legs or they can be perched on four stakes, at a height convenient for the cook. All are equipped with dampers, and spark arresters are available for use during dry periods. Stovepipe usually nests or telescopes for carrying.

My own is a Sims, made in Wyoming. It folds compactly into a heavy canvas bag, including the stovepipe, an extension shelf, and

A Sims wood-burning stove and reflector oven. Complete outfit folds and fits into canvas carrying bag. Photo by Eleanor Riviere.

a collapsible oven. Total weight is about thirty-five pounds, and despite its having been battered on countless jeep trails for close to ten years, the interlocking sections still fit well enough so that I can assemble it in about three minutes.

The most famous of the wood stoves is the Sheepherder, one model having a built-in oven at the rear of the firebox. The stove-pipe, when dismantled, fits into the stove. Another type is the Raemco, which, like the Sheepherder, is a solid, non-collapsible model, available with such accessories as a separate oven and extension legs.

These stoves are at their best in a Wall tent although they can be used in almost any type of large tent. Cooking can be done under cover in bad weather and all-night heat is possible with safety, something that cannot always be said of other types of stoves and tent heaters. Some precautions are required. Set the stove at least 18″ from the nearest canvas wall and guy the outside sections of the stovepipe with wire to prevent the wind from loosening them. Make sure, too, that the smokestack extends above the tent ridge or peak to minimize the danger of sparks lighting on the tent top and to eliminate downdraft.

When used for the first time on a trip, spread a half-inch of sand or soil on the bottom of the firebox to keep this from burning out. Also, don't be too diligent about cleaning out the ashes, once they start to accumulate. Leave an inch or two. This helps hold the fire.

When loading the stove for an all-night fire, be sure there's a substantial bed of coals, then stack the stove well with hardwood. Close both the stack damper and the front draft tightly. Whether the fire lasts all night will depend on the wood you're using. During a winter at Nine Mile Bridge on Maine's St. John River, we were limited to spruce and poplar, both green. The spruce alone would smolder for an hour or two, then suddenly erupt with a great burst of short-lived heat. The poplar alone sizzled for hours, but produced little warmth. So we combined the two. The poplar slowed the spruce and our fires usually lasted most of the night.

Don't be dismayed if the attractive coat of paint on your new stove turns to rust after the first use. It's of little consequence. If you're the fussy type, clean the stove with steel wool and oil it lightly before storage. I've never bothered. My stove looks as if it barely survived the battle of Little Big Horn, but it's still a marvel of efficiency.

MATCHES

What's to be said about matches carried on a wilderness camping trip that hasn't already been said a thousand times? Dip kitchen matches in paraffin to waterproof them; carry them in a water-proof match safe—there's no need to repeat further suggestions.

Here, however, are some thoughts that have come from actual

wilderness experience. If you smoke, carry *two* match supplies: a handful of wooden matches in a shirt pocket, easy to get at, and an emergency supply in a waterproof case. The latter, however, are *never* raided to light a pipe or cigarette! The supply in the emergency case should be inviolate; certainly not used for anything as prosaic as smoking! Save them for a *genuine* emergency.

The bulk of the camp matches should be placed in custody of the cook and if he's wise in the ways of the backwoods, he'll have them safely stashed inside a friction-top can sealed with waterproof tape. He can dole them out as you need them, and he always has some at hand for his firebuilding chores. What's more, such a can is not easy to mislay! A pocket match safe is.

Lest you think you can fall back on fire by friction or flint and steel in an emergency, I would suggest that you try these stunts *before* they become necessary. I've never had much success with flint and steel, frankly, but I have made fire with a bow and drill. It is *not* easy!

As for techniques used in making fire by friction, there's little point to describing these here. They are aptly illustrated in scouting manuals.

Chapter 7

SMOKY POTS

There's nothing like hickory smoke to flavor food and I've no serious objections to a few bits of charred maple in my corn chowder. The ultimate in food, I'm convinced, is produced over a wood fire. However, the camp stove can't be discounted completely. A backpacker, for example, who must often cook above timberline *needs* a stove—one that is light and compact, on which he can rely to provide maximum heat from minimum fuel. There are such stoves, all made in Europe, the best of them burning gasoline or naphtha interchangeably.

Among these, the Optimus is a favorite. Mine weighs less than two pounds, requires no pumping, boils a quart of water in about seven minutes. When closed it measures a mere 5″×5″×3″. A slightly larger version is made, weighing about three pounds. It must be pumped but its one-quart boiling time is only four minutes. Another excellent import is the Svea stove, rivaling the speed of the smaller Optimus yet weighing barely over one pound. These stoves are miniatures, of course, and they limit the size of utensils. Compact one- and two-man cook kits are available. The Svea stove, in fact, fits into a nesting kit that includes two kettles and a lid that doubles as a fry pan, the entire outfit measuring a bare 8½″ in diameter and 5″ high. Other miniature cook kits include Teflon-lined fry pans. And for carrying fuel, there are one- and two-quart spun-aluminum bottles with leakproof caps.

The variety of ultra-lightweight utensils matches that of standard camp cooking gear in every way except size and weight. Miniaturization has come to canteens, collapsible water carriers, provision boxes, food containers, egg carriers, even tubes from which you can squeeze peanut butter or jelly! Catalogs issued by mountaineering outfitters describe dozens of practical miniatures. Nor must these be limited to backpacking trips. They're handy in any backwoods camp as auxiliary utensils.

COOK KITS

Most professional outdoor cooks—the western pack train food wrangler, the northwoods canoe-trip guide, big-game outfitters—all of these invariably have assembled cook kits of their favorite utensils. I've never known an expert campfire cook to use one of the so-called camper's cook kits exclusively. Generally, such kits have great sales appeal but mighty little practical application. Most are made of aluminum. The kettles are excellent—and that's the extent of my praise for aluminum cook kits! For meals with a high liquid content such as soups or stews, aluminum kettles are fine. Their covers, which are supposed to double as frying pans are atrocious, because they develop "hot spots" which cause sticking. Teflon linings help somewhat and some kits include these. In the past, cook kit makers were criticized for supplying aluminum cups that burned the lips when used with hot drinks; so they now include plastic cups that give coffee a polyethylene flavor! Aluminum dinner plates are standard, too, but they cool foods so rapidly that sausage patties become mounds of cold, jellied fat before you can finish eating them. Except for kettles and their lids, when Teflon-lined, nesting kits can be considered failures.

The best cook kit is one which you assemble yourself. The utensils to be included depend upon the type of backwoods camping you're headed for. A cast-iron dutch oven, for example, is a favorite on western pack train jaunts, but it's hardly suitable for an extensive canoe trip due to its great weight. In this chapter you will find described just about every utensil used by professional, or expert/amateur outdoors cooks. Choose your cook kit items from among these suggestions and you'll soon be known as a camp cook who knows his way among pots and pans!

You won't have to buy a nesting aluminum kit to acquire the kettles. These are available separately, with flat lids which do *not* convert to skillets. Sizes vary from one to fourteen quarts and there are cloth bags for each size. The kettles will nest even when "wearing" the cloth bags, so that the kettles need not be washed free of soot each time they are packed. Be sure that kettles have wire bails, not wood or plastic handles which burn or melt over a fire.

Fastidious campers go to a great deal of trouble to keep their utensils shining like new. They soap the exteriors or daub them with aerosol shaving cream before use so that the soot washes off easily. Others scrub for hours, all of which is needless effort. Blackened pots heat more evenly and the time used in scrubbing can be put to more interesting use in the woods! I once loaned my outfit, black as a villain's heart, to friends who expressed their appreciation by returning them shiny as Christmas tree ornaments. I had to blacken them all over again!

Most woods cooks include a five-gallon "boiler" in their kits. They usually improvise this by cutting the top out of a 9" square can about 14" high and adding a wire bail. Commercial chemicals are sold in such cans but by washing them well they can be made safe for use. They provide ample hot water and double as containers for other cooking gear. Some outfitters sell such cans which have been retinned for extra durability.

The woodsman's favorite kettle will cost you nothing. He makes a "tea pail" or "billy" from a No. 10 can, used in the hotel and restaurant trade. Adding a wire bail is a matter of minutes. I've

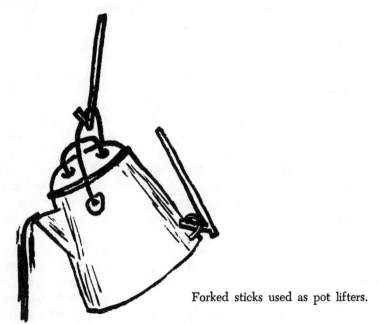

Forked sticks used as pot lifters.

used mine for boiling potatoes, making chowders, tea, coffee, and soup, and during more than one rough canoe crossing, as a bailing can! Smaller sizes, Nos. 2½ and 3, will nest within a No. 10 and are handy for minor cooking chores.

So-called "boiled" coffee can be made in any type of pot but unless using instant coffee, most campers prefer a legitimate coffee pot. In camp these differ from the household variety. The ideal pot has a wide base. Mine is 9″ in diameter at the bottom, tapering up to 6″. This lends stability and the wide bottom makes for quick heating. It has a friction-fit lid, pouring spout, bail handle, and best of all, a ring brazed near the bottom, on the opposite side from the pouring spout. This makes possible the use of a pair of forked sticks for pouring. (Figure opposite.) During the years that I worked as a guide we had such coffee pots made for us by local "tin knockers." However, an almost exact replica is now available in aluminum, equipped with a percolator basket, sold by Wearever.

Enamelware coffee pots, because their surfaces tend to chip, soon take on a battered appearance but they are, nevertheless, excellent for campfire coffee. Wide-based, equipped with a bail and pouring spout, they range from an eight-cup capacity to the giant fifty-four-cup "lodge-hall" size. They lack a percolator basket, though.

Coffee pots included in most cook kits are poor. They often lack a pouring handle and their vertical sides make for tippiness. Household pots with wood or plastic handles don't last long in camp.

Instant coffee is excellent camp fare and certainly a time- and bulk-saver. Occasionally, though, a cup of "guide's coffee" can highlight a campfire evening. Make it like this: Use one tablespoon of regular-grind coffee per cup, plus one or two "for the pot." Place in a mixing bowl and stir in one egg, shell and all, until the egg has been entirely absorbed into the coffee. In the meantime, bring the water in the pot to a vigorous boil. Dash the egg-soaked coffee into this and allow it to "roll" gently a minute or so. Then set the pot back to keep it from further boiling and add a cup of cold water. This will settle the grounds quickly.

The busiest utensil in camp is the frying pan, skillet, or spider, call it what you will. And for good reason. It's versatile—usable as a shallow kettle, grill, or baker, as well as for frying. Highly practical and the least expensive is the old-fashioned pressed-steel fry pan, selling from $1.98 and up at most hardware stores. It has a "stay cool" handle that really works. Fry pans with folding handles, or sockets into which a green stick can be inserted are sold by most outfitters. A 12″ pan will do for four persons but they're available up to 22″ in diameter!

The finest of all skillets are made of cast iron. My own favorites are 9″ square and weigh about 5 pounds each. Following our first camping trip my wife absconded with mine for use in our home kitchen. I replaced them quickly. Cast iron heats evenly and retains heat long after being removed from the fire. Larger sizes are available in the round style.

Disposable aluminum frying pans are more of a nuisance than a help. They're none too sturdy, expensive, and present a disposal problem. If you dislike washing a skillet, line a conventional frying pan with aluminum foil. The liner can be disposed of by laying it flat over the campfire flames, which will melt it into a tiny glob which can then be carried out with other indestructible waste.

To an apprentice campfire cook, frying over flames seems logical. It isn't. Heat is uneven and the flames often ignite the grease in the pan. Instead, fry on a shallow bed of coals. Rake these from the campfire if necessary. There'll be no flare-up and the heat will be constant.

A skillet is also an efficient "oven," especially for baking bannock, the old-time woodsman's substitute for bread. He made it from a thin biscuit dough, doubling the usual amount of shortening. He poured the dough into a well-greased skillet and held the latter a foot or two over the fire until the dough started to rise. When this was "set," he propped the skillet near-vertically close to the fire. When the bannock crusted, he sometimes removed it from the pan and propped it against a rock for continued baking, using the skillet for a second batch. In this manner, he baked a week's supply of "bread" in an hour. Today's bannock is more likely to be made with Bisquick and frankly it's just as tasty. I prefer a thicker dough, however, formed into a large "doughnut" in the pan so that it will bake more quickly.

During my initial days as a guide, I was amazed to see that some of the best cooks carried a cast-iron "fry kittle," a french fryer complete with basket and bail handle, used for shore luncheons during daily fishing jaunts. French-fried potatoes and onion rings, it seems, rated almost as high as a record trout! However, a french fryer isn't necessary. Deep-frying can be done in a skillet, with potatoes or onions removed with a kitchen fork. Incidentally, if you'd like to attain fame as a woods cook, dip your onion rings in pancake batter before deep-frying. When the batter is golden brown, lay the rings out to cool and drain. Then step back to avoid the rush.

Despite its weight, a cast-iron griddle has a place in a fixed camp. I've tried those of aluminum and magnesium but invariably they warped, and scorched foods. Full appreciation of a griddle comes at breakfast time, when it turns out eggs, bacon, and flapjacks, all hot and ready to eat simultaneously. I wouldn't want to tote one over Rocky Hill portage, but an excellent griddle can be improvised from a small sheet of ¼" steel plate.

THE REFLECTOR OVEN

Without a baker of some sort, a camp cook quickly acquires the reputation for being either a "boiler" or a "sizzler," serving only meals that are boiled, stewed, or fried. This leaves a gap in the menu. Carrying "store-bought" baked goods is out of the question during an extended trip. That's where the reflector oven shines, literally.

It has been around since the late 1700s, when it was a "tin kitchen" used in front of a firepace to roast meats, or to bake bread, cake, and muffins. In the woods, it later became known as a "shed baker," and despite the coming of modern stoves, it never completely disappeared. Cooks on log drives used a four-foot model for mass producing saleratus biscuits, northwoods guides used them to feed their "sports," and finally, modern campers adopted it. The reflector oven can't be considered indispensable, but I know few skilled woods cooks who don't use one.

A brisk fire is necessary, with flames approximately the height of the oven. Coals are inadequate. The heat of the flames is reflected from the sloping walls of the oven onto the ingredients placed on the center shelf. The oven is positioned 6" to 12" from the fire. Heat control is visual and easy. To increase heat, move the oven closer to the fire; to decrease it, back the oven away. It's so simple it seems haphazard. But it's not. In 1964 I ran a series of tests with various reflectors, one of which attained 600 degrees within ten minutes!

Sometimes the muffins get scorched! Note aluminum foil used to line rusted oven. Obviously it worked! Photo by Eleanor Riviere.

One of the most efficient is the Sims, with an $11'' \times 15''$ shelf, large enough for a twelve-cup muffin tray. It is made by the Sims Stove Co., Lovell, Wyoming. The Swedish Trangia oven has an $8\frac{1}{2}'' \times 18''$ shelf with a hinged back panel, which, when lifted, allows the proceedings to be viewed conveniently. All three of these fold compactly. My river driver's oven is nearly 4' long and stands 18" tall, does not fold, is rusted and battered (I've no idea how old it is). In it I've baked corn bread, biscuits, a pie, and a meatloaf, simultaneously. It's much too large for a camping trip, but it's a marvel to behold at a fixed-camp cookfire!

The more highly polished the inside reflective surfaces, the more efficient the oven will be. Because of this, aluminum is a good choice. However, tinned iron and sheet steel are sturdier, although they will discolor or rust in time. This needn't deter you. Lining the inner walls with aluminum foil boosts efficiency about 30 per cent. This is *not* an estimate. I ran tests to find out!

Northwoods guides formerly used non-collapsible ovens, made locally to their specifications with watertight seams so that they could also use their ovens as dishpans! If this seems untidy, it was a simple matter to rinse the oven, then "sterilize" it by the fire. This not only doubled the use of the oven, but it kept the interior surface clean and polished.

A solid metal shelf in the oven is preferable to a wire rack or rods on which to set baking tins. The solid shelf helps prevent scorching on the underside. Another type of oven to be avoided is one without sides. There's no problem on a still day, but even the slightest breeze will carry away heat that should be working for you. Temporary sides can be devised with aluminum foil, however. Seek an oven that does not sit too high. The taller it is, the higher the shelf must be, and the greater the blaze you'll need.

Virtually anything that can be baked or roasted in a household oven can be duplicated in a reflector. The easiest are corn bread, biscuits, gingerbread, and cakes from prepared mixes. Raised rolls and bread are a little trickier but far from impossible. Pies are not difficult if your fire is steady.

One common problem is the browning or raising of batter at the front faster than at the back. Move the oven back a trifle, until browning and rising are even. Turn the pan occasionally, too. Small cuts of meat can be roasted; meatloaf and casseroles are easy. Cooking time varies according to the oven and the constancy of your fire but averages about the same as the time required in a kitchen oven. Once cooking has started, keep the fire going steadily, with flames reaching just about to the top of the oven.

THE DUTCH OVEN

The cast-iron dutch oven is a favorite of western outdoor cooks, professional and amateurs alike. They use the oven for baking, as a soup or stew kettle, or as a bean pot; some even use it as a dishpan. These dutch ovens are not the glorified soup kettles of aluminum with glass tops found in modern kitchens. The camper's version has three short legs, a bail handle, and a cover with a flanged rim. Sizes run from 8″ diameter up to 16″; weight, from 7 pounds up to 30.

Cast-aluminum dutch ovens are lighter and there are several on the market—where they should remain. They are decidedly inferior to cast iron due to aluminum's "hot spot" trouble and because they cool too rapidly when removed from the fire.

Baking with a cast-iron dutch oven is simplicity itself. Rake a 12″ to 16″ pad of glowing coals from the campfire and set the oven over these. The three legs will keep it from resting too heavily on the coals. Heap more coals, to a depth of about 2″, onto the cover. These will be held in place by the flanged rim. Allow the oven to preheat. Estimating the temperature of the oven and the required baking time is difficult at first. This knack will come with experience, but in the meantime, it's permissible to use an oven thermometer.

Try simple recipes initially, as with a reflector oven—corn bread or biscuits. These may be baked directly on the bottom of the oven if the latter is greased lightly. Pie plates may be used even if made of aluminum. The cast iron's ability to heat evenly will counter aluminum's shortcomings in this case.

The oven can also be used for pan-broiling, frying, and deep-frying, sautéing. Casseroles, soups, and stews take on a delectable flavor. For bean-hole beans, no pot surpasses the dutch oven.

A new oven should be "seasoned" before using, and this is true of a new cast-iron skillet or griddle. Manufacturers "pre-season" them, but inadequately. Rub the interior surface with an unsalted fat such as lard, then allow the oven to stand at room temperature overnight. The iron will absorb the grease. Wipe it with a clean cloth and repeat the process but don't apply fat too lavishly—just enough to grease the surface. The more often you use the oven, the better it will become seasoned, until it acquires a smooth, glazelike finish. The flavor of food seems to improve, too, with each use!

Ideally, a cast-iron utensil should never be washed, and if used exclusively for baking, wiping is all that's needed. If used for foods that leave a sticky residue, scrape these out gently, then wash lightly with hot water and a mild dishwashing liquid. Never apply

Biscuits in a dutch oven. Note coals on cover and forked stick used to lift it. Photo by Eleanor Riviere.

a detergent or strong soap, and least of all, a scouring pad.

An old oven, or one that has become rusted, can be restored. Scour the rust gently with fine steel wool and wash. Then apply a thin layer of lard, wiping this out after an hour or so. Repeat until the interior surface is clean and smooth. Then season it.

BROILING

Broiling a steak or chops calls for the simplest of all camp cooking techniques. Simply place the meat directly on a bed of hardwood coals and turn it over when it's about half done to your liking. If this seems crude and primitive, it is. But you'll rarely enjoy meat that tastes any better! Bits of ashes and coals can be brushed off easily.

The results of broiling on a spit are almost as delicious. During a four-day woods patrol, I once lived entirely on grouse breasts, roasted on a green maple twig and washed down with tea. Spit cooking is usually of the shish-kebab variety, with meat, onion, potato or other vegetables impaled on a green stick in alternating layers. However, don't hold it *over* the fire. Mount the stick on a pair of short forked branches stuck into the earth *beside* the fire, close enough to cook but far enough away so that drippings don't drop into the flames. In this way, you can catch the drippings in a pan or piece of aluminum foil.

Spit cooking may also include whole fish, impaled lengthwise after cleaning; even chops, fillets, or steaks. Wrapping a heavy dough around a green stick results in a pretty fair "twist bread" or "wrap-around biscuit." Incidentally, use hardwood for a spit. Softwoods impart a "Christmas tree" flavor. Choose one of the sweet woods, if possible—maple, cherry, hickory, ash.

Broiling, baking, or roasting without utensils is occasionally fun, sometimes even a necessity, but the serious camp cook isn't likely to become permanently enchanted by the novelty. Certain implements are necessities for consistently good camp meals.

One of these is the wire broiler, which looks much like an old-time toaster. Newer versions can be adjusted to accommodate cuts of meat up to two inches thick, and they can be used for chicken, hamburger, chops, fish, even frankfurts, plus many cuts of wild game and fowl.

The wire broiler is at its best with steaks and chops, whether they be beef, pork, moose, elk, or deer, and a master woods chef will broil these *vertically*. He does *not* place the broiler *over* the fire in a horizontal position.

The flavor of meat lies principally within its fats and juices. Meat that is cooked horizontally over an open fire loses much of these since they have only the thickness of the meat through which to run before dropping into the flames, where they cause a "flare-up." Placing the meat in a vertical position, *with the fatty edge uppermost* minimizes this loss since the juices must then run through the *width* or *length* of the cut before dropping. Also, as the fatty edge cooks, the melting fats run down over the meat slowly to baste it and to impart further flavor. Even these juices which

Broiling a steak in a vertical broiler. Aluminum foil wrapped about its base catches drippings. Photo by Eleanor Riviere.

do escape can be recaptured by forming a drip pan of aluminum foil about the base of the broiler.

Certain meats, particularly wild game such as deer and moose, are quite dry. You can moisten these and add flavor by draping two or three strips of bacon over their top edge after placing them in the broiler.

This type of broiling calls for a brisk flame, not coals. The broiler can be leaned against the fireplace grate or propped with a stick. And the broiler can be turned easily with a forked stick "pot lifter." If there is a better method for broiling, I have as yet to run into it.

BEAN-HOLE BEANS

Canned beans compare with those baked in the ground about as well as a billboard on a barn compares to a Picasso! At a fixed or semi-permanent camp, every ounce of energy expended in the digging of a bean hole is worthwhile.

The depth and width of the pit depend upon the utensils to be used. It should provide space enough so that 6″ to 8″ of coals are under the kettle and 4″ to 6″ around it. None are placed on top. However, 12″ to 16″ of soil are needed to seal the pit. During several years I maintained not one, but three bean holes for use with 14″ cast-iron dutch ovens. After lining the pits with rocks, the opening was about 3′ deep, 30″ across the top, and 18″ to 20″ at the bottom. Rocks are not essential, but they will keep the walls from crumbling and they hold heat well. The bottom should be lined, too. Old-time bean-hole specialists in lumber camps used a length of boom chain for a bottom liner. Once the chain or the rocks are heated, they remain hot until long after the beans have been eaten!

An adequate supply of glowing coals is the secret to success. Burn a brisk hardwood fire in the pit until the coals are 12″ to 16″ deep. All but 6″ are then removed (a spade is handy for this) and the pot inserted into the hole, resting on coals. The remaining coals are then packed *around* the kettle. A snug-fitting cover is essential, lest dirt seep into the pot. Lacking such a cover, use foil to overlap the edges of the lid. At this point, place a layer of sod or wet burlap over the pot, then fill in the hole, sealing it well. This helps achieve the ultimate in flavor, since none can escape by evaporation. It is literally locked in! If a tiny plume of smoke seeps from the hole, you have a leak and your coals won't last. Repack the fill.

Excavating the pot requires care. Be gentle with the shovel. A wise precaution is to bury the kettle with its bail in an upright position so that you can grasp it with a forked stick for the lift-out.

This is not intended to be a cookbook but a good bean-hole recipe is hard to come by. Here is mine: Soak the dry beans overnight; any kind will do—pea, yellow eye, soldier, or red kidney

How the bean hole should look just before being sealed. Foil seals dirt out, raised bail will make lifting the dutch oven easier when beans are done. Photo by Eleanor Riviere.

—first culling them for impurities such as tiny stones. In the morning, while the bean hole is firing up, parboil the beans in fresh water until their jackets start to curl or peel. For two pounds of beans, mix ¾ cup of molasses, three tablespoons of brown sugar, and one teaspoon each of dry mustard and salt, stirred well into 1½ cups of hot water. When placing the beans in the pot, alternate layers of beans with layers of sliced onions and salt pork, the latter cut about ½″ thick. Pour in the molasses-brown sugar mixture, add hot water to just below the level of the beans. With the cover on securely, the pot is ready for the pit. Don't worry about the water boiling away. It can't if the pit is sealed properly.

Allow six to eight hours for baking. It would take a Lord Byron to describe the aroma that accompanies an "opening" and a Bedouin belch to voice due appreciation of the flavor that follows!

OTHER HANDY IMPLEMENTS

The handiest of camp cooking implements costs nothing. It's the forked stick used as a pot lifter. Virtually any hardwood will do, alder and maple probably the most common in the North. This can be used for lifting pots and pouring (see page 138) and I never hesitate to use one for stirring.

Every camp cook has a dozen shortcuts. He's learned that saucepans and double boilers are excess baggage in camp. A tea pail will serve as well for a saucepan, and two tea pails, one inside the other with two or three small pebbles between them, comprise an excellent double boiler. A soup ladle doubles as a dipper. A sheath knife will whittle a pot hook, slice meat, or spear a chop from the skillet. A maple shoot or pliant hazel, ash, or alder can be bent to form a pair of tongs. An overturned canoe can serve as a breadboard on which to roll or knead dough, as does a clean dish towel on a jeep hood or fender. A canister set for loose tea, coffee, sugar, flour, or salt can be improvised with an assortment of friction-top cans, each labeled with a magic marker.

Improvisation can be carried too far. I once forgot a can opener and resorted to my axe, which explains the scar on my thumb. A scoutmaster once proudly showed me his dishpan—a shallow pit lined with plastic. I didn't enthuse. I hate doing dishes on my hands and knees!

Watch the professionals at a cookfire for other suggestions. Minnesota guides, for example, use "dish-ups" (nesting metal bowls) for a dozen purposes—mixing wild salads, as serving dishes, for storing leftovers, or as dippers! And I've never seen a skilled campfire cook without a long-handled kitchen fork and spoon.

Cotton or plastic food bags are handy, too, in one-, two-, and five-pound sizes. One outfitter labels these at no extra cost. Several can be packed into a larger waterproof vinyl sack, a sound precaution for canoe travelers.

A plywood chuck box isn't out of place in the backwoods. I use one for toting utensils and grub in my jeep, and at the campsite it doubles as a cupboard while keeping out small marauders such as squirrels and mice. Some chuck boxes have rounded bottoms to fit the contours of a canoe. For mule, burro, or packhorse travel, kyacks, or panniers of canvas or plywood, are close to indispensable.

For dinnerware, I prefer enamelware to plastic, and as I've already indicated, to aluminum. Enamelware plates can be preheated, hold their heat reasonably well, and are easily washed, although rough use in the dishpan may chip them. For coffee or tea it's difficult to improve on china mugs. Enamel soup bowls double as cereal bowls or dessert dishes. Stainless steel knives, forks, and spoons are inexpensive and available in individually cased sets. Serving platters are generally impractical in camp since they won't keep foods warm while the first serving is being eaten, unless left on the fireplace. However, I once knew a guide who served meals in style—on the the covers of twenty-five-pound lard pails!

It stands to reason, of course, that not *all* of the utensils I've described can be included in a single kit. Nor have I limited suggestions because of weight or bulk. Choose those items which best fit into your type of camping and your means of travel.

CAMP FOODS

Hundreds of freeze-dried and/or dehydrated ingredients are listed in outfitters' catalogs, along with innumerable prepackaged meals. There is little point to duplicating this information here except to point out that, as a rule, these foods are far tastier than might be supposed. During the summer of 1964 I lived for a week—twenty-one meals—on such foods, including orange juice crystals, scrambled eggs, sausage, beef stew, pork chops, chili con carne, chicken stew, shrimp creole, hash-brown potatoes, and other grub prepared essentially for backwoods consumption. My only disappointment was a steak which proved tougher than poverty down East!

Such specialized camp grub is more expensive than conventional supermarket fare but it must be remembered that waste has been removed, much of the preparation done, and in many instances, precooked, merely requiring reheating. Complete meals can be prepared in as little as ten minutes, although some dishes such as stews may require up to forty-five minutes. My only criticism is that portions are usually skimpy among the prepackaged meals. A four-man dinner, for example, is easily gobbled by three men and a boy!

For this reason I usually supplement them with additional fare from the supermarket shelves. This does not necessarily mean weighty canned goods. Food chains don't cater to campers specifically, but their shelves are literally loaded with grub suitable for backwoods cookery. You'll find no "freeze-dried" or "dehydrated" labels on them. They are now termed "instant" or "minute." You have only to stroll down one aisle and up another to see that the menu can be varied and interesting without your having to tote high-water-content canned foods. You can add the water yourself, at your campsite.

REFRIGERATION

At best, refrigeration during hot weather is a problem in the backwoods. Portable ice chests, insulated with urethane foam, are efficient, but ice dispensers are rare once you leave the paved road. Mountaineers use snowbanks and some campers are lucky enough to have access to a cool cavern. However, even the Far North can be extremely hot during parts of the summer. As a result, "bush fridges" have evolved. One of these consists of a box, screened against marauding raccoons and mink, weighted with rocks and partially sunk into a cool-running stream. Perishables are placed in the box just above water level. Another type of "refrigerator" is a box hanging over a stream or lakeshore, preferably in the shade, and draped with burlap which hangs into the water. Theoretically, the burlap draws up water just as a lampwick soaks up kerosene. The rising water evaporates, thus cooling the box and its contents.

For semi-perishables such as summer sausage, slab bacon, or margarine, this type of refrigeration is marginal at best. If foods are highly perishable, such improvisations are inadequate. The only solution to the backwoods refrigeration problem is to carry nonperishable foods, supplementing this fare with fresh fish or game in season.

Chapter 8

A BACKWOODSMAN'S TOOLS

It's traditional to point out that the axe represents warmth, shelter, food, even survival in the forest. But there's more. A kinship develops between a woodsman and his axe. No implement is so much a part of himself. His brawny arm and his axe handle share the same sinews. Maybe it's like a security blanket: always there, comforting, familiar, reliable. I suppose this is why I never leave the campyard without my Snow and Nealey three-pounder. I'd feel naked without it, and I don't give a hoot what any psychiatrist might make of this!

When it comes to choosing an axe, many newcomers to the outdoors are unduly influenced by writers, some of whom are not sure which end of the tool does the cutting. Recommendations are usually in the following order:

(1) the hatchet with a light head, 12″ to 18″ handle;
(2) the Hudson's Bay axe, 2- to 2½-lb. head, 24″ to 26″ handle;
(3) the poleaxe, 3-lb head, 26″ handle;
(4) the full axe, 3½- to 5-lb. head, 32″ to 36″ handle;
(5) the double-bit, either hatchet or axe.

The hatchet is not only the first to be recommended but it gets the most votes from pseudo-experts. Yet it's the *least efficient* and the *most dangerous* of all chopping tools used in the woods. Its short handle makes a two-hand grip difficult, if not impossible, thereby lessening control; it forces the chopper to stand or kneel dangerously close to his work, where a glancing blow can mean a gashed shin or crunched kneecap; and because of the light head, the hatchet does not bite deeply unless driven with considerable force. This makes for hard work, especially since only one arm is doing it. In fact, most logs cut with a hatchet appear to have been gnawed by a beaver with a toothache!

Hatchet users argue that they cut only small wood; the hatchet is adequate for this. True. But this wood can generally be broken by hand, so why bother with a hatchet? I've never known an

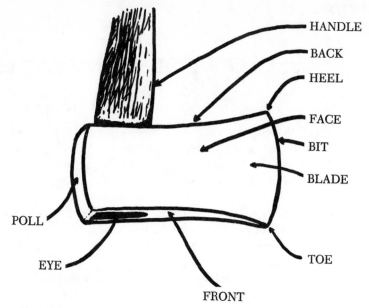

The parts of an axe.

experienced backpacker to carry one, because he can find ample firewood which can be broken with a twist of the wrist. A hatchet can be used for splitting, too, some users claim; but not if the block of wood is much more than 4″ to 6″ thick. Then there are youth leaders who insist that the hatchet is the only practical tool for youngsters. Actually, in the hands of most girl and boy scouts, the hatchet is doubly dangerous and inefficient because scouts generally receive notoriously poor axemanship training.

The final telling blow against the hatchet is the fact that no professional woodsman—guide, trapper, timber cruiser, logger, or woods surveyor—carries one. Only the romanticist—inept, and bungling at the woodpile—hangs one on his belt and walks like a sidehill gopher.

The Hudson's Bay axe is an improvement, as are the so-called stamp axe and the canoe axe with their 2- to 2½-pound heads and 24″ handles. In fact, these are pretty fair campers' tools for light work and often carried by professionals. But don't let anyone convince you that you can build a log cabin with one! For limited work such as you might encounter on a canoe trip or for clearing an

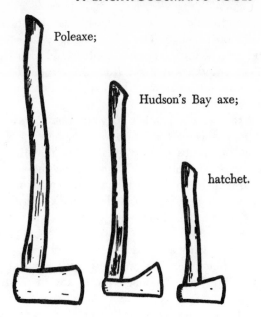

Poleaxe;

Hudson's Bay axe;

hatchet.

overgrown section of trail, these axes do well. The Hudson's Bay model has one slight drawback, though. Because of its narrow poll, the handle tends to work loose.

Once the techniques of axemanship are understood, the advantages of a heavier axe become apparent. Watch an amateur chopping with a hatchet. He uses the "grunt and groan" method, *driving* the axe head downward, usually with enough force to transmit a definite shock to his arms and shoulders with each blow. He wears himself out quickly and cuts relatively little wood. A skilled woodsman, on the other hand, swings his longer axe in a leisurely manner, *allowing the weight of the falling axe head to do the work.* He doesn't lean into each blow, nor does he grunt with each chip.

The longer handle and the heavier axe head give the cutting edge greater momentum with less effort. The chopper merely raises the axe, aims, and swings, letting the head fall as it completes a wide arc.

A 3-pound poleaxe with a 28″ handle is often referred to as a "pulp" axe since it is popular in the pulpwood cuttings. The term "poll" applies to any axe which has a flat hammer-like surface opposite the cutting edge. The longer handles of such axes afford a two-hand grip, which increases control and accuracy. And best of all you can stand safely away from the target area. A miss with a poleaxe *can* result in injury, this can't be denied, but the likelihood is minimized.

Critics of the poleaxe point to its weight as a drawback. Frankly, a 3-pound poleaxe *is* heavier than either the hatchet or the Hudson's Bay, but the difference isn't so great that I'm willing to forgo its efficiency to save a pound or so. The extra weight—and I'm referring to woods travel now, not backpacking or climbing—is hardly enough to wear out a rugged male. What's more, when I want to chop or split a log, I don't want to nibble at it. I want healthy chips to fly!

In the Upper Midwest and in the Northwest, 4- to 5-pound axe heads are not unusual, along with 32″ to 36″ handles. These are known as "full" axes. I can't criticize any man who can handle one well. For my taste, it's a mite too much axe for a camping trip. I settled long ago on a 3-pounder, and even in British Columbia, the domain of big axes, I found it more than adequate.

As for the double-bitted hatchet, it is hardly a camper's tool. George Washington Sears, the famed "Nessmuk," described his two-edged hatchet glowingly in his book *Woodcraft*. However, he failed to include specifications. Willis O. C. Ellis, writing in the May 1949 issue of *Field and Stream* described a hatchet similar to Nessmuk's. It had a 15½″ handle and weighed 1¾ pounds! Having had the effrontery to disagree with Nessmuk in the past on the matter of canoes and packbaskets, I might as well go on to further disagreement regarding hatchets. In Nessmuk's hands—he was a superb woodsman—the double-bitted hatchet was probably a good choice. In the hands of the average backwoods vacationer, it presents double jeopardy; the excellent possibility of injury on both the up *and* down swing!

There is some justification for a double-bitted axe with a 3½- to 4-pound head and a 30″ to 34″ handle, but only for use by an expert. Such an axe is useful in cabin building, the production of firewood, and for other heavy woods chores. One edge is ground thin for chopping; the other is beveled more thickly for splitting. The popular fallacy that it is used "in case one edge is nicked" is not correct. Each edge has a definite purpose.

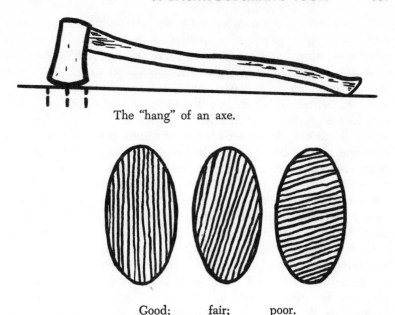

The "hang" of an axe.

Good;   fair;   poor.

Chances are your new axe will have a second-growth hickory handle, rugged yet resilient enough to absorb shock. How the handle is "hung" is important. To check this, hold the axe on a flat surface so that its bit and the knob at the end of the handle both touch. If the axe is well hung, the bit will touch at midpoint of its width. (See above.) Next, sight along the cutting edge, over the handle. Your line of sight should bisect the entire length of the handle, indicating that it is not warped. A crookedly handled axe is like a rifle with its sights out of kilter.

Avoid a handle that has been daubed with paint or lacquer. This probably hides defects. A handle that has sharply contrasting layers of light and dark wood is a candidate for splitting. Seek a clear, all-white wood with its grain vertical to the handle. A cross-grain handle is also likely to split.

The shape of an axe head is pretty much a question of geography. For instance, in the mixed hard- and softwoods of the Northeast, the Half Wedge, Michigan, or Dayton patterns are popular because their narrow bits bite deeply into hardwood. In softwood country, the wider bits have more appeal, the Jersey, Ohio, or

Western Crown, for example. A Cedar pattern has an extremely wide bit for chopping very soft woods.

Some woodsmen grind down the bevel that lies just back of the cutting edge on a new axe, grinding the axe so that it is thinner at the heel than at the toe. Such an axe will make chips fly without binding. However, once the factory bevel is removed from an axe, the guarantee is nullified.

A dull axe is a vicious tool, quick to glance, ever seeking a shin to gouge. What's more, it will double your labors. Getting an axe sharp enough to shave with may be a bit of theatrics, but even a slight nick along the edge will slow your work. An axe should be sharpened on a grindstone, not with a power grinding wheel. The latter's high speed will quickly ruin the temper in the steel cutting edge. Keep the grindstone wet and hold the axe so that the stone turns *into* the axe. Move the latter from side to side slowly so that grinding is even. Flop the axe frequently, too. The job is then completed with a hand stone, also kept dampened. Loggers carry a round pocket stone, about three inches in diameter, coarse-grained on one side, fine on the other. Preliminary honing is done with the coarse grit; a finished edge is applied with the fine one. To keep hand stones damp, loggers spit on them.

A flat file may be used in place of a grindstone. Lean the axe against a small log, edge uppermost and file *downward* along the edge. Don't draw the file back and forth. Use only a downward stroke. Finish the job with a hand stone.

Removing the remains of a broken handle from the eye of an axe can be a tedious chore. To while away a rainy afternoon at my lookout tower, I once shot the remains out with a .22 rifle but it required several boxes of ammunition! There are more practical, if less amusing, methods. One is to bury the axe in the ground, the poll protruding. Over this, build a small fire. This will char the remains of the handle, which, when cooled, will slip out easily. Burying the bit in the damp earth keeps the fire from destroying the temper.

You can then insert the new handle, striking the knob end of it with a wooden billet. If you use a hammer or another axe, you may split the new handle, or damage the edge of the knob. Striking the handle will drive it into the eye until it starts to bind. The high spots which cause this binding will be revealed by tiny shavings curling from the handle. Whittle these with a knife or cut

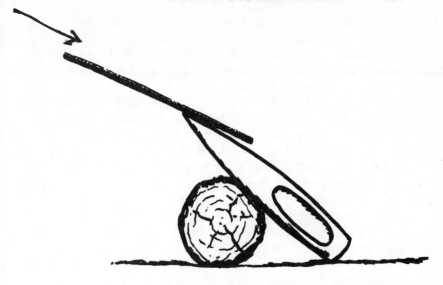

Stroke file downward only to sharpen an axe.

them down with a rasp. Repeat the process until the handle slips through the eye firmly and the "shoulder" of the handle is about ¾″ from the rear of the axe head. Be sure the "hang" is correct, then cut off the handle flush with the front edge of the head. Insert a wedge, either metal or wood. Drive this in until the handle is securely locked in the eye.

Tightening a loose handle calls for an additional wedge. Soaking the axe head in water until the handle swells, as often suggested, will tighten it only temporarily. Once dried out, it will be looser than ever.

No expert "plays" with an axe. I've never seen a professional woodsman pick one up needlessly. Only greenhorns swing an axe into a log "just to try it out," and only genuine "dubs" will cut down a tree "for practice." Axes are not playthings and they are not props for demonstrations of manliness. Nor are our forest reserves so vast that we can afford to play at being lumberjacks. Before you cut down a tree, be sure that you really *need* that tree and, of course, chop only where it is permitted. Then, when you approach with your axe, know what you are doing.

Before your first swing, check to see which way the tree is

leaning. Clever lumberjacks may fell trees uphill, but this is a tricky process which few non-professionals can handle. Fell the tree in the direction of its lean. Be sure, too, that once it is free of its stump, it will fall freely to the ground. If it hangs up in another tree, you're in trouble.

All brush and low-hanging limbs which might interfere with your axe swing should be cleared. Even a maple twig can deflect an axe. And if you want to live to see your tree fall, examine it for broken limbs. These are known in the logging woods as "turkeys," "widow makers," or "fool killers." Striking the tree with your axe may bring one of these down on your head. Choose another tree if this danger is apparent overhead, or try to drop the loose limbs with a long pole, standing away while you dislodge them.

On the subject of woods accidents, I don't have to theorize. I have personally known no fewer than eight lumberjacks who were killed or seriously injured in the woods. One, working on the same job with me, died when a "widow maker" struck him on the head. Another cut his foot so badly with an axe that he will limp the rest of his life. Still another was struck by a maple that "kicked back," and he died almost instantly. An early grave, disability, or permanent scars are par for the course in the lumber woods. Logging isn't a Ping-Pong match!

If it's safe to go ahead, start your undercut. This is the notch which will direct the fall of your tree and it is made just above the swelling of the stump. Don't make too narrow a cut or you'll find yourself chopping directly across the grain of the wood. Make this notch wide enough so that you can chop at a 45 degree angle. Cut approximately one third of the way through. Now, sit down and rest a few minutes before starting the falling cut, or notch. This one is made on the opposite side, about two inches higher, and in line with the undercut so that a thin section of wood remains between the two to serve as a "bridge" or hinge. As the falling cut deepens, listen for the crackling of wood fibers. The trunk will start to lean imperceptibly, at first. You'll hear it before you see it. Quit chopping. Only a greenhorn keeps swinging once the tree has started to fall. Step *to one side*, never to the rear. Move away without hurrying, but get to a safe distance without delay. Don't run. You may trip and fall. If you have gauged the tree well, and cut it properly, it will fall free and clear.

Never stand at the rear of the butt as a tree starts to drop.

Undercut at right; backcut at left.

It might hang up into another tree and shoot back across its stump with the speed and force of a cannonball. Hardwoods occasionally "slab" or split at the butt, then kick across the stump. One of my Maine neighbors died on a November afternoon when a maple did just that, catching him in the midriff.

Even experts "hang one up" occasionally. A favorite remedy among greenhorns is to walk up the trunk of the leaner, hoping their weight will drop the tree. It may. It may also cause it to roll, throwing the climber down, with a good chance of the trunk rolling over him! At best, a leaner is a dangerous proposition. Prying the butt backwards with a heavy sapling will often free it, but this means working close to the base of the trunk and it calls for a quick getaway when this drops. A more efficient method is to roll the butt with a peavey. This is really just as dangerous but it *is* easier. There is no quick, sure, easy, and safe method to handle a leaner. Except, perhaps, to make sure that it doesn't happen!

Once the tree is down, rest again. If these "rest spells" seem overly frequent to you, I suggest them because they are the habit of the professional. He "stops often and sets frequent," so that he's alert and fresh for each stage of the job. The next stage is limbing.

Start this at the butt end, striking each limb on its *underside,* cutting it off flush with the trunk. Stand on the opposite side of the trunk, too. In cutting branches which are lodged under the trunk, watch that they don't spring out at you as you cut them. Hardwood limbs especially are dangerous in this respect. Keep an eye on the trunk as you pare limbs from it. It may roll or settle. As you cut branches, toss them to one side.

Trim limbs from underside.

"Bucking," or cutting to length, comes next. For this a saw is far more practical than an axe: it produces squared ends, is faster and easier to use, and it reduces waste. If possible, roll the log up onto a set of "skids," saplings laid flat on the ground. Several such skids may be needed, depending upon the length of the log. They help to prevent the saw blade from binding.

Assuming you're using an axe to buck the log, make your notch— this is known as a "cow's mouth"—half as wide as the thickness of the log, chopping into each side of the notch at a 45 degree angle. When the notch is halfway through, roll the log over and notch it on the other side. If the log is so large that you can't roll it, double the size of the cow's mouth and chop it all the way through.

Splitting firewood is the axe's most common chore. If the firewood log has been cut to length with an axe, the pointed chunks won't stand on end for splitting. So lean them in the crotch of a "schoolma'am," a heavy, forked log. Lacking this, notch another log and lean the stick to be split in it. Never brace a chunk of wood with your foot.

When bucking a log with a saw, save the butt end for a chopping block. Chunks that have been cut with a saw can then be stood on the blocks for splitting. Don't aim at the center of such a chunk;

"Schoolma'am" keeps wood from rolling when splitting.

drive the axe in near its outside edge, giving the handle a slight side twist. This increases the splitting action of the head.

Hard-to-split chunks should be set aside for night wood, or for the evening campfire. Twisted, gnarled, or heavily knotted chunks are hard to split, requiring more work than they are worth, but they are excellent for a slow fire. Split only the straight-grained pieces for cookfire fuel.

Use the limbs for firewood, too. Up to about three inches in diameter, these need not be split, nor is a saw needed to cut them. Hold a limb flat on the chopping block with one hand, and with a short grip on the axe handle with the other, strike the limb at about a 45 degree angle. A single blow will generally cut clear through.

I've accorded the axe considerable attention in this chapter. It deserves this emphasis. Give a skilled woodsman a choice of· one implement with which to enter the woods—axe, gun, compass, knife —and he'll choose the axe. It virtually guarantees survival. So give it good care. Keep it sheathed or driven into a log when not in use. And touch up the edge a mite after each chopping chore.

CAMP SAWS

Over the years, camp saws have gone from the sublime to the ridiculous. The best of them all for camping purposes, the wood-frame bucksaw, is virtually extinct, a victim of our plastic-aluminum civilization. You might locate one in reasonably good condition in a secondhand store or antique shop. The beauty of this saw was that it could be easily taken apart to make up a compact bundle for carrying; what's more, any part of it, except the blade, could be improvised in the woods!

Fortunately, its modern counterpart, the "Swede saw" or steel bow saw, is commonly available. It does not provide for adjusting the tension of the blade, which should be taut as a violin string, and it cannot be dismantled for easy carrying, but it is nevertheless an efficient camp tool. I have several such saws, one of them with a 48" pulpwood frame, much too large for camping purposes, and two smaller ones each with a 30" blade, ideal for the camp woodpile. These frames are so shaped that a full stroke of the blade is possible on logs up to about 18" in diameter.

Another excellent camp saw is a shortened version of the lumberman's one-man crosscut saw, resembling a carpenter's saw except for its coarse teeth. About 27" long and weighing under 2 pounds, it is equipped with a canvas carrying case. No special skill is required to use it effectively.

Virtually all other so-called camp saws are playthings, designed to cut wood which could be more easily chopped with an axe. Many of these are folding models, or with frames angled so that a full stroke of the blade is impossible. Hand grips expose the knuckles to constant abrasions, too. Their inventors should be condemned to a year at the woodpile, working with their own saws! The best choice for a camp saw is either the 30" bow saw, or the shortened crosscut.

A dull saw blade will bind, so be sure that its teeth are filed and set periodically. "Setting" the teeth consists simply of bending them slightly, alternating to one side then the other. Filing is the sharpening of the teeths' cutting edges or points, done with a triangular file. Some blades have a "raker" tooth, which does not cut

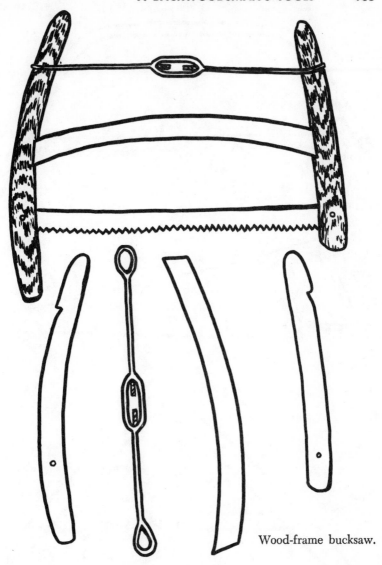

Wood-frame bucksaw.

but rakes out sawdust. Filing and setting is usually a chore for a professional, but once or twice a year is usually sufficient for a camp saw.

A saw will out-cut an axe three to one, and with greater ease. The secret is not to bear down on the blade as it is drawn back

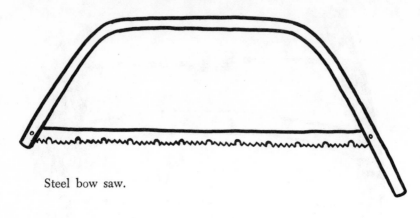

Steel bow saw.

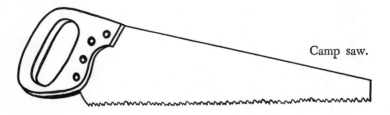

Camp saw.

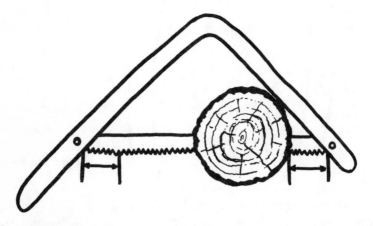

Angled frames prevent full use of the blades.

Woodsman's sawhorse.

and forth. Keep the saw frame vertical and allow the weight of the saw to do the biting. If you bear down, your saw will "run," or stray off course and bind.

If you're going to be in camp for more than a few days, building a sawhorse is worthwhile, and this can be done without nails and with only a saw and axe as tools. Cut four stakes about 3′ long and 4″ in diameter, sharpening one end of each. Drive these into the ground at an angle, over a log 10″ to 12″ in diameter, two at each end but no more than 2′ apart. Such a sawhorse will support any log you can lift into it.

THE CHAIN SAW

Some campers may gasp in horror at my suggestion that a chain saw has a place in a backwoods camp, but I refer to a camp that is being set up for several weeks' occupancy. Power equipment should be minimized in the wilderness—banned in some cases —but a small chain saw, used judiciously, is not inappropriate. For transient camps the bucksaw is adequate. Two miles of abandoned logging road lead to within a few hundred feet of my remote cabin. The wind continually drops trees across this road. Then, I must maintain log culverts to keep the jeep tracks from washing out; sections of "corduroy" have to be repaired or replaced, or even the jeep could not pass. And each year I must cut firewood for the following season. Without my little twelve-pound chain saw, my chores would be endless.

I use the power saw because it frees me from long hours with a bucksaw, time which I can then devote to more worthwhile projects such as fishing. Strangely, the raucous snarl of the saw doesn't seem to bother the deer, bear, and moose around the cabin. Beaver and raccoons remain our neighbors, too, apparently understanding that if we are to live among them for four to six months each year, we must cut wood and repair our road.

I always hate to start the saw, knowing that it will blast the soul-filling stillness. I've spent too many years in the logging woods to entertain any qualms about dropping trees; it's the noise that bothers me. However, I try to finish the chores quickly and nothing delights me more than flipping the switch to OFF position, and then listening to the peace settle back around me.

Basically the same techniques and precautions apply to chain saw use as govern woods work with an axe and bucksaw. Clear the cutting area of brush that might interfere. A maple shoot, for example, becomes a flesh-lacerating whip if caught in the whirring chain. When felling a tree, a safe escape route is doubly important because the weight of the saw will slow you somewhat. Determine your retreat path beforehand and shut off the saw once the tree starts to drop. Hurrying with a "live" saw can result in serious injury should you fall. In making your backcut, resist any temptation to cut all the way through to the undercut. The tree may slip from its stump and pinch the saw bar. Leave a "hinge" on which the butt can swing as the tree falls.

Limbing starts at the butt end but differs from axe limbing in that a chain saw cut is made *in the crotch* of each limb, cutting *toward* the butt. This eliminates the chances of the chain skipping on sloping branches. In bucking the log, position it on skids so that the chain won't buzz into the ground when each cut is completed. If this isn't practical, cut through as far as possible from one side at several points along the log, then roll it over to complete the cuts from the other side.

Always stand slightly to one side of a chain saw, never directly back of it, and with feet firmly implanted for good balance. Standing back of the saw can result in injury to your legs or knees should the blade suddenly bind and the saw kick backwards.

Heavy-duty chain saws are unnecessary for most backwoods camping purposes. The little 8- to 12-pound models with 16″ bars are more than adequate. You'll rarely have occasion to cut a tree they can't handle. If necessary, though, you can make two cuts, one from each side, through a 32″ log.

Keep your shirttail tucked in and your cuffs buttoned or roll up your sleeves. Loose clothing might catch in the chain. Loose, flopping shoelaces are treacherous, too. A "hard hat," while not as romantic as the lumberjack's battered felt, is a wise precaution. In complete honesty, though, I can't bring myself to wear one.

Carry your gas/oil mixture in a suitable metal container with a flexible pouring spout. Shut off the engine when refueling and avoid spillage. Remember, the hot muffler is mere inches from the filler cap. When gassing up, check the oil reservoir at the same time, to save a stop later. Once refueled, move the saw a few feet before starting it. A sudden burst from the muffler among the fumes might start a fire.

A complete discussion of the chain saw is impossible in a single chapter such as this, but that doesn't nullify the importance of knowing your saw and its maintenance requirements. Read the manufacturer's instructions carefully and observe them. Back in the woods several miles, the best chain saw in the world is useless if it won't run.

THE BROAD AXE—THE ADZE

Like the chain saw, the broad axe and the adze are tools of the backwoodsman who maintains a remote cabin. Particularly if this is built of logs will he find these tools useful. Their basic use is for hewing flat surfaces along a log, for making a bench, or replacing a sill.

The broad axe is exactly what its name implies; its bit is broad, up to a foot wide, and, with the handle, may weigh up to eight pounds. Some are equipped with an offset handle so that hewing can be done safely while standing on the opposite side of the log.

The adze differs in that its handle is set at a right angle to the cutting edge, like a hoe. Hewing with an adze is done while straddling a log, swinging the tool carefully between the legs. Neither the broad axe nor the adze are implements to be used care-

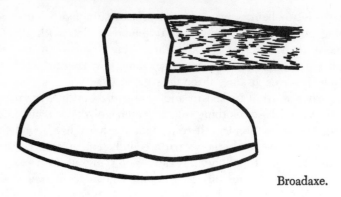

Broadaxe.

Hewing a log with an adze.

lessly! However, learning to use them can be accomplished only with actual practice. Use them, but with great care.

Hewing a truly flat surface on a round log requires the skill of a master. But there are tricks. One of these is to peel the log, then mark parallel guides with a chalk line. Next, saw or chop notches down to the level of the chalk lines, a foot or so apart. Hewing is then in short sections. The notches allow for corrections should you bite too deeply, or unevenly.

A dull adze or broad axe is not only useless but dangerous. With such a tool you'll be inclined to swing too vigorously to compensate. This is when glancing blows and injuries occur, to say nothing of sloppy workmanship. Keep a sharp bit and swing gently.

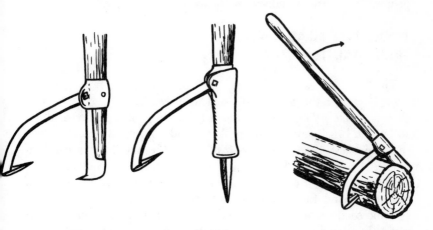

Cant dog at left; peavey at right. Either can be used as a "log wrench."

THE PEAVEY—THE CANT DOG

Ironically, it's in the state of Maine, where Joseph Peavey invented this clever "log wrench" in 1858, that the peavey is better known as a "cant dog." Yet the two names are not synonymous. Each has a curved hook, or "dog," swinging from a socket on the lower handle. The peavey, however, has a pike at the foot; the cant dog has a protruding lip. Originally, the peavey was used on log drives, hence the pike. It could pull, push, or roll a log in the water. The cant dog was a dry land tool, designed for rolling logs on a skidway or in a logyard. However, either is effective on land.

The term "log wrench" best explains how the tool is used. Rolling a heavy log by hand or by means of pries is backbreaking work, and dangerous. With either a peavey or a cant dog, one man can roll a log which three men could not otherwise budge, and best of all, he can keep that log under control.

A peavey or cant dog is a rugged implement. I've seen runaway logs splinter a handle but I've never known a lumberjack to break one. Handles vary in length but those 3½' to 4' are best for general use. These afford ample leverage yet are short enough to work in close quarters. Around any backwoods cabin, a cant dog or peavey is almost as indispensable as an axe or saw.

TOOLS FOR ROAD AND TRAIL MAINTENANCE

The arch nemesis of our jeep trail for about one mile is sweet fern. It chokes the road if allowed to grow. Using an axe on this growth is like trying to beat back a heavy fog with a canoe paddle, so I use a brush scythe, not unlike an old-time grass scythe except that the blade is shorter—about 18"—and the handle (it's called a "snath"!) is sturdier. With long, swinging strokes, the blade whizzing close to the ground, I can cut sweet fern as if it were alfalfa. No other hand tool can do this as well.

Some sections of the road produce alder clumps seemingly overnight. I've tried an axe on these with a notable degree of failure. Alders attract stones, at least they seem to, and chopping results in nicked axe bits, with relatively few alders dropped. We resorted to lopping shears, those long-handled scissors-like cutters often referred to as pruners. From then on, we "walked" through alder growth, toppling the pesky bushes right and left. We also found the lopping shears ideal for pruning trees in the campyard and along the trails we maintain. Pruning trees can be done effectively with an axe, but too often the trunk is slashed of its bark. The lopping shears trim the limbs neatly with no damage to the tree.

We deliberately maintain several large mudholes in our road. Our jeep can get through them but they do discourage "tourists" or cruising troublemakers in conventional cars. We're not antisocial. But we built this cabin to get away from traffic, hence the mudholes. However, some of the wetter stretches must be drained. Otherwise, even the jeep might bog down. At first we tried filling these with "corduroy," logs laid parallel and close together, across the road. They sank out of sight when the jeep crossed over them. So we resorted to draining the worst holes, at least partially. (We didn't want to make a boulevard of the road!)

Mattock for trail or road maintenance.

Here, the mattock came into its glory. This is not a particularly sociable instrument. It's heavy, cumbersome, tiring to use, but marvelously efficient. It's a two-bladed tool, much like a heavy hoe on one side, the other much like an axe. The hoe edge digs into the hardest clay, muck, sand, or gravel. The axe edge cuts tree roots like a hungry beaver. It was the mattock that made possible the small drainage canals across low spots in our road. Water trickles through now, the road still looks impassable to the casual prowler, and the jeep has no problems.

Also indispensable is the long-handled shovel with a pointed blade, also called a spade. Technically, it's a "shovel," but whatever you choose to call it, match it with a mattock and a pair of brawny arms, and the roughest wilderness jeep trail can be kept passable.

Another type of shovel that should be standard equipment in jeeps is the GI trench tool with a folding handle. It's too short for major ditchdigging, but for emergency use it's a worthwhile tool.

In maintaining roads and trails, each of these several tools comes into play. Each has a task it does best and each is an asset in the toolshed.

KNIVES

The hunting season annually brings forth a laughable assortment of "hunting" knives. Hunters stride into the forest with knives that range from Nazi daggers to marine bayonets, including some large enough to double as machetes! One thing is obvious. The bigger the knife, the less its owner knows about using one. Dexterity of fingers and a sharp edge will accomplish anything that can reasonably be expected of a knife. Brute strength and oversized blades are unnecessary. In fact, a large knife is clumsy to handle in tight spots, difficult to guide, and on fine work it becomes a "wood butcher's" tool.

My own sheath knife has a blade barely 3″ long and a mere ⅜″ wide at the hilt. The point has a long, gradual taper. Its handle is 2¾″ long, hardly large enough for me to wrap three fingers around it. For twenty years it has served me well, gutting deer and bear, cleaning fish, whittling prayer sticks and pot hangers, slicing onions and summer sausage, and prying spruce gum for canoe repairs.

Many woodsmen prefer a pocketknife with a small blade or two. My only objection is that I dislike carrying anything in my pockets. Nonetheless, this preference for small knives by professionals should be a hint to beginners that large knives are not a wise choice!

Combination knives which include a can opener, corkscrew, marlin spike, screwdriver, pipe reamer, and for all I know, a backscratcher are useful beyond a doubt, but they should be of high-quality steel. Otherwise, the price of the knife may lie mainly in the number of gadgets included.

Leather or wood handles are best. They're not likely to warp or chip. However, they should never be soaked in hot, soapy water for more than a moment. Long, thin, gradually tapering blades, not over four inches are a good choice.

A sharp knife, like a sharp axe, is more efficient than a dull one. A dull blade pulls hard and a slip can occur. However, a knife blade should never be ground on a grindstone or an emery wheel. These are quick but ruinous to the fine edge. Use a hand-stone. Hold the blade so that it lies almost flat on the stone's surface and rotate it with a circular motion, applying a light pressure, and turning the blade frequently. Keep the stone wet and touch up the edge often.

On TV and in motion pictures, knife throwing seems to be a necessity of life, but in the big woods, it's not likely that you'll have to defend yourself in this manner. Throwing a pocket or sheath knife can damage it. Consider your knife a fine tool, not a plaything.

For serious whittling, investigate the "crooked knife" of the northern Indians and Eskimos. They now buy these from the Hudson's Bay Company, but formerly they made their own. At first glance it appears to be an awkward tool but it is a marvel of primitive engineering. Regrettably, they are difficult to find. The Hudson's Bay Company stocks them only in its northern stores.

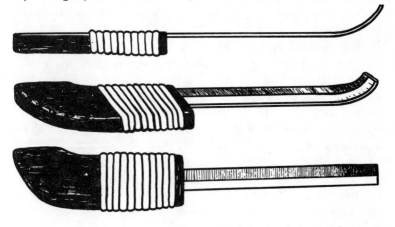

The crooked knife of the north country.

Chapter 9

WILDERNESS CAMPSITES

The specifications for a perfect backwoods campsite have been enumerated frequently in camping literature, but they bear repeating:

(1) An ample supply of firewood and water close at hand;

(2) a screen of trees to ward off high winds;

(3) a degree of exposure so that breezes will keep down insects;

(4) no dominant trees to attract lightning;

(5) sunshine in the morning, shade in the afternoon;

(6) no threatening limbs overhead;

(7) no rocky outcroppings to gouge your backbone during the night;

(8) an elevated spot out of reach of flash floods;

(9) a suitable landing and shelter for your craft if you're traveling by canoe or boat;

(10) a scenic outlook, plus good fishing, hunting, or swimming.

Only once during the life span of a good Plott hound will you run into such an idyllic spot. After all, Mother Nature is not in the campground business. It's not likely that she will assemble all of these desirable features at one convenient location, let alone a series of them along a canoe or jeep trail. A bush campsite is almost invariably a compromise.

Of course, it makes sense to seek as many good features as possible. Don't wait until too late in the day. Start looking for an overnight spot by midafternoon but no later than two hours before suppertime. And don't pass up a fairly good site at 4 P.M., in the hope that the perfect spot can be reached by five. Such a gamble may result in a night of misery. By late afternoon, accept the first reasonably suited campsite you find. After all, if you locate wood and water, a safe spot for a fire, and a relatively flat area for the tent, you have the basic requirements. Anything else is luxury by wilderness standards.

When you're looking for a semi-permanent campsite, one that you'll occupy for several days or longer, you may have to accept one or two mediocre stopovers during the search. Sometimes establishing a temporary base camp from which to explore a region makes this search easier.

Emergency campsites may be crude but they can be made livable for one or two nights. Eleanor and I were once driven ashore by a squall on Umbagog Lake in northern New Hampshire—the sort of squall a canoeman doesn't challenge! The nearest shore turned out to be a rocky beach fringed with a seemingly impenetrable thicket of young spruces. It was a struggle, getting the canoe out of reach of the waves, hacking out a campsite, and cooking among the rocks after the squall simmered down. We should have spent a miserable night, according to the standard specifications for a campsite. However, we ate well, slept well; the canoe was safe; we were sheltered. What more did we *really* need?

When traveling by boat or canoe, your choice of a campsite is more critical than if you're roaming afoot. A heavy boat that can't be hauled up onto a beach should be sheltered in a cove, where it can be moored or anchored safely against the wind. Finding such a cove may take time. A smaller boat can be pulled up on a beach, even a rocky one, once emptied of duffel. Pull it up high enough so that waves won't slosh against it, or into it.

After paddling all day and feeling weary, you may be tempted to flip your canoe over at the water's edge. Don't. A night wind can roll it away. If possible, choose a campsite where you can shelter your craft among the trees. Otherwise, tie it down.

There's even a knack to parking a car or truck at a backwoods campsite. Especially if it isn't equipped with four-wheel drive, leave it on a downhill pitch if the ground is grassy. Otherwise you may find poor traction in the morning when the grass is wet with dew. And don't leave a car—not even a jeep—on hard-packed clay or dried mud. These may be as hard as concrete when you arrive but a night's rain can change the surface into a gooey quagmire. On a remote road, don't think for a moment that no one else is likely to drive by. Where *your* jeep can travel, another can follow! Park *off* the road.

A small knoll is ideal for the tent site although a slight slope is also desirable. Either permits rain water to run off without puddles accumulating under or near the tent. The need for ditching, traditionally emphasized, has been exaggerated. In my files I have "instructions" for ditching a tent which call for a small moat lacking only a drawbridge! I can't recall the last time I ditched a tent. Most forest campsites have a highly porous surface—thick, absorbent duff that soaks up rain water and drains it away. If you *must* ditch, confine the digging to the uphill side of the tent, running the water *away* from it, rather than around it. And when you leave, refill the ditch, tamping down the earth to eliminate the possibility of erosion.

Pitching a tent in any sort of gully or depression is folly. A sudden rainstorm can wash you out. An arroyo in the West is especially dangerous. Bone dry when you arrive, it may seem a convenient campsite. However, a violent storm, as much as fifty miles away, may send a flash flood to carry away your outfit.

When I operated a commercial campground, I repeatedly failed to convince campers that they should set up their rigs away from the lakeshore. I pointed to the shelter of birches and firs a few feet back from the shore. It was no use. Everybody wanted to camp close to the lake. As a result, I spent at least one day a week helping campers to salvage their outfits. Storm winds, roaring in off the lake, flattened tents as if they were tissue-paper doll-houses! Give me a campsite in the shelter of trees; the lake will always be there when I want it!

On the other hand, there's something to be said for a gentle breeze. For one thing, it soothes overheated woods travelers; and it is supposed to keep insects at bay—mosquitoes, black flies, "no-see-ums," deer flies, and other minuscule flying pests. A breeze seems like a natural solution to the bug problem. *It is not.* Only a steady gale keeps bugs down! True, a momentary gust will sweep away the little stingers, but the moment the breeze dies down, they're back, with reinforcements! Fly dope or pipe smoke is far more effective. Errant breezes have been overrated.

In a high wind certain trees are a hazard. Balsam fir, for example, is brittle and breaks off, sometimes several feet from the ground. The severed tops are carried some distance, too, in a gale-force wind. Spruces, on the other hand, rarely break; they are uprooted. Pines, as a rule, resist wind quite well. Healthy hardwoods, particularly when they have shed their leaves, are seldom a hazard in high winds. However, the threat of the woodsman's "turkey" is ever present. Check overhead before pitching your tent. Dead white birches are treacherous. Even when bare of leaves and limbs, they often appear sturdy because the bark is intact. This hides interior rot. Some dead birches, in fact, can be pushed over by a child. They stand only because they have no branches or leaves which the wind can grasp!

"Firewood close at hand" is a standard requirement, but how close? You may find a dead hardwood and a few softwood blowdowns on the immediate site. If not, what's wrong with walking a short distance into the woods for fuel? Firewood can be bucked into four-foot lengths and carried into camp for further cutting and splitting. This preserves the natural beauty of the campsite. However, even in this day of so-called "conservation concern," this is an extreme view. Campers continue to slash campsites until there's isn't a decent stick of fuelwood within 300 feet. Then, because the campsite is barren, they *must* go deeper into the woods for fuel. Why not do this in the first place?

"Sun in the morning, shade in the afternoon," seems like asking Mother Nature for air conditioning. I'll grant that warm sunlight in the early morning is welcome, but is a chilly dawn *really* such a hardship? And I've too many interesting woodland occupations to want to sit in the afternoon shade. As long as the tent is comfortable at night, or during a heavy rain, this is all I ask.

A campsite with a stream running through it, or with a spring near the fireplace, is a prize find. However, if the water supply happens to be 300 feet away, what's wrong with enjoying the leisurely chore of "going for water"?

Springs and brooks far removed from man's "improvements" are usually safe to drink. However, be sure of what lies upstream. I once worked in a lumber camp where the hovel (the horse barn) was located within seventy-five feet of a mountain stream whose waters I drank before the camp was built. Now piles of manure have drained into it, along with diesel fuel and drippings from logging machinery. Unless you're certain that no such pollutants lie upstream, treat your water with Halazone tablets, add a drop of iodine to each quart, or boil it at least five minutes.

Clearings along wilderness rivers may be tempting campsites. They may be abandoned Indian villages or trapping camps, log landings, or simply natural openings in the forest. More often than not, however, a thick growth of tall grass harbors swarms of insects, and in the late summer and fall, when the grass is dry, there is a serious fire hazard. During a rain, such places are as wet underfoot as overhead. This isn't to say that *all* such clearings may be poor campsites; simply that you should check the possibility of these shortcomings.

Sand bars along river routes are often attractive sites, if only for the delight of sleeping so close to babbling water! When stream levels are not likely to fluctuate suddenly, such campsites are especially convenient for canoe travelers. Examine the waterline in the gravel or sand, or look in the nearby brush for signs of flooding. Erratic water heights leave telltale signs—dried grass hanging in alders, or small sand bars several feet from the normal stream.

Camping by a waterfall seems idyllic at first glance. However, if the wind is "wrong," your outfit may get a thorough soaking from fine mist or spray. Rapids, too, are attractive, but you'll have to shout when asking your partner to pass the salt.

Climbers and hikers are more limited in their choice of campsites. They can't range very far in search of the ideal spot, and above tree line wind becomes a major adversary. Mountain tents resist tremendous gusts but even routine chores become difficult. Naturally, your route will dictate the location of overnight stops, but it's often worthwhile to detour a short distance to reach the shelter of boulders, the lee of a ridge, or the stunted growth at tree line. This makes more sense than spending the night trying to keep your outfit from blowing away.

Even on the relatively "small" mountains of the Appalachian chain, a campsite below tree line is preferable. "Sleeping on top," I suppose, may be some sort of a triumph, but it is risky; in fact, downright foolhardy on such peaks as New Hampshire's 6,280-foot Mt. Washington, whose barren summit has recorded winds of up to 230 miles per hour! There are dozens of such eastern peaks, each a challenge to the climber but dangerous as campsites —Marcy and Whiteface in New York, Katahdin in Maine, Mitchell in North Carolina, to name just a few. Camping above timberline is justified only under experienced mountaineering leadership and then only when you're suitably outfitted. Keep your summit visits brief and confined to periods of favorable weather, then head for timber to pitch camp.

Until recently, campers were urged to burn their waste and

bury the residue. In many cases, burning is not feasible. Backpackers often depend upon tiny stoves for cooking and may not even bother with an evening campfire. As for burial of trash, this is no longer advisable in many backwoods areas. Even so-called wilderness trails now see so much foot traffic in some regions that for each hiker to bury his waste would mean trail sides pockmarked with tiny dumps. Rain often washes these out, unearthing ugliness. Squirrels, raccoon, skunks, and bear frequently dig them up, too, scattering everything that isn't eaten. That's why a new philosophy is spreading among those campers, hikers, and climbers who want to help the situation. It is short and concise: "Carry it in/carry it out!"

This makes sense. Certainly a can of beans weighs less empty than full. Plastic waste-can liners are ideal for fixed campsites where a trip to the nearest dump may occur only once a week. Smaller versions of these bags are available for backpackers. These can be closed tightly at the neck so that odor is confined. Tin cans are bulky, so cut out *both* ends and flatten them. They'll take up less space in the waste bag. Naturally, if you're using a campfire every day, there is no reason why inflammable trash can't be burned. Air pollution in the backwoods is not yet so serious as to call for a ban on this!

Trash can be minimized before leaving home. Go over your supplies and discard—at home—unnecessary cartons, wrappers, and plastic packages. Freeze-dried foods, for example, are often packaged in waterproof envelopes on which are printed directions, then inserted into a small carton. Why tote the latter into the woods?

Food wastes can be burned in a campfire, but don't do this at the last minute just before you leave and the fire has burned down. It takes a healthy blaze to consume such waste. Nothing is quite so disgusting as to arrive at a campsite and find the fireplace littered with half-burned garbage! And if other campers are nearby, don't commit a nasal affront by burning waste when the wind will carry the odor to their campsite.

In the backwoods, I rebel against "proper procedure." I prefer to discard food wastes in the woods a short distance from camp, deliberately to attract and feed wildlife. This includes *only* food wastes. Few human foods are unpalatable to wild things—although we once had a rabbit refuse offerings of lettuce!—and it's fun to observe the tracks of the critters who come to feed. We've had woods mice, rabbits, bobcats, fox, deer, raccoon, bear, mink, weasel, and skunks at our "table." They are neat creatures, leaving few crumbs, and somehow I believe that each muttered a "thank you" for the handout. Naturally, this is strictly a wilderness practice. Organized campgrounds are already surrounded by wild things turned pests who come to raid dumps and garbage pails!

Dishwater seemed such a trivial matter only a few years ago. We dumped it into the bushes, the rain diluted it, and it simply disappeared. In the deep woods, at a safe distance from streams, I still carry on this practice. However, lowly dishwater has taken on a sinister cast. Most of the magic suds which perform startling miracles with dirty T-shirts before your very eyes on TV commercials, contain phosphates. When these find their way into ponds and lakes they cause eutrophication (I had to look it up, too!), a process which encourages the growth of algae in the water. This, in turn, kills off other forms of life. The ponds and lakes literally "die" in time: fish, frogs, turtles, even pond lilies disappear. Algae can become so thick that the water looks like green paint.

Algae is a natural substance in water; we can probably never eliminate it. But to allow dishwater—or sudsy water of any kind containing phosphates—to reach a stream or a pond is an ecological crime. For years, campers have been portrayed washing dishes and clothing in a mountain stream—romantic nonsense since *hot* water is required to cut grease—but that day is, hopefully, over. Whatever you wash in camp, with hot or cold water, dump your wastes as far from a stream or lake as you can walk in three minutes—and don't dally on the way. In fact, don't even brush your teeth near a stream. You can't be too sure what's in modern toothpaste! Nor is this sarcasm. We know too little of the effects of modern chemicals on our environment.

The disposal of human waste requires even greater care. It must be buried. There is no alternative in the wilderness. Dig a suitable latrine—a narrow trench will do, deep enough to accommodate your needs over the length of your stay, and at a safe distance from the nearest water. Some experts suggest 100 feet. Pace this off, and you'll be shocked at how short a distance it is! I vote for 200 feet. Toilet tissue can be perched on a forked stick and covered with an inverted No. 10 can to protect it from rain. A tarpaulin around the pit is usually suggested for privacy, but unless there are finicky ladies in the party, what's the sense, when you're surrounded by 10,000 acres of woods providing a natural screen?

Some campers can't resist "improving" a campsite. When they see two trees three feet apart, they rush to build a bench between them. They set up crude chairs, tables, even camp kitchens. A wilderness campsite isn't a suburban patio. It needs no furniture. Such campcraft is out of place; it detracts from the wilderness spirit. I make a hobby of dismantling such rigs wherever I find them, using the poles for firewood. An overturned canoe serves admirably as a table and there is no seat more comfortable, or better fitting, than the butt of a tree. It's beyond me why some folks go into the wilderness to "get away from it all," then try to convert it into a rustic version of suburbia!

On the other hand, the inflexible teachings of some ultra-conservationists are carried too far. They often insist that *no green growth whatsoever* be cut. This is almost like eating a pork chop without injuring the hog! There are some species in our woodlands which can be spared without detracting from the aesthetic values—alders, for example. I have no compunctions about cutting these to make dingle sticks, fireplace cranes, pot hooks and lifters, tent poles, or clothes dryers. And, occasionally, I will cut a maple shoot or a spruce pole.

The bough bed, especially, has come under fire as the luxury of irresponsible campers bent upon destroying the wilderness. This criticism comes from those do-gooders who have never traveled in the wilderness. Every tree, every branch, every shoot, they insist, must be saved. Nonsense. True conservation calls for *selective cutting*. A twisted, gnarled spruce, a badly broken fir, a damaged maple, surrounded by healthy species, might just as well be cut and used by a woodsman who needs one or the other. I have as yet to enter any extensive softwood forest that did not reveal a number of fresh blowdowns, particularly firs and spruces. What is wrong with using the still green limbs? Every defective tree that is removed allows sunlight to reach the forest floor, where dozens of fresh sprouts—even hundreds—are eager to replace the tree you cut. Only those campers and woodsmen who know the wilderness can understand that judicious axemanship is *not* detrimental to forest growth. Sound conservation, at a campsite or in the deepest forest, calls for *wise use*, not blanket restrictions.

How should you leave a wilderness campsite, either one that you've established or one that you found ready for your use? Some backcountry campers insist that you destroy every vestige of human occupancy. "Leave only footprints," they say. "The rain will wash these away." I like this philosophy up to a point. Bough beds should be dispersed into the woods; bits of paper, bottle caps, foil, even matchsticks should be made to disappear. Leave nothing that is man-made.

But how about the fireplace? Should you leave it for some fellow camper to enjoy, or dismantle it to leave the site completely "natural"? Several friends of mine—and they *are* experts in the wilds—insist that a fireplace be dismantled, the rocks distributed away from the campsite, and gravel scuffed over the ashes, leaving the site "primitive."

I feel that this is a hollow and futile attempt at disguising human presence. After all, when I find such a "restored" campsite —and they're easy to spot—I know that someone was there before me. I can readily perceive that somebody kicked gravel over the ashes and soot-blackened rocks are not easy to hide. Any woodsman who can spot a bull moose at thirty feet can see the signs of human occupancy. What's more, I don't resent the fact that someone was there first, if the campsite is not littered, and has not been despoiled.

To me, a fireplace is *not* an effrontery to the wilderness. It represents warmth and companionship for those who passed here before me. There are few places in North America where man has not traveled, camped, eaten, cooked, and told tales about a campfire. Why try to delude ourselves that we are travelers in a virgin wilderness? A campsite fireplace, crude or well built, *is* a part of the wilderness. I like to sit before it and wonder who sat there before me. I try to imagine the tales that crossed the firelight, the chuckles, the laughter. To me, wilderness fireplaces are eloquent. Let them stand.

Chapter 10

MOTORIZE THE WILDERNESS? NO!

We are on the verge of trampling our verdant backcountry to death, not with hiking boots but with knobby rubber tires. Fire is still the greater danger but machinery is closing the gap rapidly with Big Business cheering from the sidelines.

The ultimate threat comes from merchandising experts who have dollar signs for eyeballs but little regard for a pine that casts a shadow over a trout pool. Financing the rape of the countryside are the manufacturers and importers of backwoods-geared vehicles. They have dedicated themselves to overrunning every last acre of our remaining woodlands, prairie, and mountain slopes with jeeps (and I use the term generically to include all recreational four-wheel drive cars), trail bikes and mini-bikes, all-terrain vehicles —those ugly little unstoppable six-wheel mechanical frankensteins popularly know as "ATVs"—and snowmobiles. The final, and lasting, infamy, however, belongs to the who-gives-a-damn-so-long-as-we-don't-have-to-walk "sportsman."

It's not that the culprits got together at a Mafia-like family session to plot the extermination of all that is green and serene. It's simply that violated tranquillity adds up to fat stock dividends and "time-saving, exciting, glorious adventure in the unspoiled Outdoors."

Like the near extinction of the buffalo, the catastrophe is easy to rationalize. "You can't blame the machine," nor can we criticize all off-the-road drivers. "It's only a few spoiling it for the rest of us!" The fact is, of course, that there's more than one fox raiding the henhouse. "The few that are spoiling it for the rest of us" include the makers and importers of these rigs, their advertising agencies, their salesmen, and, especially, those who use the machines.

Advertising is the initial culprit. After all, "ads create demand." And, in this case, advertising emphasis is on "unstoppable power," and a "go anywhere with ease and speed" theme. Drivers are shown in triumph over Nature, bathed in glory for scaling a steep hillside at thirty miles per hour. "Buy our machine," the hucksters scream, "and you'll be a hero who can tame rugged terrain with a twist of the throttle!" Like chips in a beaver cutting, the claims fly—economy, comfort; the envy of neighbors, and all of the other ego-building drivel that goes with selling techniques. By sly implications and half-truths, big trout, giant bucks, primeval campsites are promised. However, no advertisement has yet pointed out the hell of a mess automotivated idiots create in attaining a back-of-beyond Shangri-la, nor does any mention how long this dream spot will last once probed by rubber tires.

Advertising does not suggest that where one off-the-road vehicle can go, another can follow, and another—until a "road" or a set of wheel tracks is pushed to a wilderness bog, up a mountain slope, through a cathedral of trees. Tracks branch from tracks, and more tracks from these. Knobby tires spew up mud, gravel, sand, chewing their way over terrain so that, come the next rain, the raw earth spills up its guts.

No ads cry out against this. No operators' manuals urge restraint, reason, consideration. And, as a result, no off-the-road driver walks where he can ride! The most persuasive people in the world, advertising copywriters, never suggest: "For God's sake, leave your machine at the roadside once in a while and walk!" Instead, they hammer away: "Here's the horsepower. Go to it. Nothing can stop you!"

If I seem to be bitterly hostile to machinery in the wilderness, it's because I am! It's not that a single jeep, a stray trail bike, an occasional ATV, or a lone snowmobile is about to erase the grandeur of the backcountry. What frightens and angers me is the cumulative effect of repeated intrusions by power vehicles. They are simply pushing the suburbs just a little farther out of town! A wheel track is nothing more than an extension of a freeway. How far can we push it? Until it starts coming out the other side, facing another freeway? How much noise from a snorting exhaust does it take to convert a wilderness into an outlying suburb? And isn't an ATV, bulling its way through backcountry brush, doing essentially the same work as a bulldozer clearing a site for a new shopping center? Because, sure as porcupines climb trees, freshly opened wheel tracks invite other wheels to follow. At the rate we are producing and selling backwoods-type vehicles, we must in short order overwhelm and crush the fragile backcountry.

Congress defined "wilderness" when it passed the Wilderness Act of 1964 as an area "where the earth and its community of life are *untrammeled* by man, where man himself is a visitor who does not remain." (The italics are mine.) The key word, of course, is "untrammeled." There are frighteningly few such places remaining in the United States and, thankfully, those regions qualifying under the Wilderness Act are protected from motorized intrusion. You may enter these only on foot, with pack animals, or by canoe.

To many city dwellers, however, "wilderness" is not necessarily primeval. A few square miles of second-growth forest is "wild country." Generally, the public concept envisions as wilderness any large forested area away from roads, whether they be in state or national parks. Then, too, there are millions of acres of commercial forest which, because of their vastness, may qualify as "wilderness."

All too frequently, off-the-road vehicles travel pretty much where they please. Some limitations are in effect in state and federal parks and forests, and private timberland owners usually restrict travel in the vicinity of logging operations. Other than this, the gasoline engine is fast gnawing away at the wilds.

JEEPS

The jeep is not directly as destructive as the trail bike or the ATV, but its threat is serious by virtue of sheer numbers. More and more four-wheel drive rigs are bringing outdoorsmen *to* the wilderness. How deeply they penetrate depends only on the conscience of individual drivers and the too few regulations that exist.

I own a jeep. It's a delight to drive. With it Eleanor and I have hauled canoes, pulled a lumber-loaded trailer when we built our cabin, and we now supply the camp by four-wheel drive. Exploring back roads is our favorite pastime. However, we have never driven it more than a few feet from an established wheel track. We prefer to do our wilderness prowling on foot. We can't bring ourselves to crush young growth and to gouge the earth by opening new sets of wheel tracks.

Obviously, the jeep isn't about to be outlawed because it's incompatible with a wilderness environment; nor should it be. There

is no reason why it cannot be used to reach backcountry regions
and to travel there on existing roads and jeep trails. But to take
it off the road is to eat at the wilderness, acre by acre, mile by mile.

Jeep operation entails techniques not associated with the operation of conventional cars. For example, if yours is not equipped
with front-wheel variable hubs, have a set installed. With a twist
of the wrist you can disengage the front wheels for highway
driving. Without such hubs, undue wear is forced upon the entire
front-wheel assembly, the wheels cannot be balanced, tire wear is
uneven, and mileage per gallon is decreased.

Following a backcountry trip which has involved travel through
mudholes, pull the wheels and wipe clean the brake drums and
linings to remove grit which may have worked its way in. If
allowed to remain, this may score the drum or damage the linings.
Chances are, too, that after fording a stream or deep puddle, you
may find yourself without brakes. Drive slowly a few minutes,
applying the brakes lightly. This will dry the linings quickly and
restore braking power.

Regular servicing and inspection of a four-wheel drive vehicle
should be more frequent that those of a conventional car if much
backcountry driving is done. After all, you can't call the automobile
club if you break down ten miles the other side of Two Skunk
Brook! Depending upon your ability as a mechanic, certain spare
parts should be carried during trips far from highways. My own
experience has shown that trouble is most likely to require the
replacement of a spark plug or two, points, condenser, coil, fan
belt, or the addition of brake fluid. A few basic tools are required,
of course. For more commonplace emergencies, take along spare
motor oil and extra gasoline, plus water for the radiator if your
prowling takes you into arid regions.

Some jeeps roll thousands of miles without trouble. Ours is
not one of these. Our laughter is a little hollow, but Eleanor and
I refer to it as our "cheep jeep," with lower-case letters, too! It
seems to have spent as much time in repair shops as in the woods,
with accompanying monumental bills for parts and mechanics' labor. Despite glowing advertising claims, jeep troubles are not
uncommon.

Driving slowly on rough terrain will pay dividends. You may
get a thrill out of hot-rodding over backcountry wheel tracks, but
the rough ride will jar your backbone, jumble your camping gear,

and possibly break a spring or spring hanger. Use low gear for slow speeds, uphill and down, and don't feel sheepish about crawling in four-wheel drive. That's what the jeep is all about.

A front-end winch is useful in extremely rough country or where deep mudholes block backwoods roads. By anchoring the cable to a tree or boulder, you can probably pull yourself out if four-wheel drive fails to do the job. Too, you can help fellow jeep users who might be bogged down. My sole objection to the winch is that it encourages off-the-road travel over terrain which should not be traversed. Forest duff, for example, is soft and spongy and some winch owners will risk travel over this knowing that their power drum will pull them out. Use the winch for genuine emergencies, not as a means of propulsion through areas where no jeep should travel.

TRAIL BIKES

Ecologically speaking, the trail bike is *designed and intended* to be destructive whenever it leaves the road. This is the nature of the beast. Tranquillity disappears for a mile around when one charges up a sylvan valley. No bike rider has ever observed, close at hand, a mink rummaging along a streambank, a grouse drumming on a log, or a trillium standing shy in the shade. And, here again, advertising stresses off-the-road travel without consideration for what the knobby tires on spinning wheels do to the forest floor or fragile trail surfaces.

Trail bikes and mini-bikes are lightweight motorcycles, capable of being geared down for travel almost anywhere a man can walk. Cross-country travel, even through woodlands, poses few problems to the operator. If he's skillful, knows when to ease up on the throttle or when to "gun 'er," no glen or slope is sacred. And his trail is easy to follow. Look for forest duff scattered backwards, raw earth upturned, mudholes where goldthread used to grow, and hillside trickles hurrying to form gullies.

The presence of the trail bike is irrevocable. We can only hope to contain it. Already it is restricted from certain hiking trails in national parks and forests, and in some state areas. In Maine's 201,018-acre Baxter State Park it is banned outright, even from park roads! Some timberland owners have also banished them.

However, in a democracy, we must make room for motorbikes. Most wilderness devotees have no objection to them on roads; and certainly any realistic outdoorsman should concede that certain trails be designated for them. But to continue to allow them to travel, even in private timberlands, on self-made cross-country routes, will simply hurry the day when our out of doors will consist of rutted and washed-out trails crisscrossing like the cracks in a broken windshield!

ALL-TERRAIN VEHICLES (ATVs)

This is the peacetime General Sherman tank, minus cannon and machine gun. Its purpose is to bull its way through or over natural obstacles without regard for the environmental chaos it leaves behind. Among all of man's backwoods machines, the ATV is the most indiscriminate and callous defiler of our woodlands. Worse yet, the monster is amphibious! Its driver can gouge out a steep bank and nudge his machine into a stream or beaver bog.

Its lugged tires—and six of them at that!—under low pressure, crush into the earth every bit of growth over which they roll, while the machine itself fells saplings which Nature intended for the forest of the future.

I can see no redeeming features in the ATV, no justification for the environmental havoc it can bring about. It can only convert our remaining wilderness into an idiot's playground, gobbling up the few remaining silent places. It should be banned from *all* public lands, and certainly, when private timberland owners view their first set of ATV tracks through young growth, they'll fence it out!

You may notice, at this point, that I am offering no suggestions for the use and maintenance of trail bikes and ATVs. I have no intention of doing so. While the greatest danger from them still lies in the future, when their use becomes common, the initial destruction is already underway. I have investigated these and even turned down manufacturers' offers of the free use of machines, both trail bikes and ATVs. I want no part of the mechanical despoliation of our wilds!

SNOWMOBILES

When it comes to snowmobiles, you're either Republican or Democrat, atheist or believer, bad guy or good guy, cop or robber! There seems to be no middle ground. Few people are objective about snow scooters.

The snowmobile is an instrument for family fun—clean, wholesome excitement that comes with zipping over a snowscape; it's a means of exploring backwoods areas, otherwise inaccessible; it makes distant ice-fishing ponds easy to reach, puts hunting country within minutes of leaving the highway. This is one version.

The other differs somewhat. The snowmobile spews carbon monoxide where the scent of balsam fir used to prevail; it deafens with a cacophony of a million unleashed decibels; it lacerates the tops of tree plantations; it depletes backwoods bogs and ponds of trout and other fish; it runs down deer in the deep snow until they drop from exhaustion, then die of pneumonia.

There's some truth in both versions, but from a wilderness preservation viewpoint the snowmobile is hardly an asset. Even if the machine were as benevolent as its makers would have you think, the sheer weight of its numbers increasing like barnyard rabbits, must soon be reckoned with. During one afternoon last winter, there were fourteen snow sleds zooming back and forth across four-acre Lily Pond in New Hampshire's White Mountain National Forest. I would rather have ventured across a freeway during the rush hour than to try snowshoeing across, and as for the noise level, I later found the companionship of a jackhammer soothing! It's only a matter of time before a snowshoer must wear a red, flashing tail light if he wants to stay alive.

I bought a snowmobile three years ago, against Eleanor's wishes. Our first ride was thrilling; we buzzed over a snow-covered golf course. We couldn't speak, of course, not even in sign language, since my hands were busy keeping the contraption under control. Our second excursion was along a woods trail, less exciting but the noise level higher among the trees. My enthusiasm decreased; Eleanor's was never great. I then made a trip to our cabin, eight miles over our snow-covered "road," and eight miles back out. Tracks were everywhere—those of deer, moose, wildcats, rabbits, grouse, mink—but not one critter did I see. And the winter land-scape was little more than a blur of evergreens. During the three-hour trip, I had accomplished nothing more than guiding my monster over the snow. Nature was there, but not for me. I was too busy handling the horsepower; going too fast to read the stories in the snow; and deafened so that I couldn't hear the chickadees. I sold the machine and bought a new set of snowshoe harnesses.

Frankly, the snowmobile will provide rapid transit from Point A to Point B. Unfortunately, Point B is all too often a bit of back-country that once knew silence. It no longer does.

MOTORIZE THE WILDERNESS?
NO!

Our backcountry, whether it be a national forest or park, a state area or private timberlands, is already sufficiently crisscrossed with enough jeep and bike trails to put virtually every fishing hole, scenic outlook, or mountain peak, within hiking distance. The time has come for us to park our vehicles and walk. If every owner of a jeep, trail bike, ATV, or snowmobile were to agree to park his rig at the trail head, if he were to agree never again to punch a new trail or wheel track into the wilds, we could well be on our way to saving, perhaps even enlarging, our existing wilderness. However, I'm enough of a cynic to believe that this won't come about volun-tarily. We need strictly enforced regulations. Otherwise, what's left of our verdant countryside will become a tired, overused, beaten neighborhood park.

Chapter 11

CHILBLAIN CAMPING

The more I delve into cold-weather camping literature, the colder the winters seem to get. "Experts" toss below-zero descriptions about like squirrels dropping acorns from an oak. Some writers make camping out at 60 below sound like a March sugaring-off party in a sunny Vermont maple grove! When it comes to implying that 50- to 60-below-zero campouts are a joy and a delight, I draw the line. In fact, at 30 below, it may well become a question of survival, pure and simple.

During our northern Maine Border Patrol jaunts, we couldn't go home if it was too cold; we couldn't always reach a trapper's shack or a lumber camp; and our packs had to be light so that we could snowshoe the international boundary and its adjacent trails. Our daily assignments didn't include pleasant campsites, steaming stews over a campfire, not even a gay song at evening. This was the reality of true winter camping. Our day-to-day schedule called for two goals: cover the ground, and stay alive!

Certain periods during a northern winter can be a delight, but first understand what you're up against. Temperature is not the complete story. Consider the "wind chill factor," which enhances the chances of frostbite, or worse. For example, with the wind blowing at 20 miles an hour, and the temperature at 20 degrees *above* zero, the effect is that of a 10-*below* day in a dead calm. At 30 below, with a 15-mile-per-hour wind, your face will freeze in one minute! As for the 60-below campouts so often described, a 15-mile-per-hour breeze is the equivalent of 110 degrees below zero![1]

With a proper awareness of what awaits you in the northern winter woods, there's much to be enjoyed. The crowds are gone,

1 The U. S. Air Force has prepared a wind chill index chart which indicates the effect of various temperatures when combined with varying winds. See: *AF Manual 64–3*, Survival Training Edition, 1969, U. S. Government Printing Office, Washington, D.C. 20402.

that's certain; with the leaves off the hardwoods, visibility is greater, game is easier to approach, and there is a quiet serenity that is lacking in the relatively noisy summer woods. Too, there's a sense of adventure, even on a short trek; a knowing that at this time of year, Mother Nature is rarely in a benevolent mood and that you are on your own. However, break into winter travel and camping gradually.

The first time out, try a day hike with a noontime campfire meal during a period of moderately cold, but not extreme weather. No below zero heroics. Temperatures of 15 to 20 degrees *above* are excellent "testing grounds." Next, try an overnighter under similar conditions but be prepared for a dip in temperature during the night. Test not only yourself but your equipment and clothing. Learn to operate your gasoline stove if you plan to carry one (they're sometimes trickier in cold weather!); check the zippers on your clothing to be sure you can manipulate them easily and smoothly. Can you get a fire going quickly? Does your tent go up without a hitch, especially since you can't drive stakes into the frozen ground? Check the fit and durability of snowshoe harnesses, the fit of sunglasses, the warmth of boots and jackets. Make these trial runs with a partner, never alone.

Two or three such trips will pinpoint the shortcomings of your equipment if any exist; they'll point out needs you may have overlooked; you may find some gear is excess baggage. Once you've proven the suitability of your outfit and convinced yourself that you can handle refrigerated camping, you're ready for more extensive winter adventure.

Before venturing into a state or federal area, check with the authorities first. Access to Maine's Baxter State Park, for example, is by special permit during the winter and such permits are issued only to qualified winter travelers, whose equipment may be subject to examination by park rangers.

Make your plans known to someone, preferably a ranger or other official. Tell him exactly where you plan to travel and when you expect to return. When something goes wrong in the winter wilderness it's comforting to know that someone will investigate if you fail to appear on time. Once you're back out, report this, too. Otherwise you may set off an expensive and needless search and rescue effort.

WINTER TRAVEL—BY CAR

Remote campsites are often accessible over plowed forest roads, sometimes on private timberlands. If you're using a conventional car, don't depend entirely on snow tread tires. Carry chains for additional traction in emergencies. And here's a tip that will make you welcome in logging country: when you meet a heavily loaded log truck, take to the ditch! The truck can't leave the center of the road; its weight will bog it down on the soft shoulders. Also, no trucker can afford to jam on his brakes on a snowy surface. He plans on gradual stops. So give him the right of way, as near the middle of the road as possible. How about your car, its hood buried in a roadside snowbank? The truckdriver will stop to pull you out. During thirty years of driving on winter logging roads I've never known it to fail!

When using my jeep on snowy roads, I use four-wheel drive; not for the added power but rather for the stabilizing traction afforded by the front wheels doing their share of the pulling. Skids are rare then. And, of course, I use snow treads on all four wheels during the winter.

In the north country, it's considered a cardinal sin to pass a stalled car during cold weather. A dead engine means no heat and many people have died along remote wintry roads, for lack of help. An experienced traveler will burn his spare tire in an emergency, but this will supply heat for barely a half-hour, unless he can add firewood from the roadside forest. Stop to help!

Equip your car for winter emergencies. Include an extra five gallons of gas, a rugged snow shovel, a full-sized axe, a tow chain, a sturdy under-the-axle jack (bumper jacks are treacherous bear traps on icy surfaces!), a gasoline lantern (flashlight batteries go dead quickly in extreme cold), a spare mantle, and a can of gas line de-icer. These, coupled with a willingness to lend a hand, will get almost any vehicle out of trouble, including yours.

Once you've arrived at trail head, pull the car completely off the road to clear traffic. Back in the woods this will be light, but if a logging truck happens along, its driver will prefer shearing off one of your fenders to swerving his heavy load on an icy road! Park the car heading out, too, for an easier departure. Leave a spare key hidden where both you and your partner can find it quickly.

It's sad commentary on our "civilization," but today's roads, even in the backwoods, are often patrolled by "tourists" looking for something easy to steal. If your spare tire is mounted outside, attach some sort of a lock. This won't discourage a professional but it will dissuade the casual thief. Remove your car-top carrier, too, and lock it inside the car. And don't leave attractive items like cameras, guns, radios, or tools in view within the vehicle. Jam them under a seat and generally make your car look as barren as possible.

BY SNOWMOBILE

While I refuse to encourage the use of trail bikes and ATVs, the marvelous flexibility of the snowmobile as a winter camping vehicle can't be denied. With driver-education programs underway, and the possibility of better mufflers in the near future, the snowmobile may become at least as acceptable as the jeep when used conscientiously. Its image can be improved by driving as if *you* owned the land and the young trees growing on it. Seek permission to cross private property and respect posted areas. Leave gates as you find them, open or closed. Avoid traveling close to summer cottages, where you might damage cultivated plants or annoy occupants seeking the quiet of a winter weekend. Stick to trails, roads, or open country. Driving through heavily forested areas, dodging among trees, is not only difficult, but it damages young growth extensively.

Frozen riverways may seem like ideal routes and ice-covered ponds and lakes obvious shortcuts. However, currents flowing under river ice often create thin spots that won't bear your weight, yet are not evident under a cover of snow. Inlets to lakes and ponds, too, are often thinly frozen. Plunging through into such icy waters on a cold day has been the end of the trail for a number of snowmobilers. And there's another hazard. There may be slush under the snow cover. This may jam your drive track, freeze it solid, in fact, at your next stop. Except where river and lake routes are known to be safely frozen over, few waterways can be trusted.

Before any trip of more than a few miles, check your machine thoroughly. Carry an extra drive belt and know how to install it. An extra spark plug (two if you have a twin-cylinder machine) should be included, the gap preset. Be sure of enough gas for the travel you contemplate, and at least an extra quart beyond that. Become adept at analyzing trouble and repairing it quickly, possibly even while wearing gloves or mittens in bitter weather. Have a pair of snowshoes along for each member of the party, plus an axe, matches, map, and compass. At least one machine, when traveling in a caravan, should have a tow rope.

Except for short pleasure spins, we have found that two persons aboard one machine make for crowding and discomfort. For extensive trips, one person to a machine allows room aboard for camping gear.

For overnight trips I have strapped a sleeping bag and tent, along with snowshoes, to the seat with the remainder of my gear in the backpack. The tent and sleeping bag provide a cush-

The author's winter camping outfit before he became disillusioned with snowmobiles. Outfit includes everything necessary for a weekend in the woods. Photo by Bill Riviere, Jr.

ioned ride but they raise the machine's center of gravity and make it slightly tippy. However, this arrangement eliminates the need for towing a sled.

For heavier loads of gear, sleds become necessary. Some of these, although more sturdily built and heavier, are patterned after dog-racing sledges. Another type resembles a Fiberglas bathtub on skis. A toboggan, or woodsman's folding sled can also be towed, but with these you'll need to wrap your gear in a tarpaulin to protect against snow and snapping branches. Whatever type of sled you haul, it should be equipped with a tow bar which will keep it from ramming the snowmobile when you slow up, stop, or run downhill.

Another type of sled incorporates a folding tent, similar to that on a family camper's tent trailer. When opened it unfolds two small bunks and there is even a removable panel in the floor for ice fishing.

Without protective glasses, snow blindness is a serious risk. Glasses also protect against slashing branches, give better depth perception on undulating snowfields (it's surprising how deceptively smooth some of the snowy bumps appear without glasses!), and keep your eyes from watering excessively. Should you lose or break your glasses, improvise a set with a band of birch bark into which two narrow slits are cut at eye position. Tie it in place with a piece of string, fine wire, or even a shoelace. If bark is not available, blacken the cheeks just below the eyes with a piece of charred wood to help cut the glare.

Two men can lift most snowmobiles into the body of a pickup truck but it's easier to back the latter into a snowbank. You can then drive the snowmobile into, or off, the truck body. The tilting trailer is also popular. These usually tilt in either direction, for driving off or on. If you're a boat man, you can probably convert your tilting-bed boat trailer by adding a sheet of $\frac{3}{4}''$ plywood. A road cover for the snowmobile is a necessity to protect it from road grime.

Up to this point I have assumed that you can handle your snowmobile expertly, that you are familiar with techniques for sharp and sudden turns, that you're adept with the throttle and brake, that you can drive it as well as you drive your car. If there is some doubt, make a few day trips along woodland trails for practice, before undertaking a back-of-beyond jaunt.

ON SKIS

Cross-country skiing is backpacking at a slightly faster pace, downhill at least. Skis allow you to move almost soundlessly; wild things remain close at hand as you pass; an uphill struggle brings an exhilarating downward run; on the level, each gliding step gains you several feet. A minimum pack and spartan fare—in essence, those of the backpacker and climber—are a part of this form of travel in the wilds.

You'll need no ten-dollar-per-hour skiing lessons and cross-country equipment sells for about one quarter the price of downhill gear. Boots are light, flexible at the sole, and generally more comfortable. The skis are narrower and longer, about one foot greater than your height, and they are lighter than downhill skis. Poles are longer, too, since they are used for propulsion as well as balance, and their rings are wider to keep them from probing too deeply into soft snow. Special waxes are inexpensive.

No book can teach you cross-country skiing but the technique is not difficult to learn. The basic move is a gliding stride, pushing with the right pole as the left foot moves forward. Turns are gentler and slower than those of the slalom or downhill skier. Uphill travel is generally a zigzag, tacking course. A more direct climb is possible with a side step, or the "herringbone" stride.

Alone or with other skiers observe the precautions that apply to winter travel on river and lake ice. Ski under control, avoid dangerous pitches. Carry matches, a compass, and a map, and a few trail snacks.

At this point I should advise you never to travel alone but I am going to break a rule. Once in a while, take to the nearby hills with skis and your pack, *alone*. There are days in a man's life when companionship is irrelevant, conversation unnecessary, caution a hindrance to the spirit. Go revel in the silence. Few travelers have better access to it than cross-country skiers.

ON SNOWSHOES

No means of winter travel brings you closer to Nature during her hushed moments than snowshoeing. The pace is slow, so you can observe closely; movement is nearly soundless and you can hear the snow-muffled tones of the wild. You are a part of that day's life in the silent places.

But you'll pay a price. Snowshoeing is strenuous, especially in powder snow. And don't be surprised if you contract "mal-de-raquette," the snowshoers ailment which brings aches to hip joints and crotch, the result of unnatural straddling of the legs. But once conditioned to this—it takes a day or two—you'll stride with grace and ease. The average beginner will falter during the first few hours but he can soon cover four miles an hour.

There are three basic types of snowshoes, the oval bear paw, the Maine or Michigan pattern (one very similar to the other), and the Alaska. The latter is also known as the Arctic, Cree, or "pickerel." And there are slight but unimportant variations from these.

The bear paw, because it has no tail, is a favorite in brushy country; trappers like it. Mountain climbers choose it because it is light and compact to carry, and because its flat toe can be kicked into a snowy slope to form a step. It is generally a good shoe for beginners, or for those who will confine snowshoeing to short walks for an afternoon's fun.

The traditional snowshoe is the Maine or Michigan model, differing slightly in toe design, each having a slight front upturn and a tail. Each offers a greater bearing surface than most bear paws, especially ahead of the foot harness, and they are favored for use in the deep, unpacked snows of forest regions. In thick brush, they may be somewhat awkward to "kick around."

The Alaska, or pickerel, is a long, narrow shoe with marked upsweep of the toe. Originally designed—we're not sure by whom—for use on the wind-packed snows of the Arctic, this is the fastest of all three types. Because it is narrow, very little straddle is required, but because it is longer, your stride will need to be lengthened. Speed evolves from a long stride. The pronounced upturn of the toe acts like the upsweep of a ski. It minimizes lifting so that you can shuffle along. However, in soft snow this upturn acts as a brake on the forward thrust and this effect, trifling as it may seem, proves tiring on a long trek.

Which type of snowshoe is best? Frankly, I chose a pair of pickerels many years ago because I found brand-new war-surplus shoes of top quality selling at $3.45 a pair! Prior to that, I had

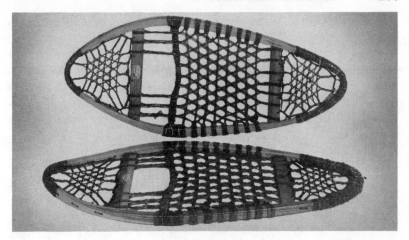

Bear paw snowshoes, well adapted to use in brushy country. Snocraft photo.

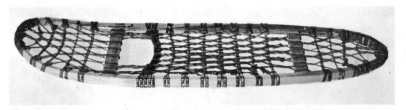

Modified bear paws known as Green Mountain style. Somewhat narrower and longer than conventional bear paws. Tubbs Snowshoe Co.

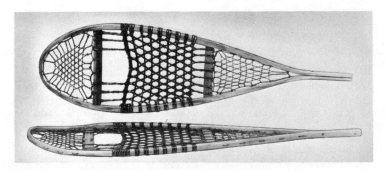

The Michigan pattern, much like the Maine pattern, is popular in wooded country where there are trails. Snocraft Photo.

always used the Maine pattern. For beginners, the bear paw—especially the slightly narrowed Green Mountain version—is a good choice. In the woods where brush is thick, use the regular bear paw; on woods trails, the Maine or Michigan; on windswept barrens, such as along the shore of a frozen river, the pickerel is superior. Does this mean that you'll need a separate pair of snowshoes for each type of snow? Hardly! Once you've learned to "swing the webs," you can travel anywhere on any style.

All-plastic and aluminum-framed snowshoes are on the market. These are primarily low-cost emergency shoes for snowmobilers. Few experienced snowshoers take them seriously.

Snowshoe fillings or webbing are usually of rawhide, which can be preserved almost indefinitely with an annual coat of spar varnish. In recent years, neoprene fillings have appeared but I have not tried them.

There are two commonly used harnesses, the H-type and the Howe, both of heavy leather. The H style has an over-the-toe housing, a strap that encircles the foot, and another which wraps about the instep. For most purposes this harness is excellent. The Howe harness, however, will give you more lateral control, because it is attached to the wood frame rather than to the heavy rawhide crossbar. Also there is a cuplike heel unit and a wide toe band that fits over the front of the foot. This combination virtually eliminates forward and backward sliding of the foot within the harness. All harnesses are adjustable and held in place by buckles which, when they ice up and freeze, become a devilish chore to undo with bare fingers, but up to date no one has improved on this arrangement.

The Beck harness, patterned after both the H and the Howe, is made of neoprene-coated nylon, and while it appears flimsy, it is a decidedly rugged hitch. Tom Lyman, a noted mountaineer, used a set of these for an entire high-altitude summer on Mt. Logan.

Early snowshoers used a 4' length of lampwicking, running this over the toe, around the rawhide crossbar, then crossing it under the arch before winding it around the ankle and tying it snugly. I used a similar hitch for many years, except that mine was made from a 4' length of ½" rawhide. Such rigs provide less control than commercial hitches, but they can be kicked off with a single pull on the knot.

A man's weight governs the size of his snowshoes and the chart on page 207 gives a rough indication of this relationship. The chart isn't a hard-and-fast rule, however. Snow conditions, terrain, experience, and duration of the trips are also to be considered. Manufacturers' capacity ratings are a little overenthusiastic in some instances. If in doubt, buy shoes slightly large rather than too small.

Remember two things and you can learn to snowshoe in five minutes: (1) don't straddle your legs sideways needlessly; (2) take long steps. It's that simple! Spreading your feet far apart is unnecessary if your stride is long enough. One shoe will step over the other. In other words, walk as naturally as possible except for a lengthier step. Otherwise a painful case of "mal-de-raquette" awaits you!

A tendency of beginners is to lift the shoes too high at the front.

The author "harnessing up" his pickerel snowshoes with a Montagnais rawhide hitch. Photo by Bill Riviere, Jr.

Lifting the snowshoe unnecessarily high wastes energy . . .

. . . it should be shuffled along, raised as little as possible. Photos by Bill Riviere, Jr.

In deep, soft snow this *is* necessary to a degree, but lift as little as possible. Shuffle along, dragging the snowshoes' tails.

Climbing a steep, wind-packed snowslope is tricky. If the snow has been hardened enough by the wind, you can probably navigate without snowshoes. If not, backsliding is a common problem on an upgrade, skidding on a downgrade. Climbers attach crampons to the underside of their bear paws, directly under the foot. Lacking these, an ice axe or pole can be stuck into the snow through the toe hole. This keeps one shoe from sliding while the other is moved. This is slow, tedious work at best. And many a climber has tripped on his alpenstock!

How far or how fast can you travel on snowshoes? Stamina and snow conditions determine this, of course. My best coverage was forty-five miles in two days, by no means any sort of a record. French Canadian racers have sustained a seven-mile-per-hour pace for considerable distance, but a four-mile-per-hour speed is "good going."

Leave your snowshoes outside at night as warming will cause snow to clog on them the next morning. Put them out of reach of woods mice and porcupines, to whom rawhide is a delicacy. For summer storage, clean them with a brush, then apply a coat of spar varnish to the frames and webbing. Again, hang them out of reach of critters! A little neat's-foot oil or leather dressing applied to the harness is a good preservative.

A snowshoer's outfit can be much the same as that of a backpacker or skier, carried entirely in a pack. However, for a long-haul camping trip, you may need a toboggan or sled on which to pull your gear. At least three persons should make up such a party. Two snowshoers are required to break out a smooth snowshoe "float" or beaten path. The first breaks trail, using a normal snowshoe stride. The second man *does not* step in the leader's tracks. Rather, he steps *between* them. Thus they pack down a smooth, even trail over which the third man can haul the sled or toboggan with some ease. Breaking trail is arduous work, so swap over frequently.

Choose as level a route as possible, even detouring to avoid steep pitches. Frozen streambeds may seem to be natural snowshoe trails but steer clear of untested ice.

Boots with sharp-edged heels will quickly wear through the rawhide filling, which is why old-time snowshoers wore soleless and heelless larrigans or soft-soled mukluks, either type of shoe padded with two or three pairs of wool socks. The home repair of snowshoes is difficult but some manufacturers will sell ready-cut rawhide if they can spare it (snowshoes are in big demand nowadays!), or during off-season lulls, some will accept snowshoes for repairs.

Repairing snowshoes in the backwoods is a matter of ingenuity. Broken filling can be rewoven with rope or rawhide bootlaces; a cracked or broken frame, spliced or splinted and then reinforced with fine wire, even fishline. And a harness can be improvised with rope. Crude snowshoes can be made by bending pliable saplings into a rough hoop, then filling these with interwoven green sticks. On such snowshoes, you'll have to walk tenderly.

Type of Snowshoe	Dimensions (inches)	Capacity (lbs.)
Bear Paw	13×33	175–200
"	14×30	150–175
"	15×30	175–200
" (Green Mountain, modified)	10×36	up to 225
Maine (Ladies)	12×42	100–125
" "	12×44	125–160
" (Men's)	12×48	125–150
" "	13×48	150–175
" "	14×48	175–200
Michigan (Maker A)	13×48	150–175
" "	14×48	175–200
" "	14×52	200–250
" (Maker B)	12×48	up to 190
" "	13×48	150–200
" "	14×48	175–250
Alaska (Maker A)	10×48	125–150
" "	10×56	150–175
" (Maker B)	10×56	up to 225
" (Children's)	8×40	up to 80

WHEN YOU'VE ARRIVED

The ideal winter campsite is a small clearing within a dense thicket of softwoods, preferably not much over thirty feet tall.

These will serve as a windbreak, yet they are not large enough to hold great clumps of snow to be dumped on your tent, or worse yet, your fire. Water is rarely a problem. Even if there is no spring or brook close by, melted snow will do, although it requires a bushel of snow to produce a pint of water! Keep a bucket over the fire, adding snow to it now and then. You'll need dry wood for kindling, but once your fire is underway briskly, even green, frozen wood will burn, especially in a stove.

For a one-night stop in a small tent with a sewed-in floor it isn't necessary to clear the snow from the actual tent site. You will find that the warmth in the tent will melt this somewhat, and your weight will compress it, so that the floor may sag before morning, but this is rarely a problem for one night.

To pitch a tent for a lengthy stay use your snowshoes as shovels to clear the snow. You won't be able to clear the site perfectly, of course, but the less snow under the tent, the less slush and water will materialize. Don't bank the tent by piling snow directly against the canvas. Heat will melt this away and you may get seepage through capillary action. Pile boughs around the base of each wall, then heap snow on these.

Once the snow is cleared, you may find the ground frozen to a depth of only 2″ to 3″, hence you can probably drive steel tent stakes. Wooden ones won't do. As an alternative, anchor guy lines and beckets to bushes. If this isn't feasible, attach the lines to short logs, then bury these in the snow. To "cement" them solidly, pour water on them so they'll freeze in. You may have to chop them out when breaking camp, but at least your shelter won't topple in a high wind.

Virtually any enclosed tent can be adapted to winter camping, but the ideal shelter is a Wall tent, set up with a shear pole rig as described in Chapter 3. This presupposes that you're traveling by jeep or snowmobile, as such tents are somewhat heavy. Inside, you can set up a wood-burning stove such as the Sheepherder, Sims, or Raemco (see Chapter 6).

Keep a supply of kindling and dry wood in the tent for an emergency. Your main woodpile is likely to be too large for such considerate treatment, so stack it outside near the door and cover it with a tarp or sheet of plastic. Keep the axe and saw inside, too, when not in use. Extremely cold weather makes axe and saw steel brittle.

If the weather isn't too rambunctious, cooking and eating meals outside can be fun. This, in fact, isn't much different from cooking out during a cold spell in the spring or autumn. However, when the temperature plummets and the wind snaps the canvas, move the kitchen indoors. Handling pots with mittened hands, and gulping food before it cools is a form of camping pleasure I choose to forgo. Too, an outside fire consumes a veritable mountain of wood in a high wind and it's too erratic for cooking purposes. Any one of the wood-burning stoves I suggested will handle both heating and cooking very nicely.

The wood stove, too, is the only one I consider using for night-time warmth. Set up solidly there is little danger of the fire escaping. With gasoline, propane, or alcohol heaters you may encounter the problem of inadequate heat output, malfunction, even poisonous fumes. These serve well among family campers who use them to ward off morning and evening chill, but for all-night purposes in a winter-bound tent, give me wood.

Winter camping is hard on sleeping gear. No matter how neat you may be, you'll track in snow, possibly mud, or fireplace ashes. During the day, roll your bedding loosely and stash it in a corner to avoid soiling it. A "doormat" of softwood boughs will cut off some of the grime at the entrance.

Up to this point, I've described *woods* techniques. Out in the open, above timberline, or in a barren region, you'll need the special gear described in earlier chapters dealing with back-packing. A mountaineer's tent is ideal—windproof, light, with sewed-in floor, and a self-sustaining frame needing few, if any, guy lines. For cooking, a small gasoline stove—two one-burner units, or possibly a double-burner model if more than two persons make up the party. However, don't use this type of stove for night heat as carbon monoxide poisoning is possible. Alcohol or kerosene stoves are no safer for this purpose. Depend on a suitable sleeping bag instead. If a single mountain tent isn't large enough to accommodate your encampment, there's no reason why two or more tents shouldn't be used: one for cooking, another for sleeping, a third for supplies and equipment, or any other arrangement that's convenient.

Commissary planning in a winter camp is quite specialized. Your body's calorie requirements are greater in cold weather; they may jump as much as 40 per cent. And you should maintain proper

Not all winter campsites are in the woods! This winter climbing expedition has set up on a plateau, close to summit routes. Porta Co. photo.

balance between protein and carbohydrate intake. To a dietitian, this is all quite clear; to a layman, it sounds like just another weight-watcher's diet.

A cold-weather diet can be a delight to an active man who is restricted at home because of overweight tendencies. Extra fat and protein can be supplied by such foods as butter, margarine, pork, ham, sausage, salted nuts, rich stews, and breads. To this list you can add bacon, macaroni, noodles, potatoes, sugar, eggs, cheese, salami—eaten in proper balance, of course.[2]

Hot liquids—soups, chocolate, tea, or coffee—should be plentiful, extra welcome at the end of a cold trek. One-pot meals are the most practical: stews, for example. Cooking is simple, especially the freeze-dried variety. Too, the concentration of food in one large pot delays cooling, and there's only one vessel to wash. A pot roast, complete with potatoes and vegetables, can simmer over the fire or on the stove while you're busy with other activities, and provide a virtual banquet at suppertime.

A reflector oven, long thought of as a summer camping implement for use before an open fire, works beautifully when placed against the side of a wood-burning stove. There's no reason why you can't have hot biscuits, muffins, even cake. What's more, you can "bake off" an extra supply and freeze it. Fresh meats, too, can be frozen. Pre-cut them into individual portions and wrap separately. Otherwise you may have to cut meat servings with an axe on the chopping block.

The "trail snacks" already mentioned—salted nuts, candy, chocolate—are doubly important in winter for quick energy, but they may make you thirsty when water is scarce. Eating small amounts of snow is harmless but only negligible quantities of water can be extracted from a handful. Mouthing snow continually, or excessively, can make the mouth sore.

"Siwashing"[3] in a winter camp is an easy rut to slip into. Cold weather seems to justify sloppy housekeeping. Pots go unwashed, dinnerware remains caked with food bits, drinking cups become gummy, altogether an unattractive environment, and an unpro-

---

[2] Calories, carbohydrates, protein, and other diet factors are explained in layman's terms in *Food Packing for Backpackers*, Gerry Cunningham, Colorado Outdoor Sports Corp., P. O. Box 5544, Denver, Colo. 80217.
[3] A "siwash" camp is one that is unkempt, sloppy, haphazard.

fessional one. Hot water is not *that* difficult to obtain, nor are a few minutes spent with a scouring pad an impossible chore. Take the time to be neat. If you want to save dishwashing energy, take a cue from the lumber camp cook. He serves *all* foods in only two utensils: a tin pie plate and a one-pint tin cup. Soup, stew, vegetables, meat, and dessert all take turns in the pie plate, which is then wiped clean with a slice of bread. Washing dishes in a logging camp is kept simple. It can be in a woods tent, too.

Siwash campers heave trash into the woods, rationalizing that the next snowstorm will bury it. However, this litter will "blossom" in the spring. Treat the environment in the winter as carefully as you do in the summer.

One problem is human waste. The only solution to this I've ever encountered is to use a small pit dug in the snow. Just before you leave, build a brisk hardwood fire over the waste.

The ability to read weather signs, described in Chapter 13, may head off becoming snowbound beyond your intended stay. However, once a storm strikes, or is immediately imminent, stay put. Build up the wood supply, snug down the camp, and wait for the blow to pass. Even if you have to ration food, you can outlast the worst nor'easter so long as you keep warm and dry. Attempting to "run for it," is an amateurish reaction, one that can lead to disaster. Visibility in a blizzard is usually near zero; drifts pile up, trail signs are obliterated; and the wind can be literally breathtaking. Afoot your chances of survival are negligible; on a snowmobile, only slightly better, dangerous at best. In a jeep, you may find that four-wheel drive is not invincible. Clear weather following the storm will enhance your chances of getting out, no matter how deep the snow.

During day-to-day activities, watch for signs of frostbite, checking each other for telltale spots of whitening flesh on the chin, cheeks, ears, nose, eyebrows. If your feet start to become numb, even while you're active afoot, return to camp immediately, or build a quick fire to warm them. Don't risk frozen feet! Working with bare hands—emergency repairs on a snowmobile, for example—pause occasionally to warm your fingers. Don't rub frostbitten spots vigorously, on the face or elsewhere; only gentle, gradual heat should be used. Hold a warm hand against the area. Do not rub a frostbite injury with snow. This out-dated practice damages flesh tissue and blood vessels.

Breaking through ice into 32 degree water is an occupational hazard of northern trappers. Some survive. Body stamina, length of time in the water, air temperature, and subsequent warming facilities, all affect the chances of survival. Generally, these are slim, so quick action is called for. Get the man out of the water quickly. Death can come within fifteen minutes of immersion. Remove wet clothing and seek warmth at once. In the winter woods, how does one do this? Frankly, only speed and luck can save a man under extreme weather conditions.

Have the best firebuilder in the group conjure a blaze in a hurry; share dry clothing with the victim; massage him through these. If he appears fairly strong, he should walk about the fire, but be careful of this. Don't let him convince you that he's "all right." The shock and warmth-draining effects of cold-water immersion continue for quite a while after rescue. One other tactic may save a man's life if you have a blanket or two handy, or a sleeping bag. Two partners can strip and sandwich the victim's bare body between them, all three wrapped in the blankets or sleeping bag.

Frankly, the above remedies seem inadequate to me but this is about all that is possible away from civilization. The prospects for survival can be frustratingly slim, which justifies a repetition of the warning: Keep away from unknown ice covers!

In order not to end this chapter on a lugubrious note, let me point out that the joys of winter camping are limitless, once you've acquired the knack, and when you observe common-sense rules. Only when you are at home in the woods all year round can you truly call yourself a skilled woodsman. The others are just "summer folks"!

Chapter 12

WHICH WAY IS NORTH?

"I've never been lost, but a couple of times I was so badly turned around I was a half-mile from my own tracks." This was a backhanded, but honest, admission by Eddie Demar, a Maine guide who helped me get started in the profession years ago; his way of admitting that he *had* been lost "a couple of times." Anyone who claims that he's never been "turned around" is either a liar or else he hasn't prowled the puckerbrush long enough for the law of averages to catch up with him. Spend sufficient time in the woods and you *will* get lost!

Standard advice is: "Carry a compass and map," but even these won't save you if you can't read the map, decipher the gyrations of the compass needle, or correlate the two. There's more to finding your way in the woods—and remaining alive if you *do* get lost— than merely carrying a map and compass.

THE COMPASS

Another guide with whom I worked used to scoff at my "fancy compass." His wasn't "all cluttered up with figures," the dial being inscribed only with the cardinal points N, S, E, and W. Jake was a superb woodsman, and because he rarely traveled out of his home territory, which he knew as well as the path to his henhouse, his fifty-nine-cent compass was adequate. It gave him the *general* directions he occasionally required.

In the hands of a less skilled woodsman, such an instrument is an invitation to a night in the woods. It will guide you out of a mile-square wood lot, but on a six-mile cross-country trek, your chances of reaching your destination "on the nose" are about as good as those of knocking down a high-flying crow with a .22 handgun. Having several times been "a half-mile from my own tracks," I can't understand the thinking of outdoorsmen who buy $75 sleeping bags, a $200 rifle, and a seventy-nine-cent compass!

Mine is a Leupold. It cost ten dollars in 1960. It's a professional-quality compass, a miniature, in fact, of a timber cruiser's instrument. The case is rugged and the cover automatically locks the needle in place to prevent unnecessary wear of the pivot. It has an azimuth scale, from which I can obtain a bearing with close to one-degree accuracy, utterly impossible with a simple N, S, E, W dial. The azimuth scale is graduated from 0 at North running counterclockwise through E, S, W, and back to N. Incidentally, "azimuth" is derived from the Arabic and means "the way" or "direction." The Leupold also has quadrant scales with 0 to 90 degree graduations for each quarter, N to E, E to S, S to W, and W to N. There is a township plat embossed on the inside surface of the cover, a handy reference for use with detailed maps. A sighting device facilitates the taking of a bearing. With an inexpensive compass, you will have to compensate for declination, the difference between True and Magnetic North. This leads to errors, since the compass must be rotated. The Leupold compass has a slotted pinion which can be adjusted with a fingernail to compensate the instrument precisely to the declination in your area, whether it be Vermont or Texas!

With such a compass a truly accurate bearing can be obtained; you can even run a rough survey with it! Less sophisticated instruments are solely for *approximate* direction finding. They'll do in a wood lot; in the big woods, you need greater precision.

No matter how refined your compass may be, it will not point the way to camp or to any particular landmark, except by coincidence. Certainly it will not point to True North unless you're standing along a thin line that runs roughly from Florida to northern Minnesota. Elsewhere, the needle is believed to be attracted by the Magnetic Pole, which, in 1960, was located roughly at 75 degrees North, 101 degrees West,[1] or in the general area of Canada's Boothia Peninsula and Prince of Wales Island. However, the compass needle is *not* attracted to this so-called Magnetic Pole.

In regions comprising about half of the United States, the compass needle's direction misses the Magnetic Pole by as much as 10 degrees; up to 12 degrees in parts of the northern Great Plains.

[1] James H. Nelson, Louis Hurwitz, and David G. Knapp, *Magnetism of the Earth*, (Publication 40–1, U. S. Coast and Geodetic Survey, 1962), p. 8, available from U. S. Government Printing Office.

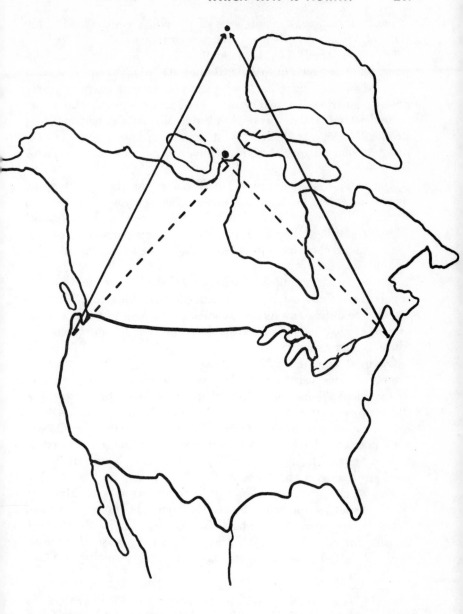

Solid lines indicate True North; dotted lines show that compass needle
does not always point to Magnetic North.

In northern Maine, it points west of the pole by 4 degrees; in the state of Washington, 8 to 10 degrees east of it.

Obviously, then, the Magnetic Pole is not a geographical pinpoint like the True North Pole. Rather, it's a large *area*, elongated in a NNW–SSE direction, and including several magnetic poles and irregularities in magnetism. The compass would be easier to understand if there were a tall, red pole on the horizon at 75 degrees North, 101 degrees West, magnetized to attract compass needles from all over America. However, no such exact attractor exists.

The actions of the compass needle are governed, instead, by overall magnetic fields in the earth, wherever you happen to be standing. To make matters worse, these fields undergo almost constant shifting.[2] For land surveys requiring pinpoint accuracy, the magnetic compass is of questionable value unless the surveyor has the latest data on these shifts.

Despite misconceptions about the Magnetic Pole, and the irregularities of the earth's magnetism, don't discard your compass. As a guide during any sort of backwoods camping trip, it is reliable and much like a fine rifle—capable of greater accuracy than the average man using it!

On most maps of wilderness regions you'll find a "declination symbol" in one margin, a slightly offset V with one leg pointing to the map's True North, the other to its Magnetic North. The difference in degrees is usually indicated. The Magnetic North on a Maine map may not be precisely the same as that on an Oregon map but it is the Magnetic North *for that area*. In the eastern United States, Magnetic North lies *west* of True North; along the northern Pacific coast, it lies *east* of it.

The declination, or difference between True and Magnetic North, varies as you move across the continent, except along an agonic line where the compass, by coincidence, points to True North. This line runs roughly along the east coast of Florida, through eastern Georgia, Tennessee, Kentucky, southwest Ohio,

---

[2] *Magnetic Poles and the Compass,* U. S. Coast and Geodetic Survey, Serial 726 (second edition, 1961), available from U. S. Government Printing Office.
[3] Based upon a U. S. Coast and Geodetic Survey isogonic chart of the United States for 1960. Slight changes occur along this line but they are of little consequence to a sportsman's use of a compass.

northeast Indiana, southwest Michigan, the northern part of Minnesota, into Ontario.[3] Along this line you need not concern yourself with declination. It is zero.

Most compasses are *not* compensated for declination. You will have to do this each time you use it with a map. When the needle has settled on its Magnetic North course, turn the compass gently until the number of degrees on the map's declination symbol appear on the compass, between the needle's pointer and the N on the compass dial. In the eastern United States, the needle should point to the *left* of the compass N; in the western states, to the *right*. Here the advantage of a compensated compass becomes apparent. You get a declination reading automatically.

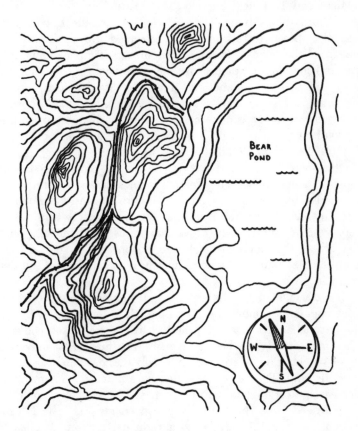

Compass compensated for declination.

Don't confuse "deviation" with "declination." Deviation is localized distraction of the needle, possibly by an iron-ore mine, a steel bridge, or even your gun or axe if these are close at hand. Keep the latter several feet away when taking a bearing.

MAPS

The best-known maps among sportsmen are the "quadrangles" or topographical sheets published by the U. S. Geological Survey, and, along coastal areas, the U. S. Coast and Geodetic Survey. Their Canadian counterparts are available through the Department of Mines and Technical Surveys. Maps issued by the U. S. Forest Service and the National Park Service are excellent, particularly those of national forests. Also well detailed are the maps available from the Army Corps of Engineers. Timber management firms and logging companies use maps showing even minor landmarks and these are sometimes available. State conservation departments, and some county agencies issue maps, too. Those put out by chambers of commerce, aimed primarily at tourist trade, are too often garnished with leaping fish and water skiers, crowding out more important detail.

In the eyes of a skilled woods traveler, a good map becomes almost an aerial photo on which he can spot roads, trails, lakes and ponds, streams, fords, waterfalls, rapids, campsites, mountains, cliffs, canyons. He can tell from the map whether the trail ahead is steep, whether rapids may prove dangerous, or if an area on the other side of the mountain is cleared or forested. A good map is a picture of the country; knowing how to read one brings the detail into focus.

Obviously a map that is several years out of date won't show recent man-made innovations, although the topography will probably be unchanged. You may find roads or trails not shown on such a map or a lake where a river used to flow! This may throw you off in plotting a course, so check the date in the margin.

Scale is vital. The larger it is, the more detail is shown. On the other hand, a large-scale map encompasses a relatively small area, so you'll need more sheets to cover a given region. Scale is generally expressed on the margin as a ratio or fraction: $\frac{1}{24,000}$, for example. This means that 1″ on the map is equal to 24,000 inches, or about 2,000 feet, on actual terrain. This is considered a large-scale map, which will probably encompass between 50 and 70 square miles, in the case of Geological Survey quadrangles.

Rural areas surrounding small towns may be scaled at $\frac{1}{62,000}$, or 1" to slightly less than a mile, and portraying 200 to 280 square miles. A still smaller scale is applied to maps of wilderness regions or to areas where development by man is sparse. These may be scaled at $\frac{1}{250,000}$, or even $\frac{1}{1,000,000}$, and may cover up to 100,000 square miles.

Canadian maps are often scaled at $\frac{1}{250,000}$, while maps of settled regions calling for greater detail may have a scale of $\frac{1}{1,000}$. With *any* map that includes a ratio or fraction form of scale symbol, remember that the numerator and the denominator are *always* the same unit. Don't misinterpret, for example, a scale of $\frac{1}{24,000}$ as one inch to 24,000 feet! It is correctly 1" to 24,000".

Estimating travel distance isn't always a matter of transposing "one inch into one mile." Trails rarely run in a straight line, nor do rivers. A pair of compass dividers will help you in figuring actual travel distance. With a map scaled at $\frac{1}{62,000}$, for instance, set the dividers at 1", roughly equal to one mile, then "walk" the distance on the map, conforming to turns in the route. Better yet, obtain an inexpensive map measurer, which, when run over a trail on the map, transmits an approximate mileage to a dial. At any rate, use scale with care. What appears to be an easy two-hour jaunt on the map, may prove to be an all-day struggle over the earth's surface!

Contour lines portray elevations and valleys. Shown in brown on Geological Survey quadrangles, these are imaginary lines which remain constantly at the same elevation, thus outlining contours of the terrain. One *never* crosses another. Better to visualize a map's contour line, note the waterline on a beach when the lake level drops. The "contour interval" is the vertical distance between two contour lines. If your map indicates a twenty-foot interval, you will have climbed or descended twenty feet vertically every time you cross a contour line.

Contour lines describe terrain quite vividly. When they are crammed tightly together on the map, you have a very steep hill or a cliff. If they are wide apart, the land is relatively flat. If several of them cross a river close together, you can bet your best larrigans that you'll find rapids at that point; but if they cross widely spaced, chances are you'll come upon smooth water, possibly a few shallow riffles.

USING A MAP AND COMPASS

To be of any value in setting a course or determining your position, a map must be "oriented," or aligned to correspond to the country about you. Lay it flat and place your compass, as level as possible, near the map's declination symbol. When the needle ceases to waver, turn the map gently until the Magnetic North leg of the symbol is parallel to the compass needle. Be sure, too, to compensate your compass for declination as explained earlier. Your map will then be oriented.

Mapping and compass work can be practiced at home. Try orienting an assortment of maps in your living room, for instance; take imaginary bearings, trace probable routes. When you come up against the real thing in the woods, you'll find it easier.

Once you're in the backwoods and want to take a bearing, center the compass over your position on the map. Now locate your destination—say it's Backland Pond, roughly to the northeast. Sight across the center of the compass to the pond. Where your line of sight crosses the azimuth scale, note the degree reading. This is your course. Let's say it is North, 35 degrees East; in other words, 35 degrees east of North.

Now take a 35 degree reading, again sighting across the center of your compass, to a landmark to which you can walk without its disappearing from your view. This may be a boulder, an unusual tree, even a stump or blowdown. Walk to this point. Repeat the process, taking another 35 degree reading on another landmark. Don't pick interim objectives which you may lose from sight when you dip into a valley, for example.

In taking bearings, place the compass on a solid object to eliminate needle wobble. If you have a steady hand and the compass is equipped with a sighting device, it may be hand-held. The reason for a series of interim bearings is simply that walking an accurate course while reading the bearing is impossible. The needle will be jostled and lead you off course. Individual sightings, however, give you a fairly accurate reference point.

Certain detours are inevitable in the woods. You can't follow that 35 degree course across a lake, of course. You'll have to swing around it, either compensating for the change in course, or taking a new bearing.

Locating yourself on a map is relatively easy if you can identify at least two distant landmarks. Mountains are a logical choice. Take a bearing on one and transpose the bearing line to your map. Draw it in with a pencil if you like. Take a bearing on the second

FOREST SERVICE LOCATION POSTER
in unsurveyed

T *45 N.*   R *40 W.*

6	5	4	3	2	1
7	8	9	10	11	12
18	17	16	15	14	13
19	20	21	22	23	24
30	29	28	27	26	25
31	32	33	34	35	36

Tack on line indicates the location of this poster

Forest Service Section Line Marker.

landmark and draw in this line. Where the two lines cross is your position.

Finding yourself in one of our national forests—and there are 187 million acres of these—is made easy by the Section Line Marker, a sort of "street sign in the woods," in the form of small yellow posters on which township sections are graphed and numbered 1 to 36. You'll find these on trees, sometimes on a post.

Township boundaries are marked by Township Lines, usually 6 miles apart and running north and south; and by Range Lines, also spaced 6 miles apart, but running east and west. They form blocks—these are townships—6 miles square. Within each of these are 36 Sections, each a mile square. At each section corner, and sometimes at the ½- and even the ¼-mile point, you'll find the yellow Section Line Marker. A nail or tack is driven into it at the Section Lines where the marker is located. Also on the marker are the range and township numbers. Thus, by locating one of these, you can identify the township, and the nail or tack will pinpoint your exact position.

Logging companies run surveys through their lands, often marking boundaries, sometimes outlining areas to be cut. Generally these lines are marked by paint spots on trees. Following such a line will eventually bring you to a road or trail.

Rough surveys are possible with a hand or pocket compass. My woods partner and I once hired out to clear land for a dam project. We were paid by the acre. When the company surveyor couldn't make the rounds for several weeks, our pay was held up. So with a pocket compass and a 100′ steel tape, we ran our own survey and the paymaster advanced us money on it. When the final audit was made, our surveys proved to be off by only 8 per cent—in our favor!

If you have a description of the property and can locate one corner marker, you can establish lines with fair accuracy. Sight from the known corner according to the bearing given in the description. A partner can act as "rodman," walking your line of sight with a tall pole, guided by your hand signals. Distance along this line can be measured with a steel tape, or even by pacing. An average man takes 26 paces to equal a surveyor's 66′ chain. Once a second corner is located, repeat the procedure to find the third and fourth to circumvent the property. Such rough surveys are not legally acceptable, except possibly for staking a claim in undeveloped country, but they can establish the approximate boundaries of a cabin site.

Errors in compass reading occur—under mental stress when you're lost, or when time is short—but they can be reduced by using the utmost care in orienting a map and by taking slow, deliberate compass bearings.

A knowledge of surveyors' dimensions is helpful. Some of these follow:

> $30\frac{1}{4}$ square yards$=1$ square rod;
> 40 square rods$=1$ rood;
> 4 roods$=1$ acre;
> 640 acres$=1$ square mile;
> 36 square miles$=1$ township
> Surveyor's chain$=66$ feet, or 100 links;
> 1 link$=7.92''$.

Have you ever wondered what an acre looks like? It's a square, 208 feet, 9 inches to a side, or 43,560 square feet. Or try a football gridiron. Not including the end zones, the playing field comprises 1.1 acres.

Maps which are exposed to weather, or handled repeatedly can be protected by cutting them along township lines and attaching the segments to a cloth backing, with margin for folding between the sections. Such backing is available from some map firms and can be applied with a flatiron, like a press-on patch. A clear plastic bag will protect such a map, even when it's open to the section you're using.

The "Watch Method" of determining direction has been standard fare in outdoor books since the day Daniel Boone took to the woods! It goes something like this: Point the hour hand at the sun. Halfway between this and the "12" on your watch is South! But if the sun is out, who needs a compass? If it's cloudy, hold a wooden match so that it casts a shadow across the center of your watch. Now you can still point the hour hand toward the sun, with the shadow to guide you. You have found South. Maybe.

Actually this "direction finder" may lead you miles off your course, even in the opposite direction. In most of the continental United States, the method works fairly well in the winter, but in the summer it may be worse than useless. North of the Canadian border, it works quite well year-round except during the late spring and early summer.[4]

Although the U. S. Air Force survival manual describes numerous direction-finding systems, the Watch Method appears to be absent.

NATURAL TRAIL SIGNS

Finding directions at night takes on an exciting urgency but the need for this is rare. Polaris, the North Star, is never more than one degree from True North and on a clear night you can easily establish this, but it will be of little use to you come daylight. You can, of course, mark a rough northerly course at night by pointing a stick at the North Star, but following this course once you leave the stick, will be tricky at best!

The "moss on the trees" has become so famous as a natural trail sign that it is now virtually a joke. Which is just about what it *really* is. So-called moss is often nothing more than lichen, which may grow on all sides of a tree. Occasionally, in a hardwood forest, you may find a few trees with lichen or moss growth on the north side but this alone is *not* a reliable sign. You should look for supplementary signs.

Where the prevailing wind is from the northwest, the tops of pines tend to lean or grow in a southeasterly direction. Old-time woodsmen used to say that spruce gum picked from the south side of a tree had a clear, amber color; from the north side, a soiled-grayish tint. The pileated woodpecker is said to nest only on the east side of a tree. And if you can find a stump, the growth rings are wider on the north side.

If you could gather one of each of these natural signs—presuming they are valid—at one point for comparison purposes, you might be able to obtain a rough bearing. Most of these signs are unreliable, although, given a choice, I would bet on pines with their tips reaching to the southeast.

Following a stream—downhill of course—is said to lead to civili-

[4] See: Robert Owendoff, "How to Get Lost in One Easy Lesson." *Izaak Walton Magazine,* January 1963; and Harold Gatty, *Nature Is Your Guide* (New York: E. P. Dutton Co., 1958).

zation. In the United States this is generally true. In Canada you may find yourself walking to Hudson's Bay or to the Arctic Ocean! However, where following a stream *will* lead you out of the woods, don't walk along the immediate bank. Here you'll run into alder thickets, side streams, swamps, and bog holes which may prove difficult if not impossible to cross. Instead, follow a brook or river along the usual ridge which parallels almost every watercourse. The walking will be easier.

Old woods roads, while not natural signs, can be helpful or deceitful, depending upon which way you travel them. Downhill will usually lead to other roads, possibly a lumber camp. Uphill, you may end up in a maze of "twitch roads" and brush-piles from which extricating yourself can be a horrifying experience. In logging country, remember that loggers haul logs *downhill* whenever they can.

SURVIVAL

Outdoor books are top-heavy with survival suggestions. Gather watercress, plantain, wild tubers, and concoct a wilderness salad; make a deadfall and trap an edible critter; roast it on a fire conjured up from bits of bark, a bow and drill, all whittled with a stone knife scrounged from a streambed! And like the Mounties of old, signal for help with a pocket mirror.

The truth is, not one outdoorsman in 10,000 is sufficiently learned as a botanist to know watercress from skunk cabbage. And the sportsman who can successfully rig a deadfall is as rare as a whooping crane.

To acquire the skills for this type of survival calls for years in the wilderness, plus substantial exposure to "book knowledge."[5] However, the genuine need for such spartan effort to survive arises during the life of no more than one man in a million. With such odds, an outdoorsman is better off first acquiring the basic skills which will prevent the need for such survival effort. If he can live through the first forty-eight hours in the wilds, the average sportsman—however hopelessly lost *he* may think he is—will probably be back in camp within another forty-eight.

[5] One of the most authentic writings on the subject is Bradford Angier, *How to Stay Alive in the Woods* (New York: Collier Books, 1956).

All types of emergencies arise in the wild. A canoe flips over in the rapids and equipment may be lost, but this almost invariably occurs along a known canoe route. A cabin burns, but a trail or road leads to the highway from the ruins. A plane crashes, but a flight plan filed before takeoff will direct search planes. A storm overtakes mountaineers, so they "hole up" until the blow passes and the sun again reveals their route. I am not making light of wilderness emergencies, and certainly not the ability to survive them.

My point is that all too often there is no real need to survive; merely to *avoid!* The most common emergency, of course, is the lost person. And usually he's within an easy day's walk of camp. Nevertheless he doesn't know where he is; nor does anyone else.

True survival in the backwoods begins anew every morning, at the moment when you step from the campyard or leave an established trail, not when you discover you are lost. This includes never stepping into the woods without the "basics"—map, compass, matches, knife, possibly an axe. More elaborate survival kits are incessantly suggested, including water purification pills, plastic water bag, plastic sheet for shelter, surgical tubing (for a slingshot!), candle, nails (I suppose with which to build a cabin if you must spend the winter!), flexible wire for snares, hooks and a fishline, dehydrated foods, steel wool for tinder, a flexible wire saw, first-aid kit, flashlight, mirror (those signals again!), plastic tape (with which to bind the splint on a broken leg, I presume), police whistle, safety pins, sewing kit, aluminum foil, rope, razor blades, flint bar, and a hone. Lest you think I have my tongue in my cheek, this is a survival kit actually suggested by an "authority." With such a kit, it's not a question of survival. The problem is carrying it!

Frankly, I have no idea what I'd do with this assortment of cultch. A true survival kit needn't fill a knapsack. Pick items of *genuine* value, not far-fetched possibilities—add to the map, compass, knife, and matches, such luxuries as trail snacks (candy or raisins), a few extra shells if you're carrying a gun, plenty of tobacco if you smoke. Anything else is burdensome clutter. Stow the *basics* in your woods clothes and you'll probably never have use for the more exotic junk.

I have already touched upon the second step toward daily survival—tell someone where you're going and when you expect to

All you need to survive in the big woods!

return. If you do this, rescuers will know where to start looking and you'll be safely back in camp long before you can snare yourself a rabbit barbecue.

The third step is to condition your mind to the fact that someday you *will* become lost if you roam the woods long enough. Convince yourself beforehand, as you wander along known trails, that an enforced night in the forest need not be a horrifying ordeal. To experienced woodsmen, it isn't. The late Colonel Townsend Whelen, one of the greatest outdoorsmen of recent times, once wrote that a "compulsory" night out ". . . is an experience you will enjoy and cherish for years afterwards." This sort of confidence comes with time spent in the wilds.

Learn to love the wilderness, in the sunshine and in the rain, in the heat and in the cold. Take a truly personal interest in the small things about you as well as the spectacular ones. With a knowledge of the woods and a close kinship with its creatures, will come a feeling of ease, a knowing that you are "at home." Especially, put aside fears of the woods at night. After all, there is nothing there after dark that wasn't there during the daylight hours! A walk on a starlit trail, sitting in the dark and listening to night noises near camp are good conditioners of the mind. A true woodsman's environment is the forest. Getting lost holds no real fear for him. He's psychologically ready for it.

The tired adage: "Indian no lost, teepee lost," makes sense. After all, the red man was *at home* in the wilds; he knew nothing else. That he rarely became lost can be attributed to well-developed powers of observation, not to a "natural sense of direction," which neither white man nor Indian ever possessed. He noted, perhaps unconsciously, strange tree trunks, rock formations, bends in a stream, even a deer track within a moose print. His trail signs were all about him, every day, *because he noticed them.*

Short of becoming genuinely lost, deliberately spending a night out under simulated "lost" conditions is an apt way to condition your mind. Choose a small area of woodlands, close to your home or camp, and wander alone into it, moving erratically without concern for directions. Take along a candy bar or two (but not full rations), tobacco if you smoke, a few matches, and clothing appropriate to the season. As night begins to fall, gather enough firewood to last until morning, then gather as much again. You'll burn more than you think. Settle yourself as comfortably as possible by the fire—a small one to keep you warm, and to save on wood.

You'll get little sleep; the ground will be hard, you'll be lonely, like the last man on earth. But come morning with its sunshine, you will have joined the ranks of at-home-in-the-woods experts who look upon a night out as merely a slight change in plans. Naturally, before attempting such an experiment, alert your family.

If this suggestion seems far-fetched, consider that teen-agers attending the famed Outward Bound schools undergo similar tests during at least two nights out, virtually without food or equipment. Following such a trial by loneliness, the outdoors—day or night—holds no terror for them.

Standard advice to a lost person is: "Don't panic!" This is like telling a woodsman not to fret while he's being treed by an ornery bull moose. Unless you've felt the grip of panic, it's difficult to

This hunter got lost. When the search party, which included the author, found him, he was dead. In his pockets were dry matches and ammunition.

describe, and certainly no advice tempers the wild fear that accompanies it.

A search party of which I was a member once tracked a lost hunter for three days. We never caught up to him. We did find his rifle, his cap, his jacket, and *one of his boots.* That was all.

Following a four-day search for another hunter, we found him dead. In his pockets were dry matches, his rifle functioned, he had ammunition and a compass. His body lay close to a dry stub which would have burned at least twenty-four hours, and less than 100 feet away was a tumble-down tar-paper shack which, if he had fired it, would have produced a smoke signal visible for ten miles! In both cases, "panic" was eloquently inscribed along their trails.

Panic doesn't erupt suddenly. It's little more than annoyance at first, much like your feeling as you watch the last bus pull away at midnight, four miles out in the suburbs. Your eyes probe the woods; you wonder where you made a wrong turn. You try to wish a familiar stump into view. Maybe it's a few yards back along your trail. You backtrack and there, at last—tracks in the mud! Joy elbows worry aside. The trail to camp can't be far. Suddenly the tracks are familiar. Your brain reels from a bludgeoning blow. The tracks are *yours*. You've walked in a circle!

Now your heart pounds; your mouth is dry but sweat oozes through your clothing. You find yourself hurrying a little. Maybe just ahead, over that knoll . . . Your stride lengthens; faster, faster. A gut-gnawing fear twists at your vitals. Mind and body slip out of control as a reason-robbing monster takes over. You're running, dodging trees, thrashing through brush, hurtling over logs. *This* is panic.

It's most likely to happen to the part-time outdoorsman who is fundamentally afraid of the big woods. He's at ease in the sunshine, by his campfire, in his canoe, or along a familiar trail. But because he has not made the wilds a second home; because he is not a living part of his environment; because he has failed to accept the frailties of man in the woods; because he's hamstrung by civilization's standards for comfort—he becomes a pitiful, pathetic, unreasoning creature when he becomes lost, running in abject and uncontrolled terror of . . . what?

What's to be done then, when you find yourself "turned around"? Sit down; and stay down for at least five to ten minutes. Standing, you'll be poised for flight. Review in your mind your day's wanderings; try to remember the last familiar landmark. While doing this, light up a pipeful, or munch on a candy bar. If you cannot reconstruct your route, and you still have no idea of which way to travel, make a note of the time. If you still have more than two hours of daylight, try to locate a known landmark. Move slowly, deliberately. Don't act on impulse. Reason your choice between two courses.

Naturally, if the sun is out, your prospects are improved. At noon it's roughly in the south; it sets in the west. If this seems overly elemental, many a panicky man has forgotten to use the sun. And even if it's cloudy, a match stick will cast a faint shadow, indicating the sun's position.

However, when all has failed, you've located no familiar objects, and only two hours of daylight remain, admit that you're lost for the night. To wander further may well find you still disoriented at dark. You'll have too little time to gather firewood. Settle down sometime before sunset.

In most parts of the United States and in much of southern Canada, you'll be located within twenty-four to thirty-six hours, if you co-operate with the searchers. And there *will* be searchers. There is something about a "lost person alarm" that surfaces compassion in men who live close to Nature. They may cuss and growl, but no ranger, warden, or guide will fail to answer the call. They'll have you out before you can find a porcupine to eat! But you *must* co-operate.

Once you've concluded that you really *are* lost, stay put. If you travel, you may head away from civilization and your rescuers. Give them a chance to find you. At least, don't make a foot race of the search.

Find a lakeshore or riverbank for your campsite if possible; or a woods clearing. Sparse hardwood growth is a good third choice. Devote the remaining daylight hours to gathering wood. If rain or snow comes up, a rough bough shelter will provide some protection.

Until morning your only companionship will come from your fire. Watch the devil-dance of the flames, count the stars, listen to the night noises, recall some favorite poetry, count the states through which you've traveled, or the cities whose names start with *M, P,* or *S*—anything, in fact, that will keep your mind off your predicament. Sleep if you can, but frankly, this will be fitful at best. Tend the fire, but keep it small enough so that you can sit close for warmth, and to conserve fuel. Eventually dawn will come. It always has! And never again will daylight be such a joy to you.

Now is the time to start getting yourself rescued; but *not* by traveling! Stay put. And don't expect rescuers before breakfast. It takes time to organize a search party. Build up your fire to a healthy blaze, but keep it under control. Pile on green boughs, leaves, moss, punky wood, anything that will create smoke.

Billow as much of this into the sky as possible. Smoky the Bear may not like it, but then he's never been lost! A forest fire lookout or a search plane will be seeking a smoke column. And, here again, more debunking is in order. Don't build three fires, despite the hundreds of times you may have read this suggestion. In the first place, you probably couldn't keep three smoky blazes going simultaneously, even if you scurried among them on roller skates. Secondly, a single unaccounted-for smoke in the woodlands will draw attention. Thirdly, it's impossible to keep three smoke columns from blending unless they're several hundred feet apart. *One* fire, belching smoke like a sawmill stack, will do the trick.

If you hear a plane or helicopter, boost your smoke output. If it approaches, remember that dark clothing shows up poorly against a forest background in the summer, but stands out clearly if there is snow on the ground. Wave an appropriately colored garment to signal the aircraft that you are uninjured—a walk-out case—able to navigate. The craft will radio this fact, along with your location, to the rescue party. But even if the aircraft leaves, stay put.

When you hear signal shots or voices approaching, don't run toward them. It's not only dangerous to leave your fire, but sounds in the woods are deceiving. You may actually move *away* from the searchers. Give them a chance to find you. Don't go looking for them. If you have a gun, answer their signal shots—one shot to save ammunition if you're low, or the standard three shots. Either will do. If you have no gun, shout.

All in all, true survival is a matter of prevention, of planning, of mind-conditioning. Carry the basic necessities during every jaunt into woodlands; learn to feel at home in the wilds; learn the skills of a woodsman. You can then enter the wilderness fully confident, reassured, and capable of enjoying it to the hilt. And that's the way you'll come out.

Chapter 13

WOODSMAN'S WEATHER

When Mother Nature is about to throw a meteorological tantrum it's a wise woodsman who scoots for cover. To him a "sudden" or "surprise" storm is almost as rare as a beaver with three-foot antlers. He can spot the symptoms of a weather change in advance, and while it may rain twenty-four hours instead of the twelve he predicted, he's seldom caught off guard. He'll be holed up somewhere, snug as a mouse in a mattress.

It will be said of him that he has an "uncanny" knack for predicting weather. Actually, there's nothing uncanny about it. It's simply the ability to observe and interpret natural signs. And these are all around us.

In the cities where smog hides the clouds and forty-story cave dwellings obscure the stars, we've lost this affinity we once had with the sky and the wind. To most urban dwellers, bright stars indicate a good day for the picnic tomorrow, and clouds mean that the ball game will be rained out. Neither is necessarily correct. If it were not for radio and TV forecasts, most of us would be constantly surprised by the weather.

But not the outdoorsman who lives close to the earth, the water, the sky, the wind, the animals, and the birds. These, along with fog, sound, odors, dew, smoke, even rainbows, are clues to coming weather. Almost daily there is a weather map etched in the sky and unfurled by the winds. And there are dozens of weather maxims, many in rhyme, which are part of our folklore—yet amazingly accurate.

WIND

According to an old Spanish proverb, "When God wills, it rains with any wind." The proverb, however, points up exceptions rather than the rule.

Without wind there will be no change in the weather. With winds out of the N, NW, and SW, come fair weather; while rain, snow, sleet, and other atmospheric mayhem are usually borne by winds from the S, E, and NE. And there are rhymes bearing this out, probably the best known being:

> When the wind is in the South,
> The rain is in its mouth.

Izaak Walton went into more depth on the subject—from a fisherman's point of view, of course:

> When the wind is in the North,
> The skillful fisher goes not forth;
>
> When the wind is in the East,
> 'Tis good for neither man nor beast;
>
> When the wind is in the South,
> It blows the bait in the fish's mouth;
>
> When the wind is in the West,
> There it is the very best.

Shifting winds are a hint of what you can expect. For instance, during a rainstorm accompanied by winds ranging from NE to S, you will get partial clearing soon if the wind shifts into a westerly quarter. Complete clearing will probably follow. Incidentally, a "westerly" is one blowing *from* the west; an easterly, from the east.

Under a cloudy sky, with winds shifting from NW to NE, or from SW to SE, look for squalls—showers and blustery gusts. When winds shilly-shally between SW and SE under a clear sky, wind and rain squalls are on the way.

The most deceitful of all is the south wind. It comes up as a balmy breeze and many an unknowing canoe trip outfit pitches camp on a southern exposure to enjoy the warmth at evening and a respite from black flies. By morning, tents are often flattened or sagging, sleeping bags soggy, grub and firewood soaked. This is easily explained. Low-pressure systems, which travel from west to east, bring storms. Winds circulate counterclockwise about these. Therefore, a south wind is actually the forward edge of the storm. The center of its fury isn't far behind.

Strong northwest or west winds which rise in the wake of a

clearing storm can also deceive. Such winds usually drop at sunset and probably won't rise again until after 9 A.M. the next day. The early morning calm may tempt a canoe outfit to set out across a large lake, thinking that yesterday's blow is over. A few miles out they're caught in the second day's fury. Winds out of the northwest, strong and gusty after a storm, often blow for two to three days, dropping with the sun during the summer. In the winter, they are likely to blow far into the night, diminishing somewhat just before dawn, only to rise again with the sun.

In Florida and parts of the West Coast, winds may not necessarily abide by these rules. Local weather systems in these regions frequently vary from those which follow a national pattern.

CLOUDS

Clouds are probably the most eloquent of the natural weather signs. That old-time woodsmen and sailors often cast their eyes upward is evidenced by this most famous of all weather rhymes:

> *Mackerel scales and mare's tails*
> *Make tall ships carry low sails.*

Not many of our forefathers knew the clouds by their Latin names (how many of us know them today?), so they applied their terminology drawn from life around them. The "mackerel scales" are, of course, cirrocumulus or altocumulus clouds, mottled in a pattern that resembles fish scales. Sometimes they develop into a wavy configuration, much like the ripples on an almost flat, sandy beach. The "mare's tails" are detached wisps of elongated white cirrus clouds with tails gracefully flaring upward. Also known as "hoss tails" in early times, these fly at tremendous speeds at altitudes of 20,000 feet or more. An isolated mare's tail, or a tiny stray patch of mackerel may not materialize into a storm (although they *are* symptoms), but when you observe a spread of mare's tails charging across the sky, *and* a substantial patch of mackerel, chances are you'll have rain within twenty-four hours during the summer, or snow in the winter.

The best-liked clouds are *cumulus*, usually ranging at 4,000 to 5,000. These are the white puffballs whose shadows run across fields under a summer sky. They were "sheep's backs," or "wool

Cirrocumulus clouds, more easily remembered as "mackerel skies." They bring rain or snow. ESSA (Environmental Science Services Administration) photo.

High-flying cirrus clouds, or "mare's tails." ESSA photo.

Cumulus humilis, or "sheep's backs," floating across a fair weather summer sky. ESSA photo.

packs" in the old days. They are fair weather clouds—until they start to bunch up and enlarge *upward*, forming ragged parapets or towers; at the same time lowering, with their undersides turning dark. Rain, possibly a thunderstorm, isn't far away.

The speed with which clouds change their formations and shapes is often a tip-off, too. Buckskin weathermen had a rhyme for this:

> *Short notice, soon to pass;*
> *Long notice, long 'twill last.*

In other words, a slow transition from favorable to foreboding indicates a lengthy storm; a quick change, a short blow.

Sun dogs or halos around the sun were favorite weather omens, and they still are. Caused by sunlight shining through the ice crystals in cirrostratus clouds, they forecast rain or snow. Cirrostratus clouds are a thin, veil-like canopy at great altitudes. An altostratus formation is similar except that it forms at lower altitude

Altocumulus clouds; cool, clear weather usually follows. ESSA photo.

as an opaque film (some weather experts describe this as a
"ground-glass" sky) through which the sun shines as little more
than a blob of light. This portends a warm front and rain within a
half-day or so.

Don't let the Latin names for the various clouds keep you from
learning about them. There are basically three types of clouds:
cumulus, the fluffy "sheep's back" seen on a beautiful summer
day; *stratus,* which appear in layers, hence its name; and *cirrus,*
which is a high-altitude cloud, usually containing ice particles.

Another classification system[1] divides the clouds into High,
Middle, and Low formations. The High clouds include *cirrus,*
the wispy, hairlike bands, or patches of ice crystals; *cirrostratus,*
transparent, whitish, veil-like, producing the halo phenomena; *cirrocumulus,* grainy, rippled patches, sheets, or layers, with some
development of towers and parapets.

The Middle clouds—there are only two basic types—have the
prefix *"alto." Altostratus* is the "ground-glass" sky, often stratified;

[1] See: *Clouds,* Environmental Science Services Administration, U. S. Department of Commerce.

Altostratus clouds, forerunners of rain and snow. ESSA photo.

altocumulus are often small clouds—"cloudlets"—regularly arranged, sometime seen in a parallel roll formation.

The Low clouds are: *stratus,* low-flying formations with a uniform base, opaque enough to mask the sun, sometimes formed by the lifting of fog; *nimbostratus* are dark gray clouds, thick enough to hide the sun, bringing continuous rain or snow; *stratocumulus* are layerlike formations ranging from dark gray to white, with patches and rolls somewhat like *altocumulus* but at a lower altitude.

At first glance, learning to identify the various clouds may seem a difficult chore. If and when you delve deeply into the subject, you'll find that only a fine line exists between one type and another and that frequently they overlap. However, recognizing the basic types—and these *will* help you outguess the weatherman—is not difficult, especially if you make use of the various government publications which explain in laymen's terms, and illustrate actual clouds.[2]

[2] See: free price list: *Weather, Astronomy, and Meteorology,* U. S. Government Printing Office.

Stratus clouds generally identified with persistent rain. ESSA photo.

COLOR

Color came to weather forecasting long before it was adapted to photography and TV! In fact, in Chapter 16 of Matthew is written: "And the Pharisees and Sadducees came, and to test him they asked him to show them a sign from heaven. He answered them, 'When it is evening, you say, *It will be fair weather for the sky is red.* And in the morning, *It will be stormy today, for the sky is red and threatening.* . . . You know how to interpret the appearance of the sky, but you cannot interpret the signs of the times.'"

More recently, weather observers scribbled weather rhymes dealing with color such as:

> *Red sky at morning, sailors take warning.*
> *Red sky at night, sailors delight.*

Evening gray and morning red,
'Twill pour down on traveler's head;
But evening red and morning gray,
Will set a traveler on his way.

The "red sky at morning" and the "morning red" refer, of course, to the eastern sky. A brilliantly red sunrise, according to some experts, means rain or snow within twenty-four hours. I bet on twelve to eighteen hours. The brilliance tinges the entire eastern cloud layer as a rule, although the sun may rise as a dull-red ball, shining dimly through a veil of gray clouds. Either way, a storm is coming.

The "red sky at night," and the "evening red" refer to the western sky. This omen can be tricky. The sun setting as a dull-red ball during a heat wave means more hot weather to follow. However, a lavender sky with blue showing above the clouds is almost a guarantee of more good weather, but not necessarily hot. You'll get high winds the next day, though, if the setting sun lights up the sky with golden, amber hues, sometimes streaked with green at the edges. If the sky develops into a pale, butter-yellow spread of bright light, keep your raincoat handy.

Rainbows are short-range signs and there are rhymes covering these, too:

Rainbow in the morning, shepherds taking warning;
Rainbow at night, shepherd's delight.

Rainbow to windward, foul fall the day;
Rainbow to leeward, damp runs away.

Why should a "rainbow in the morning," or "to windward" portend rain? Because storms travel roughly from west to east. A morning sun which creates a rainbow must shine through rain-laden clouds to the west of your position. These clouds are headed your way—with rain. A "rainbow at night"—actually this means afternoon, of course—has the sun in the west and the rain-laden clouds in the east. These have already passed you.

FOG

Fog and mist have more than their share of weather rhymes. For example:

> *Evening fog will not burn soon;*
> *Morning fog will burn 'fore noon.*

Early fog rhymes originated in New England and there the term "burn off" is still common. A fog does not disperse, dissipate, or drift away. It "burns off."

One rhyme, which I have heard only in the state of Maine, has a practical application:

> *When the mist is on the hill,*
> *Let the hosses be still;*
> *When the mist is in the holler,*
> *Put the hosses in the collar.*

And another, whose origin I could not trace, states that:

> *Fog that starts before the night,*
> *Will last beyond the morning light.*

Another, which I found applicable during a January thaw, seems to be valid during the summer, too:

> *When the fog goes up, the rain is o'er;*
> *When the fog comes down, 'twill rain some more.*

Although not completely accurate, this one is interesting:

> *A summer fog for fair,*
> *A winter fog for rain;*
> *A fact most everywhere,*
> *In valley and on plain.*

On the Maine coast, a beautiful summer day is occasionally transformed into a cold, damp one by a "sea turn." The sea doesn't turn, of course—the wind does, blowing ashore the cold sea air and fog.

Morning fog is generally a favorable sign. Almost invariably it *will* "burn off" by noon. I used to travel across northern lakes early in the morning to reach camps where I guided fishermen, and on many such trips I had to steer through the fog by compass. Yet by the time I'd had a second cup of coffee with my "sports," the sun had the blue sky all to itself.

A fog forming late in the day or during the evening is another matter. This one *does* last through the night, and sometimes into the next day. However, don't include local fog patches that form in low-lying pastures and fields, sometimes covering adjacent highways. I have seen general fogs that lasted four days in the winter, the result of warm air overlying the snow cover.

DEW

Dew does not "fall." It isn't a fine mist that descends. It is condensed from the air's moisture content by objects on the earth that are colder than the surrounding air. A good example of "dew" is the moisture that forms on a drinking glass containing an iced drink. This form of dew has few weather implications, but out of doors dew is a reliable weather sign, and it also has rhymes about it:

> *When the grass is dry at morning light,*
> *Look for rain before the night.*
>
> *When the grass is dry at night,*
> *Look for rain before the light.*
>
> *When the dew is on the grass,*
> *Rain will never come to pass.*

I've never maintained an orderly tabulation of the success ratio, but I do know that whenever the bottom of my canoe was dry at night, it rained before morning, or shortly thereafter! In the winter, you can substitute "frost" for "dew," and "snow" for "rain" with equal reliability.

SMOKE

Smoke as a weather sign is easily observed and interpreted. When it rises directly into the sky and is quickly dissipated, high pressure dominates and you'll have continuing fair weather. But if it rises only a short distance, then settles into low places, low pressure is in evidence, to be followed by rain or snow.

A weather rhyme that dates back to Olde England reads:

> *When the smoke goes West, gude weather is past;*
> *When the smoke goes East, gude weather is neist.*

Smoke that "goes West" is carried by an east wind and this means foul weather. Smoke going east, on the other hand, is borne by a fair-weather west wind.

SOUND

Early weather prophets overlooked nothing when it came to planning tomorrow's activities. Even sounds were guidelines, according to this rhyme:

> *A stormy day will betide,*
> *Sound traveling far and wide.*

On a calm day, with a lowering cloud canopy, sounds carry great distances, often with a hollow ring. Lowering atmospheric pressure permits this and the clouds may act as a sounding board. Train whistles, mooing cows on a far hillside pasture, the barking of a dog, the cries of children across the lake—all of these sounds travel farther than their normal range. Rain or snow will follow, probably within twelve hours.

The wilderness is likely to be quiet on such a day, most of the wild things remaining silent—all but the rain crow, the yellow- or black-billed cuckoo. When he feels rain coming, he emits throaty croakings.

SMELLS

I have not been able to unearth a rhyme dealing with odor as a weather symptom, but such signs exist. You can "smell the rain coming" if your nose is moderately sensitive. Lowering air pressure permits swamp and marsh gases to escape more freely; stagnant water in ditches, too, smells more "loudly." Cooking odors travel farther, even the presence of a skunk is more perceptible. Hunting dogs are more efficient than usual in pointing game birds. I'm amazed that the writers of those noxious TV commercials haven't latched onto these facts to hustle their deodorants!

VISIBILITY

Visibility along coastal areas can tip off approaching weather. During periods of stable barometric pressure, especially in warm weather, salt water is overlaid by a haze that reduces visibility. If this clears suddenly, so that distant islands or shore points are more visible, it means simply that unstable air is moving in, the instability created by low pressure. Rain or snow is en route.

PAINS AND ACHES

My medical knowledge is limited to bungling a Band-Aid, but it is a fact that old injuries or wounds "act up" as low pressure moves in. Don't laugh at the war veteran who predicts rain because a battle wound has started to pain him. Arthritis sufferers, too, sometimes beat the weatherman to the punch. Even corns are prognosticators!

NIGHT SKIES

A ring around the moon, formed by moonlight shining through high-altitude ice-crystal clouds (*cirrus*) indicates rain or snow within twenty-four hours. This is a commonly accepted sign but, frankly, I have not found it entirely reliable. Another version stipulates that a ring growing smaller portends a storm; growing larger, and eventually dissipating, clearing.

That the number of stars visible inside the ring indicates the number of days the storm will last is an old wives' tale. And the same is true of the number of stars stipulating the number of days before the storm arrives. Natural weather signs are rarely *that* specific! What's more, the saying "The bigger the ring, the bigger the wet," as much as I would like to add it to my list of reliable signs, seems notably unreliable.

A quarter-moon tilted so that its "horns" point downward is known as a "wet moon," indicating rain; one with the horns pointed upward, a "dry moon," predicting fair weather. This is another sign I would like to believe, but it's a fallacy. However, when the horns of a partial moon stand out clearly and sharply against the night sky, the chances of high winds are good; when the points are fuzzy, calm weather usually follows.

The color of the moon may be indicative, too. When it is yellowish or orange-tinted, rain is likely. A bright, white moon portends no change. Check this coloring when the moon is well into its zenith, however. The earth's atmosphere colors it falsely on the horizon.

Another night sign, and this one often misleads city folks, is the brilliance of stars. "It'll be a nice day tomorrow," they say, when they note a "million" stars blinking brightly. Don't be too sure. Unusual clarity at night often means rain or snow by early morning.

THUNDERSTORMS

It's difficult to believe that the violence of thunderstorms can come from those lovely white *cumulus* clouds so common on a beautiful summer day. However, when the temperature is high and the humidity oppressive, keep an eye on these formations, especially after 2 P.M. When their rounded tops begin to form towers which climb higher and higher so that the cloud develops vertically, you have a thunderstorm in the making.

As this towering continues, the cloud reaches the *cumulonimbus* stage, accompanied by a darkening of its underside. It is now a thunderstorm cloud. In a matter of minutes, its height may reach 25,000 feet and there the upper edges may flatten out to form an "anvil top"—*anvil cumulonimbus,* the ultimate in storm clouds.

The cause is moist, warm air, heated on the earth's surface and rising until it reaches an altitude cool enough to condense it into a *cumulus* cloud. Since the warming effect of the earth's surface varies from area to area, the rising air is unstable and varies in its moisture content and warmth. Hence, thunderstorm clouds develop at varying speeds and in all shapes and sizes.

Cumulus congestus—warm air from the earth develops the cloud vertically . . .

... into cumulonimbus, a thunderstorm cloud which ...
... continues its upward development into full-fledged "anvil head"
cumulonimbus—a thunderstorm now at full potential. ESSA photos.

Thunderstorms don't follow the usual SW to NE path of most
storms. They travel a more direct W to E route. Thus, once a storm
is sighted, you can determine whether or not it will strike you.
Draw an imaginary east–west line through your position. If the
center of the storm appears to lie along this line to the west, or
slightly to the north of it, you are in the line of fire. If the center is
well south of the line, the brunt of the blow will miss you. A storm
to the east of your position has already passed. It will not "turn
around and come back."

Bear in mind that a storm which appears to be a mile wide
some distance to the west, may well grow to three or four miles
wide by the time it reaches you. Allow extra time for a retreat.
Don't defy thunderstorms, particularly in a small boat or canoe, or

in an exposed position on dry land. Winds often gust up to seventy-five miles per hour. That's hurricane force!

A second type is the *frontal* thunderstorm, which may occur at any time of day, even during the winter. It is caused by a cold front moving into an area where warm air has dominated. The cold front actually lifts this warm air by sliding under it and forcing it upward to cool heights, there to form thunderstorm clouds. This sort of a storm may be much broader than an air-mass storm, since the condition may exist the entire length of the cold front, sometimes hundreds of miles. Otherwise, the appearance and behavior of a frontal storm is much like that of an air-mass upheaval, except that the frontal type usually approaches from the northwest.

Don't try to outrun a thunderstorm by dashing ahead of it. Your best chances are a southerly or northerly course, never an easterly one, except, of course, if the safety of land lies in that direction.

Estimating the distance to a thunderstorm is simple. At the flash of lightning, count slowly: One . . . two . . . three . . . , about one count per second, ending when you hear the thunder. Since sound travels at 1,100 feet per second, every fifth count is one mile. When you see a flash of lightning, and then almost simultaneously hear an electrical "click," the storm is upon you. Thunder will follow almost instantaneously—flash . . . click . . . boom! It can be a little frightening.

What are the most dangerous locations during a thunderstorm? There's a simple answer to this, too: *Any time you are a prominent object on the landscape or afloat, or any time you are close to such an object.* Specifically, danger spots are:

In a canoe or small boat (lightning *does* strike water);

Above timberline, or on an open prairie (lie down if caught here);

Under or close to a dominant tree. In the woods, keep away from logging cranes or other machinery;

By an open fireplace (the chimney type, as in a cabin);

Close to a wire fence, or woods telephone line;

Near metal pipes laid atop the ground, as is commonly done at seasonal summer resorts;

In any small, isolated building, standing by itself in the open.

Oak trees are the most frequently struck, followed by elm, poplar, tulip, pine, ash, and maple. This sounds like folklore, but it has been authenticated.[3] A belief exists, too, that the beech tree is never struck by lightning. Maybe so; I have never found one that appeared to have been hit, but I don't plan to make a personal test!

One of the most dangerous of all places is a forest fire lookout tower. In one tower which I manned, at least two visitors had been killed during prior years, each a photographer bent upon taking storm pictures.

Among the safe places is a metal-topped automobile. Some experts point out that the rubber tires insulate it, but I wonder about these when they are wet. More likely, it's the all-steel cocoon formed by the body that protects you. The fact that convertibles are not considered as safe, seems to back up this theory.

[3] E. W. Littlefield, "Lightning and the Beech Tree," *New York State Conservationist,* Oct.–Nov. 1956.

In the woods, an even stand of timber is relatively safe, the smaller the trees the better. Virtually any cabin or shack located in woodlands is a protective shelter, as is an overturned wooden or Fiberglas canoe. I draw the line at aluminum!

There is some question about the safety of a cave or ditch, as suggested by the Environmental Science Services Administration in its publication *Lightning*. The booklet advises these as alternatives when no building is available. However, some mountaineering experts disagree.[4]

The body may act as a conductor between the floor and roof of a cave, or from one wall to another in a ditch, according to some experts. They suggest that you stand *near a prominent object* which may likely be struck, but not so close that you will be injured. However, where is that fine line between safety and danger in such a case? It has been recommended, too, that a climber caught out in the open, sit on his packframe in such a manner that the frame will conduct a charge *by him*. On Mt. Katahdin, however, a climber was killed by lightning recently. He was in his mountain tent, lying down using his pack as a pillow!

The truth of the matter, of course, is that we know little about lightning, the prime consolation being that your chances of being struck are about one in a million. Yet lightning isn't to be taken too lightly, not when you consider that 600 persons are killed annually by it, and some 1,500 injured. Fatalism is not appropriate. At least take the known precautions.

There's an old adage to the effect that if you hear the thunder, lightning did not strike you; if you see the lightning, it missed you; but if you *are* struck, you did not know it! However, a near miss can be an impressive occasion. My grandfather, who logged the Wisconsin woods at the turn of the century, escaped unscathed when two horses, between which he was standing, were both killed outright!

Occasionally, when a person is about to be struck by lightning, his hair may stand on end—literally—and his skin may tingle. The only escape is to drop to the ground immediately. If it's any comfort, this is official—from the U. S. Environmental Science Services Administration. However, one in a million are pretty good odds.

[4] Alvin Peterson, "Lightning Hazards to Mountaineers," *American Alpine Journal*, 1962.

At that rate, thunderstorms are entitled to respect but there's no real justification for blind fear.

THE BAROMETER

Virtually every ourdoorsman has at some time received a barometer for Christmas or his birthday. For years, my first one hung on the wall, where I tapped it in a knowing and professional manner to see which way the needle jiggled. When this was upward, I confidently predicted good weather. No one challenged me, since it was usually already a beautiful day. If the needle flickered downward, I predicted a storm. Here again, I couldn't miss, since it was currently raining or blowing a snowy nor'easter. All my barometer ever did was to confirm, not predict. Used in this manner, it was little more than a plaything.

A barometer measures atmospheric pressure and it works equally well indoors or out. Someone back in about 1640 figured out that normal sea-level pressure will hold a column of mercury in a glass tube at 29.9 inches. The principle is still in use. When the mercury rises, pressure is increasing; when it lowers, pressure is dropping. Early weathermen, seafarers primarily, referred to their instrument as "the glass," and they came up with this rhyme:

> *When the glass falls low,*
> *Prepare for a blow;*
> *When it rises high,*
> *Let all your kites fly.*

The barometer most of us know is the aneroid type, in which atmospheric pressure activates a mechanism which, in turn, moves the needle "up" or "down" on a calibrated circular dial corresponding to the "inches" on the mercurial barometer.

Such barometers are preset at the factory for sea-level use. However, atmospheric pressure decreases with altitude at the rate of 1″ for every 920′. Some casual experts round this off at 1,000′. For every 920′ your location is above sea level, you will have to adjust your new barometer upward 1″. Most dials are calibrated at $\frac{1}{10}$″ so that you can reset it $\frac{1}{10}$″ for every 92 feet. On the back of most barometers you will find a small screw with an arrow

WIND-BAROMETER TABLE

Wind Direction	Barometer Reduced to Sea Level**	Character of Weather
SW to NW	30.10 to 30.20 and steady	Fair with slight temperature changes in 1 or 2 days.
SW to NW	30.10 to 30.20 and rising rapidly	Fair, followed within 2 days by rain.
SW to NW	30.20 and above and stationary	Continued fair with no decided temperature change.
SW to NW	30.20 and above and falling slowly	Slowly rising temperature and fair for 2 days.
S to SE	30.10 to 30.20 and falling slowly	Rain within 24 hours.
S to SE	30.10 to 30.20 and falling rapidly	Wind increasing, with rain within 12 to 24 hours.
SE to NE	30.10 to 30.20 and falling slowly	Rain in 12 to 18 hours.
SE to NE	30.10 to 30.20 and falling rapidly	Increasing wind; rain within 12 hours.
E to NE	30.10 and above and falling slowly	In summer, with light winds, rain may not fall for several days; in winter, rain or snow in 24 hours.
E to NE	30.10 and above and falling fast	In summer, rain probably within 12 hours; in winter, rain or snow, increasing winds.
SE to NE	30.00 or below and falling slowly	Rain will continue 1 or 2 days.
SE to NE	30.00 or below and falling rapidly	Rain with high wind, followed within 36 hours by clearing, and in winter, by cold.
S to SW	30.00 or below and rising slowly	Clearing in a few hours, fair for several days.
S to E	29.80 or below and falling rapidly	Severe storm imminent, followed in 24 hours by clearing, and in winter, by cold.
E to N	29.80 or below and falling rapidly	Severe NE gale and heavy rain; in winter, heavy snow and cold wave.
Going to W	29.80 or below and rising rapidly	Clearing and colder.

* From *Official U. S. Coast Guard Boating Guide*, U. S. Government Printing Office.

** Readings at sea level. Add 1/10" for every 92' of altitude at *your* location.

FOLKLORE AND NATURAL SIGNS

marked "up" and "down." Turning this makes the adjustment.

It's not practical to carry a barometer on most camping trips, but on the wall of a backwoods cabin it can be highly informative. Observe it often and as regularly as possible, jotting down the readings, and the time, on a wall chart. Make note, too, of the wind and the current weather. The speed with which the barometer falls or rises is important. A simple "up" or "down" reading means little. The wind direction is vital, though. Following is a wind/barometer chart which, combined with a barometer and regular observations, can make you wise in the ways of weather.

The fine lines between superstition, folklore, and scientifically established fact are often fuzzy. No doubt some superstition has been blended into folklore weather predictions, but generally the early weather prognosticators were keen observers from sheer force of habit *and necessity*. The pioneer livelihood was based on foot-, horse-, and sail-power. Weather was far more important to them than it is to us today. Only in extreme cases are our jets grounded, our freeways closed, our freight trains stalled, but a heavy rain—which our transportation facilities almost ignore—bogged down many a wagon train or Conestoga freight wagon. Weather was an integral part of every life, which is why the American Indian, the pioneer in linsey-woolsey, the seafarer, and the mountain man in buckskin, all were pretty good weathermen. And they left us a heritage of weather wisdom which few modern meteorologists will challenge.

That falling cockleburs can predict rain is, at first, a ridiculous presumption. And the dropping of soot from a fireplace chimney seems equally far-fetched. Yet cockleburs and bits of soot, perched precariously, on the verge of falling, may well be loosened and dropped by dropping atmospheric pressure.

Birds supplied weather signs long before the white man nosed ashore at Jamestown, Plymouth, or Wiscasset, Maine. The Shawnees believed that when birds flew low and silently "a great storm" was coming. Mourning doves perched close to the trunk of saplings predicted "great winds." Present-day seacoast dwellers have their "bird signs" too. When sea birds remain close to shore or perch for long periods on rooftops, pilings, and rocks, they look for rain.

Duck hunters know that waterfowl fly high in good weather; skim the marshes in bad. And in many parts of the country, a robin singing high in a tree means continued good weather, but stormy weather is on the way when the robin drops to the lower limbs for its songfest!

Wild animals, especially elk, leave the high country at the approach of a storm, especially if it's likely to be snow. Deer also do this. I once hightailed out of Maine's Caribou Valley when I noticed that *all* of the fresh deer tracks were headed downhill. A nor'easter struck that night and I was the last man out of the valley that winter! Deer and moose, normally morning and evening feeders, take to browsing voraciously during the day when they sense bad weather on the way. When coyotes howl at midmorning, a storm is in the offing.

Fallen spruce and pine cones open in dry weather, but tend to close as dampness nears. Hardwood leaves turn, although some experts believe this is caused by a shift in winds. But even this brings rain.

Lobstermen will tell you that in humid air rain is more likely at low tide than at high, because a falling tide lowers atmospheric pressure. I'm not enough of a seaman to confirm or deny this.

Eleanor predicts weather by the cooking water in vegetable pots. "It's going to rain!" she exclaims when she has to add water to the spinach, and I'm sure that many a pioneer woman made the same comment in her log-cabin kitchen. Water boils away faster when low pressure is present, or moving in.

When Tom Bingham, a Black Hills pioneer, discovered Wind Cave in what is now Wind Cave National Park, he *heard* it before he saw it. It was a mere ten-inch opening, so that air currents blowing in or out caused a whistling sound. When atmospheric pressure is falling, the air in the cave tends to blow *outward;* with a rising barometer, it blows *inward*. Even a cave can predict weather![5]

A perfect summer day—cloudless and warm—is known as a "weather breeder" among woodsmen. Of course their prediction can't miss. Perfect weather doesn't last indefinitely and *any* change has to be for the worse!

[5] Freeman Tilden, *The National Parks* (New York: Alfred A. Knopf, 1968), p. 250.

One yarn which *must* be labeled superstition claims that shooting a gun at a tornado will dispel it! And there's another which can't be trusted completely, but I'm fond of it nevertheless because it gives me hope for the day when I awaken to hear rain pattering on the tar-paper roof of my cabin. It's a rhyme which states simply, and optimistically:

> *Rain before seven,*
> *Stop before eleven.*

Few, if any, serious books on weather acknowledge the existence of weather rhymes or folklore but this doesn't deter me from memorizing and observing. I know that Mother Nature always tips her hand. In that respect, she's a lady. When about to throw a tantrum, she drops a cocklebur, or paints a pallid mackerel across the sky. She's trying to tell me something. And I'm going to listen.

Chapter 14

GETTING ALONG WITH
WILD THINGS

What we do not recognize, we suspect; what we fail to understand, we fear. This is basic human behavior. When this blind reasoning —or lack of it—is carried to the outdoors, we quickly take the next step. We destroy.

While deer hunting on the slopes of Maine's East Kennebago Mountain, I heard a single shot close by on a beech ridge. I made my way to it and found a hunter probing a pulpy mass of blood, guts, and fur with his rifle muzzle. There was no greeting. He simply looked up and asked: "What is it?"

He had killed a marten, a creature of the deep woods, rarely seen by man—a needless act of abject stupidity.

Had that hunter possessed the good sense to hold his fire he would have witnessed a scene observed by only one man in a million—a marten prowling for its daily meal. He might even have seen it overtake a squirrel, high in a tree, or it might have approached him had he remained still. But he had never seen a marten. So he killed it.

During my early days as a woodsman I frequently carried a gun needlessly. I like guns; I enjoy shooting; and at the time I was proud of my marksmanship—a hawk toppled from a tall elm at 120 yards; an arctic owl blasted from a fir spire; a red fox toppled at 175 yards; a woodchuck upended on the run. Today, I'm rather ashamed of these "feats." I still shoot a great deal but at paper targets and tin cans. I've learned to enjoy wild things, not as bull's-eyes, but as neighbors. Each day in the woods is now a richer than ever experience.

Hunting is a legitimate and *necessary* sport. I have no patience whatsoever with the bleeding-heart type of conservationist who howls that *all* hunting is evil. Such do-gooders are ignorant of the ecology of the woodlands and the prairies. We cannot stockpile wild animals. Just as any given acreage of pastureland will support so many beef cattle, a given area of swamp, woods, and prairie will sustain only so much wildlife. Beyond that limit, excess live-stock, wild or domestic, suffers—from malnutrition, disease, preda-tors, starvation.[1]

The real danger to wildlife is not the hunter. He is the first to protest when a species is endangered. It is his money that fi-nances the enforcement of game laws and wildlife management research. The threat comes from loss of habitat and this is so serious that some eighty-nine species of wildlife, although not hunted, are in danger of extinction. The culprit is not the gun, but the bulldozer that fills in marshes, drains swamps, levels forests, and prepares the earth for endless acres of asphalt and concrete.

Nevertheless, the only killing of wild animals which can be justi-fied today is during designated hunting seasons for specific species; as a survival measure (a rare necessity!); in self-defense (still rarer!); or for the control of certain predators. The shooting of any wild thing, whether protected or not, for the sheer pleasure of seeing it fall to the ground is as sickening a commentary on man-kind as the hunting of polar bear and wolves from a plane.

Legitimate hunting has a place in backcountry camping. In fact, most big game hunts are conducted from remote tent camps, and even small game hunting is better enjoyed for having camped out away from the mass of road-bound hunters.

"Pot hunting" to supplement the larder adds variety but don't rely on it for a food mainstay. Game animals have a knack for becoming scarce when you really need them. What's more, there are few if any places where pot hunting is legal except during regular game seasons. Enjoy a rabbit stew as an unexpected delight but don't plan on it. The backwoods are more fun when you live *with* your wild neighbors than *by* them. And you'll eat more regularly, too.

The presence of wild animals, birds, reptiles is not necessarily a hazard; in fact, it's proof that Nature's balance hasn't yet been thrown completely out of kilter. When our environment has elim-inated wild things, it's only a matter of time before we join them in oblivion.

You can't ask for better neighbors than a pair of otters cavorting

[1] E. L. Cheatum, "Too Many Deer," *New York State Conservationist*, June–July 1956; also James B. Trefethen, "The Face of Starvation," *National Wildlife Magazine*, Oct.–Nov. 1969.

in the water, a family of beaver gnawing industriously at a clump of poplars, a pileated woodpecker jackhammering a dead stub, a grouse budding unconcerned in a birch, a moose looking foolish as he lifts his great hooked nose draped with lily pads, a skunk waddling uninvited into a campsite, or a bear imitating a forty-mile-per-hour bulldozer in his panic to get away from hated man. These are delights of the backcountry, not hazards!

Not everyone feels this way about woods critters. At the campsite next to ours one night, a woman sat up until dawn in genuine fear that a bear would invade her tent. My reassurances, and her husband's, carried no weight. She was *sure* she would be attacked. Unbridled fear of wild things can bring only misery, but an understanding of them adds zest.

Bear stories always make good news copy as well as campfire entertainment. Yet unprovoked attacks by bear on campers are exceedingly rare—virtually non-existent if reasonable precautions are taken.

The three major species are the black, grizzly, and the Alaska brown bear. The grizzly is not numerous and is confined to the Far West, the Canadian West, and Alaska. Your chances of encountering one, unless accompanied by a skilled hunting guide, are slim. Nevertheless, take precautions. Give the bear a chance to avoid you. Hikers and backpackers, slinking quietly along a wilderness trail, stand some chance of meeting a grizzly. A few pebbles carried in a tin can tied at your belt will rattle sufficiently to warn a bear, certainly avoiding the possibility of a surprise encounter. Should you meet a grizzly who shows signs of standing his ground, *you* had better leave! Don't pitch camp in the vicinity of a grizzly that shows no fear.

It was one or two grizzlies which killed and injured several campers in the backcountry of Glacier National Park in 1969. Such attacks had not happened for many years but the resultant publicity renewed fear of all bears throughout America. Biologists are not in agreement as to why the attacks occurred. Some proposed that perfume, hair spray, even shaving lotion attract bear. This is theory, of course, but until it is proven or disproven, it's just as well to omit the use of these cosmetics in grizzly country.

The Alaska brown bear is the world's largest, sometimes weighing up to 1,500 pounds. He's a resident of Alaska's coastal regions and keeps to the thickets, except for occasional forays into

Grizzly bear with two cubs. Fish & Wildlife Service photo.

the open. His reactions are often unpredictable and he should be considered dangerous. Apply the same precautions called for in grizzly country and *never* let your guard down. The brown is difficult to kill. This takes a rifle with the knock-down power of a falling brick wall, coupled with skilled marksmanship.

The black bear is the one most of us know best, yet few campers have ever seen one running wild in the woods. The black is a relatively small bear, rarely exceeding 400 pounds, more likely to range between 150 and 250.

The only dangerous black bear is the semi-civilized critter who has learned to beg from tourists, or one that visits campground garbage pails and town dumps. This bear has lost all fear of Man and it's beyond my understanding that some people will hand-feed one, no matter how "cute" it may seem. One swift swipe with a forepaw will break a strong man's back! At a lumber camp I once saw a three-inch iron-bound oak door that had been torn from its hinges and smashed. The culprit was trapped the next night. It was a rather scrawny 200-pound black bear!

Attacks by black bear are rare, but when they do occur there is usually provocation. I once tracked a she-bear with two cubs and managed to get within thirty yards of them. I had no intention of shooting; I merely wanted to observe. Within seconds, however, I *had* to shoot. Even though I had intended no harm, the she-bear had no way of knowing this. My approach, in her mind, endangered her cubs, so she came at me.

Last summer, a black bear severely mauled a tot playing in the backyard of her home on the outskirts of Kitimat, British Columbia. In Michigan, several years ago, a large black bear carried off a small child. These are certainly instances of unprovoked attack, but I believe that in each instance, the bear did not identify the children as human beings because of their small size. I'm sure that had adults been involved, both bears would have retreated. Wild animals misunderstand, too.

A black bear, while he should not engender fear, certainly deserves respect. Throwing rocks at one feeding at a campground garbage pail is provocation; and approaching a cub for a camera close-up is a hostile act in the eyes of that cub's mother.

Usually the smell of Man will keep a truly wild bear away. However, don't store foodstuffs in a tent while you're away for the day—especially such favorites as meats, a can of bacon grease, or an open jar of honey. Few bear can resist such temptation and canvas is little more than tissue paper to bruin. He never has understood doors—so he's apt to avoid the tent's entrance, going through one wall and out the other, creating a disaster area en route!

Moose are seldom bothersome. But if your campsite is invaded, it's probably because you pitched camp on a lily-pad-lined shore where Mr. Broadhorns has been in the habit of feeding. In the process of reaching his favored dining area, a bull has been known to catch an antler in the clothesline and amble away with the week's washing. Too, you may find your presence disputed while fishing a beaver bog. When you see a moose, cow or bull, circling you nervously, keep an eye on it. Moose live close to water and this one may resent your fishing in its personal pond. As for meeting one in the woods, I've been trying for three summers to track one down in the large swamp near our cabin. All I want are pictures but I have as yet to catch up to one, photogenic or otherwise.

Being treed by a moose is a favorite campfire topic among woodsmen and I know several who have undergone the experience.

Alaskan moose at a favorite feeding spot, among lily pads.

A moose can trot through the woods at a good clip, despite its huge antlers, but when it comes to tricky footwork, like trying to corner a man, the moose is awkward. Nevertheless, his attempts are impressive and a wise man takes to a tree. Such encounters usually end up in a stand-off—the quarry up in the branches, the moose pawing and snorting in frustration. But even these instances are rare.

Deer are the most common of the large animals, either the eastern white-tail, or the western mule variety. A wounded deer can be dangerous; its hooves are sharp enough to disembowel a man. Otherwise, there's nothing to fear. The white-tail has a habit of approaching a nighttime campfire, sometimes sneaking soundlessly to within a few yards. Fascinated by the light, it may stand for some time. You'll be unaware that it's there. Suddenly you'll hear a "chesty," blowing sound, much like a series of throaty sneezes—the deer's cry of alarm—then the pounding of retreating hooves. Eleanor and I have never been able to figure out why a deer will share our campfire, apparently at ease for several minutes, then suddenly hightail away in fright. It has happened to us dozens of times, yet each sudden "deer sneeze" startles us off our log seats!

Mule deer, so-named because of their huge ears, like the shade of pines in the semi-open country of the West. You'll often find one or more lying down, calmly watching your approach until you get too close. Once spooked, their tremendous strides carry them over a ridge quickly.

Stalking within camera range of either the white-tail or the muley is never easy. Work your way toward them upwind since, despite indifferent eyesight, they have sharp noses. Make no sudden moves. A woodsman once described stalking technique briefly; "Stop often 'n' set frequent," he advised. Freeze when the deer glances your way, move slowly forward when it resumes feeding or looks in the other direction.

Elk favor the high country of the West in the summer and seek sheltered valleys when snow comes. They are especially wily and

White-tail deer on the Texas plains. Fish & Wildlife Service photo.

Mule deer in Montana. Fish & Wildlife Service photo.

Bull elk in its winter feeding range. Fish & Wildlife Service photo.

shy. Consider it a memorable day when you get a close-up view of a bull! I've managed to photograph a young bull but never a mature one, and even then all I got was a going-away view of the stern deck.

An elk's whistlelike "bugle" is a stirring sound. In the South Dakota Black Hills I once "conversed" with one, using an elk call, but I couldn't budge it from its hiding place. A full-grown bull is a majestic beast but none of his kind is ever a problem to backwoods campers. You'll be lucky, in fact, if you can get near one.

Next to bear, the various cats are the most feared of woods critters. Thanks to phony TV series, too many people believe that the cougar, the wildcat, or the lynx devote their lives to tracking down and pouncing upon hapless outdoorsmen. Probably no animal in North America makes a greater effort to avoid Man than the cat.

Wildcats—they're known as bobcats, too—are extremely timid. During close to forty years in cat country, I have seen only three running free, without dogs on their trail. Their tracks are common on snow in rabbit swamps. While returning to our fire tower at about midnight many years ago—Eleanor and I had been visiting in the valley and we knew the trail well—we paused for a breather under an overhanging ledge. There was a rustling overhead, no more than eight feet above us, then a hackle-raising scream. We had surprised, and frightened, a wildcat!

The largest wildcat I ever saw had been trapped near a lumber camp where I worked. It weighed thirty-five pounds, unusually large. The average is nearer twenty to thirty.

The lynx is rare, confined primarily to the North, where he keeps to the deepest wilderness. He's slightly larger than the wildcat and even more shy. I know several woodsmen who have never seen one except in a trap. I came upon my only one accidentally, spotting him lying in the snow on a woods road, about 100 yards away. I cussed myself at the time for having missed an easy shot, but as I look upon it now, I'm glad I missed. Otherwise, I would not have seen the cat's magnificent leap of more than twenty feet from a sitting position! He was gone before the echo of my shot died out.

The cougar—also called mountain lion, catamount, puma, panther, "painter," or just plain "big cat"—is a western species, weigh-

Bobcat in Arizona. Fish & Wildlife Service photo.

ing from fifty to 200 pounds, unmistakable by virtue of his size, and a long restless tail. Some biologists think there may be twenty to fifty of them in New Brunswick; an occasional "cat report" comes out of Vermont; and I once saw a photo of one reportedly killed in Maine in 1936, but I've never been able to authenticate the latter.

The cougar still stirs the minds of excitable folks. Cat legends die hard. In 1960 half the sportsmen in a Minnesota town turned out to hunt down a "cougar" which a farmer had reported. We found large dog tracks.

Cats—either the wildcat, lynx, or the cougar—may be relatively plentiful in country chosen for backwoods camping. However, when you consider that hunters cannot approach any one of them without the aid of dogs, it stands to reason that fear of them is groundless.

Canada lynx. Note pointed, tufted ears, as compared to those of bobcat. Fish & Wildlife Service photo.

A Quebec French Canadian logger I once knew refused to leave the bunkhouse at night. He had heard an "Injun devil," he said. And his fear was genuine. In his language the "Injun devil" is a "carcajou"; in ours, it's a wolverine, the most despised of all northwoods animals. Pound for pound—it seldom exceeds forty pounds—it is the most vicious, aggressive, and ferocious animal on the continent. He's been known to attack a bear, tear apart a team of Alaskan huskies, eat a porcupine, quills and all; he is a trap robber, and an apt burglar, breaking into remote cabins considered breakproof. He befouls the interior, leaves a shambles. Most northwoods trappers have a right-to-the-point attitude toward the wolverine: "Shoot it on sight!" Your chances of running into one are slim but they're not uncommon in the Canadian wilds and in parts of Alaska. The critter has only one redeeming feature—its fur will not accumulate frost, even at 70 below, nor mat and freeze to the skin. Eskimos use it for trimming parka hoods and wrists.

The most despised critter in the northwoods, the wolverine. This one was captured alive after photo was made at Auke Bay, near Juneau, Alaska. Fish & Wildlife Service photo.

Early Russian novels were rich in questionable wolf lore and the subject is still a spine-tingler around a campfire. The timber wolf is an impressive creature, weighing up to 160 pounds. It's a cliché, I realize, but "bloodcurdling" is an apt description of its howl. However, that's about the extent of the threat the wolf presents to most backcountry travelers. If you're lucky, you may hear one in northern Minnesota; otherwise, you'll have to listen for it in Alaska or Canada.

So far as campers are concerned, we can group the various foxes together—the red, gray, kit, and arctic—along with the coyote. They're interesting to watch, difficult to approach, and present no problems at a campsite. You may hear a fox yapping at night—a high-pitched, doglike bark—or a coyote may awaken you as it howls at the moon, but these will thrill you, not annoy you.

The beaver is probably the backcountry camper's best friend and most interesting neighbor. His conical house of mud and sticks, as well as his dams provide seasoned firewood; and when you come upon a beaver dam, fish the pond behind it. Trout are often trapped in these ponds and have nothing to do but grow big, fat, and sassy. Beaver dams also serve as bridges, but they're a nuisance to a canoeman.

Some persons mistake muskrats for beavers. The latter are much larger, weighing up to fifty pounds or more, while muskrats seldom exceed four pounds. The beaver's tail is flat, like a canoe paddle blade, and scaly with no fur on it. Early beaver trappers in the American West considered beavertail a delicacy. The muskrat's tail is relatively long, slightly flattened but never as broad as that of a beaver. Muskrat houses are smaller, too, up to three feet high at the most. I have seen beaver houses eight feet high.

Beaver are compulsive woodchoppers. In fact, some woodsmen claim that their incisor teeth, if not used regularly, will grow in a circular fashion, piercing the beaver's brain cavity from within its mouth. Along streambanks where beaver are working, you'll find stumps clearly showing teeth marks, and at the foot of the stumps, wood chips, some as large as a man's thumb. Beaver do not eat these chips. They *do* eat the bark of poplar and aspen, their favorite food, and I've found beaver-cut stumps of maple, black birch, ash, and even a white oak more than a foot through, but never a softwood. Beaver can't direct the fall of a tree and they "hang up" many. Occasionally, a beaver is killed by a falling tree,

Typical beaver pond, dam in foreground, beaver lodge in center background. Fish & Wildlife Service photo.

and sometimes one is pinned to the ground by a heavy butt sliding off the stump suddenly.

A beaver house is a masterpiece of engineering. The entrance is always underwater, which is why beaver build a dam in conjunction with a house. Raising the water guarantees suitable depth around the dwelling. Within the house is a shelflike area where the family can eat or sleep out of water. Few beaver dams are truly watertight. Whether this is planned or not, I'm not sure. Possibly they "build in" some leaks so that the pond won't overflow the dam. However, remove a few sticks from the top of a dam to start a small sluice and it will be repaired within a few hours, certainly by the next night.

As for beaver slapping the water with their tails "to warn other beaver," I believe this may be a fallacy. Eleanor and I have observed innumerable beaver, often at close range, and I'm convinced that the tail is brought down sharply for more effective leverage in making a quick dive. We've heard it hundreds of times, but intended as a signal "cannon shot" or not, it always startles us.

Not all beaver build houses and dams. "Bank beaver" lead an easier life, living in holes along a streambank, with an underwater entrance. When you find a floating brush pile of alders and poplars, you have come upon a bank beaver's feed bed. Although he builds no structures while residing in a streambank, he is industrious to a degree, sometimes cleaning out a large clump of alders. Both beavers work principally at night but often get in some overtime by starting in the late afternoon. Evening is the best time to observe them.

However, they're wary. You can't stroll casually into a beaver

Unusual action shot of a beaver swimming underwater. Fish & Wildlife Service photo.

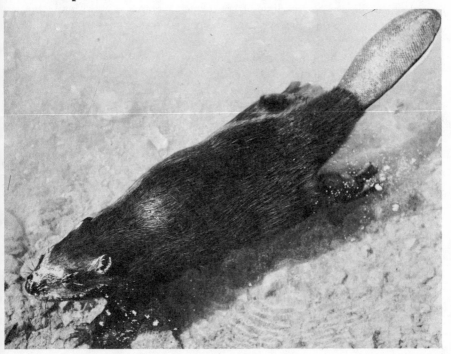

cutting to watch. They'll flee. Our favorite technique is to steal along the river in our canoe until we hear a beaver's bucksaw teeth gnawing away in the brush. We then edge the canoe silently between the beaver and the river. During several years of trying, we have succeeded in tricking only a few. But what magnificent, hell-bent rushes they make during their getaway, plopping into the river so close that they splash us!

Often found in beaver country but actually a nomad who roams from watershed to watershed, the otter is shy, timid, and difficult to approach. During the years that we've haunted waterways, we have gotten within close range of only a few. Last summer we ran into a trio on the river near our cabin. After a few minutes of hide-and-seek around the canoe—they hid and we sought—the otters clambered up onto the bank and ran upstream for about a half-mile, during which we lost them. Suddenly, there was a series of splashes back of the canoe and there they were! More hide-and-seek antics followed, then we managed to corner the mother in a small cove, while her two youngsters swam to the opposite bank. For about five minutes, Eleanor sat within paddle length, listening to the angry growling of sputtering Momma otter. Finally we realized that our curiosity and misplaced friendliness were really cruel. We edged away, the three otters regrouped, sailing away with their heads held high, resembling tiny Viking vessels. Compared to the otter, the beaver is a sluggish barge!

Too often we think of the wilderness as the north country, overlooking the great and fascinating swamps of the South. These are not the evil places so often portrayed in the movies. Swamps are interesting and beautiful. During four days in Okefenokee, we did not see a single snake, for example. Alligators, yes—more than a hundred of them. These are supposed to poise on hummocks, drooling at the prospect of gobbling a swamp visitor, but while we didn't find their behavior friendly, it certainly was not threatening. Traveling into the swamp with a small outboard-powered boat, then switching to a canoe for prowling the interior, we sneaked the canoe to within thirty-five to fifty feet of dozens of alligators. Their retreat was not the pell-mell rush of the beaver. They gave us the right of way, grudgingly, and I think condescendingly, sinking slowly out of sight and easing away in dignity. We left Okefenokee reluctantly, with a feeling of respect for alligators, but not fear.

Alligator in Okefenokee Swamp. Fish & Wildlife Service photo.

Porcupines are pests, hated by foresters because hedgehogs—porky's other name—strip the bark of softwood trees, killing them. And many a wilderness wanderer has awakened to find his canoe paddle or axe handle gnawed. Even outhouses are not sacred. Porky likes to gnaw the seat!

Quill pigs—still another name for a porcupine—have benefited from a reluctant protection accorded them because they can be overtaken and clubbed by a hunter, then eaten to ward off starvation. Frankly, this borders on romantic drivel. During forty years in the woods, I've never met a woodsman who has tasted porcupine meat.

We tolerate them near our cabin, not as possible future fare, but simply because they're interesting to watch. Last summer, while investigating a new beaver pond, we located a baby porky in a maple clump, no more than six feet from the ground. For the first time we observed one literally at eye level, doubly fascinating because of its size, barely that of a kitten.

Porcupine quills can be painful. Porky can't throw them, but he

Porcupine, stupid and destructive, but easily overtaken by a man on foot. Fish & Wildlife Service photo.

can flip his armored tail with bulletlike speed. If your dog is inclined to chase wild critters, keep him on a leash in porcupine country. He can come off only second-best in a tussle. And, of course, keep paddles and the axe out of reach; inside the tent is safe. Porky won't come in, although while sleeping out at Lost Pond in Maine, I once had one climb up and sit on my chest!

The skunk is a frequent visitor to campsites, sometimes strolling in nonchalantly to join the campfire circle. Pandemonium usually results, but there's no need for panic. The skunk is a gentleman, using his odious firepower only in self-defense. Don't harass a skunk, make no sudden moves, try to avoid surprising him, and you'll have no problems. Of course, keep an overly aggressive dog under control or he may be a candidate for a tomato juice bath. Rounding a huge boulder in an upland pasture while grouse hunting, I once came face to face with a skunk, at about twenty-five feet. We both fired from the hip, but luckily for me, my 16-gauge pellets outran his spray by a hair's width. Even though the skunk missed me, I had to hang my clothes in the woodshed that night!

A Minnesota raccoon about to gulp a tidbit. Fish & Wildlife Service photo.

Another frequent campsite visitor is the raccoon. He's harmless except for the mess he creates when he finds the waste container. I once had to chase a coon into the nighttime woods at our cabin. He was carrying off our garbage pail, the bail in his teeth! Besides raiding campsites, raccoons love to travel riverbanks, feasting on such tidbits as dead fish and fresh-water clams. It is also a nest-raider, seeking eggs, which it holds in its paws, breaking one end gently, in order to suck the contents. The raccoon *does* wash its food. It will dip the fare into the water, rub it between its paws, then gobble it.

Itinerant campers seldom see a weasel, dark brown in the summer, snow-white in the winter (except for the black tip of its tail) when it becomes "ermine." It's a tiny critter, not much over ten inches long, but especially vicious for its size. At a Border Patrol camp we had a weasel as a self-invited guest for several weeks. We had to make our grub supply secure but we didn't drive the little fellow away. In fact, we fed him bits of raw meat, which he accepted quite ungraciously, but while he was there, we had no mice or snakes.

Most of us know the gray squirrel, and its larger cousin the red or fox squirrel, equally at home in hardwood forests or in city parks. But it's the little red squirrel who is the northern backwoodsman's neighbor, and the bane of deer hunters. Try stalking soundlessly in the woods some morning, and you'll quickly have a red squirrel scolding you in a voice that carries over two townships. He's been known to gnaw his way into a frame camp, or to tear a mattress apart, and he's a compulsive camp raider, quick to find a poorly stored grub supply.

Except for some minor thievery, or raucous calling in the too early morning, wild birds are good company in the backcountry. In fact, hairy-chested outdoorsmen who scorn bird-watching are passing up hours of enlightening entertainment. Every region has one or two species of special interest. My favorite is the Canada jay, also known as "camp robber," "gorby," or "gobby." I once had lunch with one at 30 below zero!

I'd squatted on my snowshoes and unlimbered a half-frozen ham sandwich. While still struggling with the first bite, I was joined by a Canada jay who boldly perched on my extended foot! I tossed him bits and we sat for several minutes in mutual observation. According to legend, a "gobby" is the reincarnated soul of a lumberjack killed in a woods accident. Since learning this, I've often wondered whose double-bitted spirit I had lunch with that day. The gobby's title of "camp robber" is justified. He'll fly away with any small, bright object left lying about. And like any stealthy thief, his flight is almost soundless, the flutter of his wings barely perceptible even at close range.

The variety of birds—there are some 1,700 species in North America—presents an endless performance of interesting antics: a ruffed grouse successfully fighting off a hawk to protect its chicks; a kingbird plaguing a crow ten times its size; a great horned owl defying me as I poled my canoe within thirty feet; the pileated woodpecker that died even as I watched its strange dance of death; the peculiar hum of nighthawks' wings; the blackcrowned night heron who returns to the same tiny island in the marshes near our home, year after year; ugly yet beautiful red-headed turkey vultures perched atop dead trees in a southern swamp; the magnificent Canada goose, poised on spring ice in a northern lake.

Look into the skies, the trees, the brush. You'll see birds with colors that put a rainbow to shame, matching every sound made by a symphony orchestra, and performing maneuvers that are the envy of jet-fighter pilots!

Few of us can honestly claim that we *like* snakes. In fact, I've known persons, otherwise at home in the outdoors, to become terrorized by them. An eighteen-inch garter snake once sent a woman into uncontrolled hysteria while I was guiding her to a remote beaver bog for trout fishing. I had to hold her by force to prevent her dashing pell-mell into the woods.

Frankly, I'm not fond of snakes. When I conducted a camping and nature school for an eastern science museum some years ago, I often assisted naturalists in displaying live snakes, including a six-foot boa constrictor. My nonchalance was sheer bluff!

Snakebites appear to be so rare that precautions take the form of a joke. There are some 2,000 cases of snakebite in this country annually, admittedly most of these among professional handlers, zoo employees, and research workers. Of those bitten, fewer than 1 per cent die. Snakes are statistically a smaller risk than lightning. But there *is* a risk.[2]

The coral snake, because of its limited habitat in the deep South, accounts for fewer than 2 per cent of the poisonous snakebites. Pit vipers—the rattlesnakes and the water moccasin, or cottonmouth—account for the balance. The water moccasin has a limited range, running roughly 100 miles north of that of the coral snake. No northern water snakes are poisonous. One or another species of rattler occurs in every state except Alaska, Hawaii, and Maine.

In snake country—local inhabitants will tip you off to areas of concentration—wear leather shoes, at least ankle-high, preferably calf-high with loose-fitting uppers. These may be uncomfortable in hot weather but venom-laden fangs will have difficulty penetrating the leather. Loose-fitting trousers help, too.

Don't reach blindly into holes, under bushes, or onto overhead ledges. Stepping over a log without first checking the other side, you may disturb a rattler. A strolling gait, rather than a hurried stride, will give a snake a chance to make a graceful departure. Surprise it and it may strike.

Snakebite treatment is too often described glibly, as if any out-

---

[2] For a brief though well-detailed description of poisonous snakes and the treatment of bites, see: *Brief Guide to Snakebite,* Lester E. Harris, Jr., Preston Publications Inc., 1645 Tullie Circle N.E., Atlanta, Ga. 30329.

doorsman can be transformed into a skilled snakebite specialist in seven short paragraphs. Rather than rehash what has been written with more authority than I can muster, I suggest simply that you carry a snakebite kit such as that marketed by Cutter's. Read the instructions before venturing into snake country. Obtain a copy of *Brief Guide to Snakebite*, and the American Red Cross first-aid manual.

Early summer is the season for black flies, mosquitoes, midges, and "no-see-ums," the latter so tiny that you'll feel their burning stings before you see them. Mosquitoes may last through the summer, but usually the first cool night in July "puts down" the others.

A tent equipped with netting, long-sleeved shirts, pants with cuffs tucked into stockings or boots, all of these help prevent bites. Wearing a head net is worse punishment than the stings, but if you're severely allergic to insect bites, use one. Some persons become seriously ill when bitten. Any sign of extreme swelling, or puffing of the eye areas, warrants medical attention immediately.

I generally rely on pipe smoke as protection, but even without this, black flies bother me little. However, we have tried virtually every known bug dope, coming to the conclusion that none is completely effective. Cutter's is one of the more efficient. This is a cold-cream type, non-greasy and pleasantly scented, popular among women. Another which has worked fairly well is aerosol-type "Off."

I'd like to offer some magic formula, some brilliant technique for foiling insects, thereby attaining immortality among outdoorsmen, but I can't. There is no complete escape, except by planning your woods vacation for the cool weather of spring and fall.

There is one partial solution in camp. Build a smudge, burning smoke-creating grass, punky woods, etc., much like the lost hunter's signal fire. This lays a smoke screen over the campsite. Bugs can't tolerate smoke. If you build this smudge in a metal pail, you can move it about for more effective coverage. A smudge helps, but that's about all that can be said for it.

Every year when we return to our cabin for the summer, we're eager as children headed for the circus. Did the cabin winter well? Any blowdowns across the "road"? Is the swamp trail passable? We wonder about these, certainly. But our real concern is for the wild friends we left reluctantly last fall. Are the beaver still at Little Springy Brook? And the moose along the Mopang? The bear on Buck Mountain? Is that red fox still prowling the Barrens? And, if during our first night I hear my favorite night noise, a great horned owl hooting a welcome, I feel I've come home.

Our first full day in camp should be spent tidying up the place. It isn't. We hop in the canoe, or prowl our "trails," and at the end of the day we always come back to the cabin, contented. They're all there, the bear, moose, deer, beaver, even the red squirrels. We wouldn't have it otherwise!

Chapter 15

WILDERNESS, WHERE ART THOU?

If we think of "wilderness" as a virginal region untouched by Man, such tracts are rare. A semblance of unspoiled country is included in our National Wilderness Preservation System, nearly all of this acreage being within our national forests and our federal wildlife reserves. Other tracts that qualify as wilderness are in some of our national parks, in a few state parks and forests and, of course, in Canadian preserves. Except for these, there is little true wilderness left in North America.

However, there still exist vast tracts of primitive lands—the hinterlands, the backwoods, the backcountry, the bush, the puckerbrush—call it what you will. Man has been there and left his mark: roads and trails, mines and ghost towns, forests slashed then reseeded. Then there is submarginal land that will grow no crops and has no attraction for the developer and his bulldozer. Too, there are commercial forests, sections of which are cut periodically and in which logging roads are built, and often abandoned once the logs are removed. Then there are the "public domain" lands left over from the original federal holdings acquired when we were a geographically expanding nation. These are "the lands nobody wanted" although they are becoming increasingly desirable.

Much of this acreage is wild enough to please the backwoods camper. There he can still find a lake whose shores are not ringed with cottages, where fishermen don't have to wait in line to launch their trailer boats, where campgrounds are simple clearings in the woods, where some of the roads are impassable at certain times of the year. There is, in fact, more wild country than we think, albeit it is not *virginal*, merely primitive.

THE BUREAU OF LAND MANAGEMENT

There are 457 million acres of public domain land, sprawling from the deserts of Arizona to the Alaskan tundra, all under the jurisdiction of the Bureau of Land Management, a division of the U. S. Department of the Interior. These are lands which have not been incorporated into our national parks and forests, or into our wildlife preserves. It's not all wilderness, of course, but much of it is literally *backcountry*, accessible only on foot, by packhorse, mule, burro, canoe, trail bike, or jeep.

Most of this acreage lies in Alaska, Arizona, California, Colorado, Idaho, Montana, Nevada, New Mexico, Oregon, Utah, and Wyoming. In these states, the Bureau of Land Management has developed more than 100 campgrounds, most of them small and primitive. In this case, the word "campground" needn't raise your hackles. True, these represent the massing of people within a given area, and certainly where this occurs, the spirit of the wilderness *is* dispelled. However, look upon these campgrounds as jumping-off places to the more primitive, less spoiled hinterlands. On BLM lands you're welcome to roam, to camp away from the organized facilities, to hunt and fish where there are no waiting lines. All that BLM asks is that you observe a few simple rules: care with fire; leave gates as you find them; avoid off-road travel with vehicles that may cause ruts and eventually erosion; travel with equipment suitable for backcountry camping. You can't ask for more lenient restrictions!

Of course, reaching such unspoiled regions will require some effort. True backcountry doesn't lie alongside a paved highway. Leave the works of man. The wild country is there, waiting.

Some BLM lands—the estimate is as high as 50 million acres— are surrounded by private lands and this creates problems, especially during the hunting season. Some ranchers whose private roads lead to BLM acreage are not shy about charging twenty-five dollars or more for the privilege of crossing their lands. The ranchers claim the fees cover only the cost of "maintaining" the private ways and cleaning up litter. Of course, it's actually a form of extortion which legal pussyfooting by the federal government has failed to put down. The problem has existed for many years and the "toll system" is still in effect.[1]

Not all BLM lands lend themselves to backcountry camping,

[1] See: *Public Access to Public Domain Lands*, U. S. Dept. of Agriculture, Economic Research Service, Misc. Pub. 1122, U. S. Government Printing Office.

fishing, or hunting. Some areas are barren and desolate, appealing only to a lover of the desert. Logging companies cut timber on some BLM lands, mining firms probe the earth, and some of the lands are fringed by highly developed resorts. However, several vast tracts remain wild and are yours to roam in. Among these are:

Alaskan lands—283 million acres!—managed jointly by the BLM, the U. S. Forest Service, the National Park Service, the U. S. Fish and Wildlife Service, and the Alaska Division of Lands;

the Arizona Strip bordering on Utah and Nevada, with no designated campgrounds. Camp where you like;

the Clear Lake (118,000 acres) and the Cow Mountain (54,-000 acres) in California;

the Sequoia-Owens Valley region, also in California, and adjacent to the Sequoia National Park, the Inyo National Forest, and Death Valley National Monument;

the Glade Park region of Colorado, surrounding Grand Junction, and adjacent to the Grand Mesa National Forest, the Uncompahgre National Forest, and the Colorado National Monument;

southern Idaho (12 million acres), with much of the BLM land abutting several national forests, including the Challis, Sawtooth, Targhee, and the Boise;

Montana (6½ million acres), well distributed throughout the state but broken up into relatively small tracts surrounded by or abutting private lands;

the Battle Mountain district of Nevada, larger than the combined states of Connecticut, New Hampshire, Delaware, and Rhode Island! Within the region are the Toiyabe and Humboldt national forests;

New Mexico (13 million acres), distributed throughout much of the state except for the northeast;

southeast Oregon (15 million acres)—large, solid blocks, with numerous smaller units along the coastal ranges.

The Bureau of Land Management publishes several excellent maps and descriptions of its land holdings, particularly of those areas I've just mentioned.[2] Another good source of information is the bureau's magazine *Our Public Lands*.[3]

---

[2] Write to the BLM at one of the regional offices listed in the Appendix.
[3] Published quarterly, 25¢ per copy $1 per year; U. S. Government Printing Office.

THE NATIONAL FORESTS

Our national forests are under the jurisdiction of the Forest Service, within the U. S. Department of Agriculture. There is at least one in every state except Connecticut, Delaware, Hawaii, Iowa, Maryland, Massachusetts, New Jersey, New York, and Rhode Island. Don't be aghast if you hear chain saws snorting, bulldozers growling, or cattle mooing! National forests have been specifically designated to serve a number of purposes. In one or another of them—there are 154, totaling 186 million acres— you'll find ski lifts, campgrounds, mines, cattle, logging camps, swimming areas, boating facilities, hunting, fishing, trails for bikes, snowmobiling, hiking, and climbing. In addition wildlife management, watershed protection, and forestry research are carried on. Naturally, conflict arises among these varied interests. Conservationists protest some logging contracts; loggers howl when they are restricted; ski lift developers constantly seek new snowy slopes; wilderness lovers want no more roads to ski lifts. A forest ranger has a hard row to hoe!

The Forest Service has become increasingly conscious of outdoor recreation, and in some forests this is the main operational goal. Campsites number in the thousands, so many, in fact, that there is no listing of these in any one publication. Instead, regional offices issue booklets describing sites in the respective regions.[4] Backcountry sites, off-the-beaten-track spots, are not usually listed.

Some campgrounds are quite large and highly developed, including flush toilets, electric lights, self-guiding nature trails, paved roads—and crowds. These campgrounds are necessary to provide for today's mass camping boom. In New Hampshire's White Mountain National Forest, Eleanor and I once "camped" in a $12,000 motor home which had been loaned to us; in the Pisgah National Forest of North Carolina, we spent part of a Sunday afternoon watching hundreds of children slide down a natural water chute into a cool mountain stream; in Wisconsin's Chequamegon National Forest our canoe was nearly gunned down by water skiers; and in

[4] U. S. Forest Service regional offices and their addresses are included in the Appendix.

the Superior National Forest of Minnesota, we couldn't find an unoccupied campsite and had to spend the night in a motel! But these incidents are not typical—at least, they need not be. The Forest Service also maintains thousands of small, remote campsites, primitive and natural. These may be occupied when you arrive, of course, but not by the hordes that haunt roadside campgrounds.

It is possible to camp away from organized or developed facilities in the national forests. This is not publicized widely by the Forest Service; in fact, few campers are aware of it. In trying to pin down the specifics, I contacted the service and got the following reply: "The use of developed recreation sites for camping and picnicking is not required, except when necessary to protect the environment. However, people are encouraged to use developed sites where improvements for safety and convenience are available." At best, this is a lukewarm admission that backwoods campers may camp in the backcountry, except in areas that are specifically restricted due to fire or other hazards. However, inquire of the supervisor. Chances are you'll be permitted to camp away from the mobs!

Getting into the backcountry of the national forest shouldn't be difficult. The smallest unit comprises only 10,000 acres, but some of the forests range up to 3 million acres! Naturally, if you "follow the crowd" you'll be shunted into a regular campground among wall-to-wall trailers. Obtain Forest Service literature to help you locate the forest country you prefer, and its backcountry camping possibilities.[5]

THE NATIONAL PARKS

The national parks are administered by the National Park Service, a branch of the U. S. Department of the Interior. In some respects the system, while smaller, is far more complex than the Forest Service. The National Park Service is not only responsible for the administration of national parks, but also of monuments, military parks, cemeteries, memorial parks, battlefields, historic

---

[5] *National Forest Vacations* (45¢, U. S. Government Printing Office) details all of the national forests and includes mail address of local headquarters. *Backpacking in the National Forests* (25¢) lists wilderness and primitive areas.

sites, seashores, parkways, even the 18.07 acres that make up the White House grounds! As a result, no government agency guides so many tourists and vacationers.

National parks differ from national forests in that they are designated to preserve outstanding recreational, scenic, and historic areas. At the same time, the Park Service must make these accessible to as many people as possible, and provide facilities for the crowds that visit the parks. In other words, the National Park Service is in the resort/tourist business.

It operates 33 parks and 77 monuments, plus the numerous other areas I've mentioned, totaling 27 million acres. If you're bent upon a wilderness experience, choose your national park carefully. Learn to differentiate between a park, monument, historic site, seashore, and parkway. Camping facilities, for example, are provided at most *parks,* and at *some monuments,* but not at historic sites, memorial parks, or battlefields.

Wilderness and backcountry campers won't be happy at most of the highly developed outdoor areas in the national parks. During the height of the season, these are overrrun by hordes of tourists and gregarious campers. I'm not throwing rocks at the service. After all, its function is to make available these areas to as many people as possible. But after a week of elbowing tourists and being elbowed by them, I'm usually ready for a lonesome campfire as far back in the puckerbrush as I can go! The backcountry splendor of the national parks can be enjoyed without milling among the crowds, however.

Camping is channeled into four types of facilities. Type A campgrounds are for family campers and some sites may even include utility connections for recreational vehicles. Type B camping areas provide minimal facilities and may include trail camps with open-front shelters. If this sounds attractive, beware. Some Type B campgrounds are vast, perhaps with as many as 300 individual tent sites. Type C areas are for group camping. None of these facilities appeal much to backwoods campers.

Type D is not officially designated wilderness camping—on your own in remote park sections—regulated to the extent that the park superintendent or ranger must be notified of your intentions to travel away from developed facilities. You may be required to submit your equipment to inspection to guarantee that it's suitable. A fire permit may also be necessary. In case of high fire danger or adverse weather, you may be forced to cancel your trip. A national park backcountry jaunt, then, requires planning and consultation with officials.[6]

NATIONAL WILDLIFE REFUGES

In the National Wildlife Refuge System, Man is the secondary form of life. The Fish and Wildlife Service, through its Bureau of Sport Fisheries and Wildlife within the Department of the Interior, manages more than 320 units, totaling over 27 million acres, all dedicated to one purpose: to help Man keep in balance with his environment by protecting and encouraging the propagation of all species of wildlife in areas where Man can attain a true appraisal of his own position in the universe. Frankly, this is not the "official" purpose. It's mine. This is the way I feel about our wildlife refuges.

It is in a wildlife refuge that I see myself as I really am, a rather puny, limited creature, and to wild things, probably a dull, uninteresting trespasser. I can't bound like a deer and I haven't a fraction of the might of a bear; I can't soar like a hawk, dive like a kingfisher, swim like an otter, or sing like a hermit thrush. I'm even outclassed as a builder by the beaver. Wildfowl wing their way north and south annually but I have trouble keeping a compass route across a single township. At night I stumble over stumps, yet a great horned owl hunts without benefit of radar. In my bragging moments I point out that I once covered forty-five miles in two days on snowshoes, but that's routine for a wolf—and without snowshoes. I puff when I climb a ladder to change the storm windows, but the fisher scampers up a tree almost as fast as the eye can follow! Man, a superior creature . . . huh!

There are refuges in every state except New Hampshire, Rhode Island, Connecticut, and West Virginia. You'll find them in coastal marshes, in the Appalachians, across the prairies, in the southern swamps, high in the Rockies, in the arid Southwest, and in the lush Pacific Northwest. National Wildlife Refuges are not recreational

---

[6] *Camping in the National Parks* (25¢, U. S. Government Printing Office) includes the mailing address of each park office. The most complete treatise on our national parks is Tilden, *The National Parks.*

Although a northern woodsman by training, the author found Okefenokee National Wildlife Refuge in Georgia fascinating. Photo by Eleanor Riviere.

areas as such, but some provide fishing, camping, even hunting. Some are small and close to major cities; others are vast, so huge they're called "wildlife ranges" rather than "refuges," like the Desert National Range in Nevada, which encompasses over 1½ million acres.

Most wildlife refuges are day-use areas, so far as visitors are concerned. A few provide minimal campgrounds within their boundaries; Stephen Foster State Park in Georgia, for example, is seven miles inside the Okefenokee National Wildlife Refuge. If you can't camp within a refuge, do so close by and make daily trips into it.[7]

[7] See: *National Wildlife Refuges* (25¢); or *The National Wildlife Refuge System* (5¢)—both from the U. S. Government Printing Office.

THE NATIONAL WILDERNESS PRESERVATION SYSTEM

The Wilderness Preservation Act of 1964 set up the National Wilderness Preservation System, under which the National Park Service, the Forest Service, and the Bureau of Sport Fisheries and Wildlife were directed to study their roadless areas of 5,000 acres or more for possible inclusion in the system. They were given ten years to complete the task.

Areas in the system are true wilderness as defined by the Wilderness Act (see Chapter 10), where the "imprint of Man's work" *is* "substantially un-noticeable." They're not merely cut-over and reseeded forests, or unwanted "junk lands." They are essentially just as the first white man saw them. Visitors are welcome, but you'll have to enter afoot, on horseback, with burro or mule, or by canoe. No motorized equipment is permitted. Even planes are restricted in their overflights. Facilities have not, and will not be, developed; even trail signs may be lacking. Here you'll be completely on your own—for one day or for a month—in truly primeval surroundings.

The system is still in its infancy. Although there are now 57 units in 14 states, many more are still in the review stage, or awaiting congressional action. Wilderness areas are now located in Arizona, California, Colorado, Minnesota, Nevada, New Mexico, Idaho, Montana, North Carolina, New Hampshire, Oregon, Utah, Washington, and Wyoming.

Most of the present units are in national forests—the Forest Service jumped the gun in 1924 and established its own primitive and wilderness areas, some of which were later incorporated into the National Wilderness Preservation System. The Bureau of Sport Fisheries and Wildlife has also contributed. Up to date, though, foot-dragging by the National Park Service and the Congress has resulted in no national park lands being included.[8]

---

[8] The best source of information on the National Wilderness Preservation System is *Search for Solitude* (65¢, U. S. Government Printing Office).

INDIAN RESERVATIONS

Indians welcome visitors to their reservations for vacation purposes. Although under the jurisdiction of the Bureau of Indian Affairs (a part of the U. S. Department of the Interior), the various tribes on their own initiative maintain public campgrounds that range from posh to primitive. Some charge a small fee for hunting, fishing, or camping. They may also restrict pets and a few prohibit alcoholic beverages. With the payment of a fee, vast Indian lands may be opened to you. How free you are to travel, hunt, fish, or camp on Indian lands depends on individual tribal regulations and upon how friendly your request is.

Reservation lands are often vast; the Hopi reserve at Keams Canyon, Arizona, for example, encompasses 2½ million acres but the total Indian population is only 6,000. And there are only 52,000 Navajos on the nine-million-acre reservation at Window Rock, Arizona.

Among Indians who will share their lands, fish, and game with you, are tribes in Arizona, California, Colorado, Florida, Michigan, Minnesota, Montana, Nebraska, New Mexico, North Carolina, North Dakota, Oklahoma, Oregon, South Dakota, Utah, Washington, and Wisconsin.[9]

Indians are gracious hosts. Some are as sophisticated as a New Yorker, others shy and retiring. Either is entitled to respect; request permission before camping, hunting, fishing, observing ceremonials, photographing villages, individuals or community events. The Indian is a neighbor down the street, even if his home is 2,000 miles from yours!

NATIONAL SCENIC TRAIL SYSTEM

In 1966, President Johnson said: "We need to copy the great Appalachian Trail in all parts of America." This is impossible, of course. Already too much of America is sealed under concrete, burdened with hot-top, and crisscrossed with freeways. But the spirit of President Johnson's statement is commendable. We do need

[9] See: *Vacationing with Indians* (30¢, U. S. Government Printing Office).

more foot trails. And these are being attained through the National Scenic Trail System, slowly, grudgingly in some cases. But someday it may again be possible to walk across the United States without having to hike 2,500 miles on pavement between rows of billboards.

Eventually, National Scenic Trails will include many of the early routes used by pioneers. Two have so far been designated—neither of them pioneer routes but essential to the system nonetheless—the Appalachian Trail and the Pacific Crest Trail. The Appalachian extends 2,000 miles from Springer Mountain in Georgia to the summit of Mt. Katahdin in Maine. Because the trail traverses the crowded East, don't conclude that it's a suburban sidewalk or neighborhood path! It's a rugged hike, through some wilderness and generally over much terrain that is "stood on edge"! To walk the length of it is a challenge to the most virile backpacker.

The Pacific Crest Trail traverses even more rugged terrain in its 2,350-mile meandering from the Canadian border in Washington down through the Cascades and Sierra Nevadas to the California-Mexico boundary. The final 400 miles are through desert environment.

Some other trails which will likely be included in the National Scenic Trail System include the Long Trail, running 255 miles through Vermont from Massachusetts to Canada, sections of it in the Green Mountain National Forest; the Continental Divide Trail, 3,100 miles along the nation's spine atop the Continental Divide; sections of the Lewis & Clark Trail, the Natchez Trace, parts of the Oregon Trail, and segments of the Santa Fe Trail.

Unfortunately, many parts of these routes have long been obliterated by superhighways, suburban developments, and supermarket parking lots. However, along those portions which can be restored to a semblance of their original pristine beauty, perhaps we can recapture the spirit of the early pioneers.[10]

NATIONAL WILD AND SCENIC RIVERS

This program, too, is in its infancy and will probably be many years in reaching fruition, but the National Wild and Scenic

[10] See: *Trails for America*, Bureau of Outdoor Recreation ($2.25, U. S. Government Printing Office).

Rivers System will eventually provide us with a water route to, or through, regions where trees still grow tall and green.

To be included in the system, a river must be free-flowing—no dams or other man-made obstructions; it must be generally primitive and unpolluted, with land access restricted to trails or infrequent roads. It must also be designated by the state legislature having jurisdiction over it, and finally it must be approved by the Secretary of the Interior. And it must be administered at no cost to the federal government, a rather startling requirement in its own right!

Initially, eight rivers were named by Congress as components of the system:

Idaho: segments of the Middle Fork of the Clearwater, and the Middle Fork of the Salmon;

Missouri: segments of the Eleven Point;

California: the entire length of the Middle Fork of the Feather;

New Mexico: segments of the Rio Grande;

Minnesota and *Wisconsin:* segments of the St. Croix;

Wisconsin: segments of the Wolf;

Oregon: segments of the Rogue.

Along with Wisconsin's Wolf River, the Allagash Wilderness Waterway in Maine was specifically cited in the National Wild and Scenic Rivers Act of 1968. The Allagash is a state-administered wilderness park.

At least sixteen other rivers are under study as potential parts of the system. Whether or not they are eventually included, the fact that they have been considered sufficiently wild and unspoiled to warrant investigation would seem to make them potential boat or canoe avenues to backcountry adventure.[11]

STATE LANDS

State parks offer limited backwoods or wilderness camping opportunities. Most state facilities must cater to a variety of recreationists—campers, picnickers, horseback riders, swimmers, boaters, fishermen, water skiers. The result is a heavy visitor load.

---

[11] See: *Plans for Studies of Wild and Scenic Rivers,* Bureau of Outdoor Recreation, U. S. Department of the Interior, Washington, D.C. 20240.

Activities away from organized facilities may be strictly regulated, especially overnight trips. Generally, too, state parks are limited in size, so that when you consider public pressure, the variety of facilities required, it's not surprising that most of them have become crowded, overused, noisy outdoor resorts appealing to quantities of users rather than to quality of experience.

There are exceptions—201,018-acre Baxter State Park in Maine, for example. The park's campsites are deliberately kept small and few; self-contained recreational vehicles are banned, as are motorcycles and trail bikes, even from the roads. Hunting is not permitted and entry into the park during the winter is by special permit only. Essentially, Baxter is a wilderness park and will remain such.[12]

The Adirondack Forest Preserve in New York, although ringed by developed resort areas, includes thousands of acres of mountain woodlands accessible only by foot or canoe.

Still another New York area in keeping with a wilderness theme is the 50,000-acre Moose River Recreation Area in Hamilton County. Don't let the name "recreation area" mislead you. It is not a jam-packed Sunday afternoon picnic site. Trailers, motorcycles, and trail bikes are banned from traveling beyond the two entrance gates. Jeep roads and foot trails branch out from the main road. Camping, hunting, and fishing are permitted. Much of the land has been cut over, but the state is gradually restoring its wilderness character.[13]

Few other states in the East have the space for such a wilderness system but they might well take a cue from New York and Maine, and set up at least one park as a wilderness haven. In the West, state parks are all too often overshadowed by the tremendous holdings of the Forest Service and the National Park Service, but nevertheless some state parks and forest reserves are quite large, with wilderness-like hinterlands.

[12] See: *A Guide to Baxter State Park and Mt. Katahdin in Maine,* Department of Economic Development, State House, Augusta, Me. 04330.
[13] See: *Adirondack Canoe Routes, Moose River Recreation Area,* and *Public Campsites in the Forest Preserve Park Region,* N. Y. State Dept. of Conservation, Div. of Lands and Forests, Albany. N.Y. 12226.

Typical sign at entrance to private timberlands. Photo by Eleanor Riviere.

PRIVATE TIMBERLANDS

It wasn't too many years ago that, as a lumberjack, I was welcome on "company lands"—to cut logs or to haul them—but when I returned in the spring or fall to catch a few trout or perhaps to shoot a deer, my way was barred by locked gates.

Times have changed, and so have timber company attitudes. You're welcome today on close to 60 million acres owned by some 200 companies, with the privilege of hunting, fishing, camping, or, in some instances, leasing a cabin site. More than 86,000 miles of company roads are open to the public,[14] although you may have to pay a small fee to travel on some of them. Many of these logging firms and paper companies have built campgrounds which

[14] See: *Public Outdoor Recreation on Forest Industry Lands,* American Forest Institute, 1835 K St., N.W., Washington, D.C. 20006.

give access to trails, canoe routes, hunting lands, and fishing waters. Whether or not you will be permitted to camp away from established sites is a matter of individual company policy.

In Maine, the forestry department maintains some 300 backwoods campsites spotted throughout some 10 million acres of forest, all on private land. The timber companies provide the sites, and pay a wild-land tax which goes to maintain forest fire protection and to operate campsites. Most of these camping spots are available at no charge, although a few of the busier sites require a dollar-per-night fee.[15]

In my files I have dozens of rather good maps issued by timber companies, on which are shown roads, trails, streams, campsites, portages, and other landmarks vital to a backwoods camping trip. Some of the maps are revised annually so that areas currently being logged can be indicated. These are marked in red, with a request that hunters keep out. This is only fair, in view of the fact that some hunters have been known to shoot a deer that wore red britches and a yellow tin hat! Certain roads may be closed, too, where logging truck traffic is heavy. Other than these restrictions, many private timberlands are open to "poking in the puckerbrush."

CANADA

The thought of wilderness surrounding me as far as I can see sets my adrenal glands to quivering! That's why, if I were to be reincarnated as a citizen of another country, I'd choose to be a Canadian. I feel at home in Canada.

As in the United States, tourists and most campers gravitate to national or provincial parks, the latter, counterparts of our state parks although invariably much larger. These are set up to accommodate as many visitors as possible without damage to the wilderness. They fail, of course. The scenery is there, the waterfalls, the semi-tame wildlife, the rivers, but—the wilderness? It has been pushed back. You can see it, *in the distance.*

Canada's national parks are superb in their beauty, but the heavy feet and the spinning tires of tourists despoil the fringes along the

---

[15] See: *Forest Campsites,* Maine Forestry Department, Augusta, Me. 04330.

highways (true in the United States, too, of course!). In driving from Banff to Jasper national parks in Alberta, Eleanor and I gambled that the scenery would be worth the risk of carbon monoxide poisoning. It was. At a campground in Jasper, our tent was one of 100, and nearby were more than 150 recreational vehicles. Canada's national parks and her provincial parks are worthy of a visit. Gulp in the scenery, gawk with the tourists, buy a few souvenirs, then hightail away from the congestion. You can see the wilderness from the park roads and from the highways. However, zipping along the Trans-Canada Highway, or second-gearing over the Alaska Highway can hardly be termed a

The author packing in the Athabaska River Valley, Alberta. Photo by Eleanor Riviere.

wilderness experience. To benefit from *any* wilderness, you must *enter* it, not just glance at it from a high-speed right of way.

Eleanor and I are "side road probers" and "trail tryers." We can't resist a rutted back road, or a partially overgrown trail. During five weeks of such probing, we waded through snowfields in July at 8,500 feet, prowled in Indian villages, strolled through aspen groves that had been stripped of bark by starving elk, got sprayed by a 300-foot waterfall, and met a schoolteacher who commuted thirty miles every day from a backcountry log cabin and who wanted to move fifty miles farther back into the bush because "it's getting crowded around here!"

Canada's national and provincial parks are huge. Distances are deceiving on Canadian maps unless you check the scale carefully. While we indicate the size of our parks in *acres*, Canadians measure theirs in *square miles*.[16]

Roughly 90 per cent of Canada's land area remains undeveloped. To read much of today's business literature, you'd think that the entire Northland is becoming transformed overnight into an industrial complex of mines, railroads, oil fields, pipe lines, and highways. This is true to a degree but only on a localized basis. There is a growing awareness for the need to protect Canada's wilderness before it is too late. The Canadians have the benefit of our experience, proving that it is easier to preserve than to restore. Individual Canadians and organized groups are awakening Canada to this need.

Much of Canada's wild lands are "crown lands" under the jurisdiction of the ten provinces. Tremendous segments are leased or licensed to forest products industries, which, in effect, control the lands. It is this acreage, almost inconceivable in its scope, that attracts the real backcountry adventurers. Canadian travel literature says little about this—the established parks and tourists' routes are boosted instead—but under a system of fire and travel permits, much of the wilderness is open to travelers with tent and canoe, or afoot in some regions. New Brunswick and Nova Scotia, however, require that a licensed guide accompany nonresidents in their forests.

16 For information on Canadian national parks, write to the Canadian Government Travel Bureau, Ottawa, Ont.; for details on provincial parks, write to Government Travel Bureau, at the appropriate provincial capital.

The logger has swung his axe in large segments of the Canadian wilderness, but often this is the only sign of man. A cut-over area grows up again, an abandoned logging road is soon choked by the forest, lumber camps quickly fall victim to heavy snows. Once the logger has left, Nature takes over quickly. This is true of much of the logged-over lands in Canada. Too, there are seemingly endless regions on which man has left little, if any, impression—areas economically unfeasible to develop, forests not worth the cutting or too difficult to reach with heavy machinery.

A Detroit reader once wrote to me, in essence saying: "OK. You talk about the wilderness. Where is it? Specifically, I mean. If you were going on a trip this summer, where would you go?" A straightforward question calls for a direct answer:

(1) I would drive to North Bay, Ontario, then take Highway 11 northward to Cochrane. This road is the Northern Route of the Trans-Canada Highway and, even at the height of the summer season, I have found traffic light. From Cochrane westward is the land of the stunted spruce, you are *that* far north. As for campsites, they're innumerable; rarely did we find them more than half-full, usually empty. Counting the streams that crossed the road was impossible. Some are silted, but as you travel westward, they clear up into beautiful fishing waters, nearly all tributaries to rivers flowing into James Bay. Side roads are not numerous but the few that exist probe true wilderness. The towns along the route are small but supplies are available in many of them. With a tent—and, by all means, a canoe or small boat—you can spend an entire summer here without twice fishing the same pool! It's roughly 350 miles from Cochrane to Nipigon, where Route 11 rejoins the Trans-Canada Highway. This is, of course, a relatively easy "wilderness" trip.

(2) In the same general region, the Ontario Northland Railroad runs northward from Cochrane to Moosonee on James Bay. By prior arrangement, you can probably have your outfit dropped off at a wilderness stopover, to be picked up a week or two later. This suggestion is for anyone capable of handling a *genuine* wilderness campout. Amateurs should not apply!

(3) In Alberta, I would leave Route 1A at Seebe, west of Calgary, and swing southward onto the Forestry Trunk Road that runs the length of the Rocky Mountain Forest Reserve to Coleman on Route 3, well over a hundred miles south. This is not a road for

limousines or travel trailers! It's jeep country, although with care
a conventional car can navigate the route. The scenery rivals that
of Banff, campsites are numerous, and fishing streams are a dozen
per mile. And the forest growth is superb. How much of it you
can enjoy depends on how much time you have, the stamina of
your legs, and your penchant for poking around in silent places.
(4) Take Route 16 westward from Jasper National Park, through
Mt. Robson Provincial Park. After leaving Robson (we hit ninety
miles of gravel road) the country becomes relatively uninteresting
but once past Prince George, British Columbia, Route 16 is the
only major highway through a mountain and forest area larger
than the state of California. Side roads are numerous and nearly
all are dead ends deep in the wilderness. The towns of Vanderhoof,
Burns Lake, Smithers, and Terrace are not large, but you'll find all
the supplies you'll need, plus local information sources. Eleanor
and I fell in love with Smithers. When my reincarnation comes
through, I'll choose it for my hometown!

Suggestions for wilderness trips in Canada would fill a book far
lengthier than this one. You can almost play "pin the tail on the
donkey" with a map of Canada and come up with a good trip
possibility. Canoe trips, especially, can take you along river routes
that will require weeks to cover.[17] Trips like that on the Mac-
kenzie, 2,000 miles with only one portage (but this one is 16
miles!); or 637 miles on the Albany River to Fort Albany on
James Bay; or 350 miles from Norway House to York Factory via
the Nelson and Hayes rivers.

Distances in the Canadian wilds are difficult for some Americans
to grasp. Temper your enthusiasm with objective reasoning. Once
in the bush, running downstream on a brawling northern river,
you are completely on your own. If you're in doubt about your
ability to handle such a trip, there are literally thousands of less
arduous routes, wild enough to appease your hunger for the backcountry, and marvelous training grounds for that "big trip" when
you're ready for it.

Find out all you can about a region before entering it. Most
libraries have a good shelf of Canadian travel books, and the
various federal and provincial agencies issue booklets and maps by
the bushel.

---

[17] See: *Canoe Trips in Canada,* Canadian Government Travel Bureau.

But no matter where you travel, do as much as possible afoot, by canoe, with pack mule or horse. If you remain within the sound and the fury of the highway, the visitors' centers, the scenic overlooks with their parking lots, you're cheating yourself. Take to the woods, literally!

Chapter 16

SMALL TRACTS AND CABINS

If I owned every site about which I've said: "I'd like a cabin on that point," or: "That knoll is perfect for a shack," I could start my own national forest.

A permanent camp has practical aspects, even if you're a chronic wanderer. No matter how late you arrive, you can "pitch camp" simply by unlocking the door; and you can leave as conveniently. A tar-paper roof and wooden walls take some of the curse off a five-day rain, which can be utter misery in a tent. And, with a wood-burning stove, you can enjoy the cabin early in the spring and late in the fall—year-round, in fact.

While at our camp, we actually spend more time in the woods than we do while tent camping. Chores are easier and take less time. And we have only to step from the campyard into a hundred square miles of forest. The canoe waits, overturned on the riverbank barely thirty feet away. We've found moose droppings by the kerosene can, bear tracks on the path to the jeep trail; and wildfowl shuffle up and down the river. Deer nuzzle toadstools near the woodpile. "Punkin" pines and virgin hemlock tower overhead giving us shade, maples provide firewood, and there's cedar for kindling. If the spot were any more woodsy, the government would take it for a wildlife refuge.

Nor has the cabin put a crimp in our wanderings. We love every knothole in Camp Hell'n'gawn, but since building it we've bought a new tent and made trips to Okefenokee, British Columbia, Ontario, the Great Smokies, climbed Mt. Katahdin, and I've walked to Stinking Jam Brook several times for a mess of trout.

It took us three years to find the spot. Real estate agents showed us "cabin sites" on potato farms, knolls surrounded by a hundred acres of murky bog, tar-paper shacks amid forty acres of pine slash, washed gullies touted as "overlooks" and bargain-priced at $2,000, or outlandish pink and purple A-frames with swimming pool and par-3 golf privileges. One or two sites we would have bought, but they were priced to jolt even an oil tycoon.

Our specifications didn't make our search any easier. The site *had* to be on a river—not just any river, but one with rapids that would keep out motorboats and water skiers, and one that supported a reasonable population of trout and salmon. There had to be deer in the area, too, along with bear and moose, not that we planned to hunt them; it's just that we wanted compatible neighbors. The site had to be isolated—no gravel driveway just off a main road. And we specified woods, lots of them, tall and far-reaching. We might just as well have tried to buy Yellowstone National Park. We never did find this dream site, not one that was for sale, at least.

So we contacted one of the paper companies, hoping that we could lease a lot. The manager at the field office listened to our "specifications." He didn't laugh aloud. He didn't even snicker. Unrolling a map, he nodded understandingly. "I've got just the spot for you. Right here . . ." And he pointed at the map. "Here's how you get there." We were on our way.

Six miles from the highway, the station wagon began to drag bottom on the abandoned logging road. We walked from there, leaving the road after about two miles, then cutting through a swamp on a compass course—and there was the river. It looked as if no one had been there for a hundred years. Walking along the bank, headed downstream, we trod softly, not wanting to break the spell. Then—*our* campsite—just as we had pictured it for three years! The lease came through in a few days. The annual fee? Less than the cost of two nights in a motel!

Searching for a cabin site can be almost as much pleasure as spending a summer on one. We rode endless miles over back roads, walked dozens more over trails new to us, we chatted with woodsmen, game wardens, fishermen. However, our search could have been more efficiently organized. We could have eliminated much needless travel and saved countless hours "looking at a place."

For example, so-called "resort developments" were simply an extension of suburbia in synthetic buckskins and phony log cabins of aluminum siding, despite their advertisements of "back-to-nature" tracts. We should have known better than to bother with outfits that touted "GIANT ¼-ACRE ESTATES."

Ads in magazines offered "Tax Land Bargains," "Buy an island for $26," or "Wooded vacation lands at $12 an acre!" The fact is, of course, that in today's economy, few worthwhile land tracts are seized for delinquent taxes. Their owners can always sell them for much more than the overdue taxes. And when such a seizure does occur, someone on the local scene quickly snaps up any bargains. So-called "tax lands," at ridiculous prices, are generally junk lands.

Beware of "free lands," too. You will be deeded a plot, only to find that it is so small you'll need to buy two more lots on which to build an outhouse. What's more, you'll have "fees" to pay—for a right of way, for a building permit, for water; you may even be required to have the "donor" build your cabin with materials *he* sells.

Farmers occasionally dispose of outlying lands, sometimes on a river or a lake, but only rarely do farms extend into truly wild country. Too, the farmer may decide to sell other lots after you've built, and you'll find yourself in a cottage colony. Western ranchers are better possibilities. Some ranches are extensive, encompassing areas of genuine backcountry.

Logging firms and paper companies seldom sell small plots, unless they have opened a lakeshore for resort development. Nevertheless, a company land buyer might give you excellent leads on plots which have been offered the company, but were turned down because they were too small or too inaccessible for heavy logging machinery.

Small-town real estate agents, especially those with listings in hunting and fishing regions, can be helpful. We had several "near misses" among them. Most realtors made a genuine effort to locate what we wanted. Too, a rural agent may know of land that is for sale but not officially listed on the market.

Buying an existing cabin may be easier than finding a suitable lot on which to build one. If you can find such a camp, somewhere near your specifications, it may be less expensive to repair or restore it than to build from scratch.

The Bureau of Land Management frequently sells small plots from its vast holdings in Arizona, Montana, Wyoming, Colorado, New Mexico, Nevada, Idaho, Utah, California, and Washington. Lots average forty to 120 acres, but smaller and larger units are also sold, all on bids. You may bid through the mail, of course, but you won't be able to raise your offer when the actual auction

This cabin has been partially restored, near the Blue Ridge Parkway by the National Park Service. Other similar cabins can be restored as private backwoods camps. Photo by Eleanor Riviere.

takes place. All sales are handled by BLM's regional offices.[1]

BLM lands may or may not be bargains. Each parcel is appraised at its fair market value and bids must equal or exceed this. Descriptions of plots and their appraised values are published in BLM's quarterly magazine *Our Public Lands*.[2]

In some national forests of the West, sites for "private recreation residences" may possibly be leased. This program is gradually being phased out and no new residential sites are being estab-

[1] See: the Appendix for a list of these and their addresses.
[2] See: Chapter 15 for subscription information.

lished. If such sites are still available, they are in forests administered by Forest Service regions I, IV, and VI.[3]

Unless you make a lucky find on your own, leases on private timberlands are good possibilities for a cabin site. Most companies don't want a concentration of camps in a given area—"our" company, for example, will not issue leases within 1½ miles of each other. Privacy is assured and, generally, a greater choice of locations. Access is usually over private logging roads, so this cuts down traffic nuisances. All of last summer, fewer than a half-dozen cars and trucks got within a quarter-mile of our cabin. Leases are not issued indiscriminately, only to responsible applicants. Anyone who proves himself otherwise may be evicted. Most campsite leases are on a year-to-year basis, but don't let the seeming impermanence scare you off. I know of one such lease which has been renewed annually since 1888.

As for loggers moving in to strip the forest from around your cabin, this *can* happen, but it's rare indeed. Most campsites under lease are on lakeshores or riverbanks, where progressive companies now leave a permanent strip of green. Two summers ago, loggers appeared directly across the river from our cabin. We could hear heavy machinery churning and we had visions of devastation. I "moseyed" over, tactfully suggesting that they build their log landing further downstream. As it turned out, we had no reason to fear. The boss grinned. "Scared ye, didn't we! Shucks, we ain't gonna spoil yer scenery!" And they didn't. They bulldozed a landing downstream, out of sight from our cabin.

Some responsibility goes with a leased camp lot. The company expects that you'll take precautions against forest fires, and that when one starts you'll pitch in to help put it out! We keep a five-gallon Indian backpump fully loaded and ready to go.

A campsite lease generally stipulates that you cannot clear the lot completely; that you may cut firewood for a per-cord fee (this can be as little as two dollars per cord!); and that in the event the lease is terminated, the permanent developments revert to the company; you may remove the furnishing and contents, but not the building. Having lived and worked among loggers, we figure that such a lease is a good risk.

[3] Region I, Federal Building, Missoula, Mont. 59801; Region IV, 324 25th Street, Ogden, Utah 84401; Region VI, P. O. Box 3623, Portland, Ore. 97208. Address each "U. S. Forest Service."

Buying a cabin site may prove a little more involved. Be sure, before the transfer is made, that you have an unrestricted right of way. BLM lands, for example, are often surrounded by private holdings. Make certain, too, that drinking water is available. If you finance your purchase through a bank, a title search will be required to make sure that the seller *really* owns the land and that it is not encumbered. If yours is a cash purchase, have an attorney conduct this search for you. Check the boundaries, too. Real estate agents are rarely aware of the exact property lines. Ask for a description and locate these yourself.[4] Don't become aghast at the loose definitions such as "southeasterly, 108 feet, more or less." This is common practice in recording deeds. If you're still in doubt, have the lot surveyed.

It used to be that a man left his wilderness cabin unlocked as a haven for a lost woodsman, a trapper caught in a storm, or for any woods emergency. I've spent several nights in cabins whose owners I didn't know. We always replenished the wood supply, left a little money if we used food, and latched the door on our way out. This was the simple, unvarnished hospitality of the big woods. But it's no longer feasible. Crime has taken to the back-country, with thieves on the lookout for isolated camps they can raid. Plan your cabin site, then, so that it can be hidden as well as possible from roads or trails.

Each year we create a new entrance to our footpath from the jeep trail so that it can't become obvious. And when we leave for any length of time, we disguise it with old tops, limbs and other forest cultch. It's so well hidden, in fact, that woodsmen friends have been unable to find it on their first trip in! Nor are we overly suspicious. From along our jeep trail we have had equipment stolen—a utility trailer and road maintenance tools. It's beyond me, though, to understand why anyone would want to steal a pick-mattock!

In clearing your lot, cut trees with discretion. Take out dead or dying timber, or any trees that lean dangerously over the cabin site itself. But remember that heavy growth protects you against the wind, provides shade in the summer, and shields your cabin from unwelcome visitors! Overzealous axemanship might result in a barren campyard.

---

[4] See: Chapter 12 for instructions on running a rough survey.

A cabin style in keeping with its environment is not only attractive, but less costly to build than one whose design is foreign to the area. For example, don't lug cement blocks into a forest; on the other hand, lumber may prove expensive in desert surroundings.[5]

Breathes there an outdoorsman who has never wanted a log cabin? I doubt it. There are still many in the North but few are being built these days. Erecting one requires suitable logs, skill with an axe, and, contrary to what some experts say, a strong back!

The best logs are spruce, 10" to 12" at the butt; cedar is longer lasting but the natural trunk curvature makes it difficult to fit into place. For a 20'×24' cabin, you'll need 40 or more trees, depending upon the height of the wall.

Cutting this many on your lot will undoubtedly denude it, so you'll have to cut them some distance away. You'll then have the problem of "skidding" them to the cabin site, for which you may have to hire a woodsman and his "twitch horse," trained for such hauling.

The logs should be cut in the spring or early summer, when the sap is running; otherwise, they'll be the devil's own chore to peel. Unpeeled logs may seem more picturesque but they harbor borers. And the bark will eventually fall anyway, creating an unsightly mess and a fire hazard.

Log cabin construction, with the logs notched and laid up horizontally, is not a difficult chore for a skilled woodsman, but if you've never attempted such a task, don't approach it lightly. On the other hand, if you have the logs at hand, some axe skill, perseverance, and can get some help, by all means build one! Nothing so well represents the big woods, or brings so much contentment to a woodsman, as a log cabin.[6]

A pole cabin is easier to build. Logs need not be as long, or as thick at the butt. Conventional sills of milled lumber are built (or you can hew log sills). The logs are then cut to approximately

---

[5] At 5¢ each, from the U. S. Government Printing Office, you can obtain building plans: No. 6003, A-frame cabin; No. 5968, concrete block construction; No. 5928, frame construction on a cement slab; No. 5997, a 24'×33' vacation home.

[6] Detailed instructions for building log cabins are found in Bradford Angiers, *How to Build Your Home in the Woods* (New York: Hart Publishing Co., 1952).

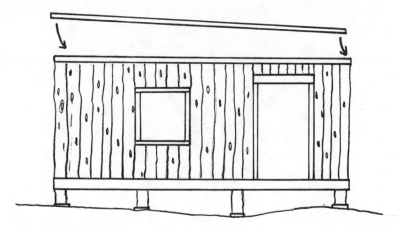

Side wall, pole cabin construction. Upper plate is in two sections. Spikes are driven through first into top end of logs.

six-foot lengths and placed *vertically* on the sill, where they are toenailed. Spikes are then driven down through the ceiling plate (also conventional construction, usually 2×4s) into the upper end of the logs. Frames for doors and windows are milled lumber. For caulking between the upright logs, use plumbers' oakum, held in place by quarter-round battens.

In areas of deep snow, A-frame cabins are highly practical, even if not "woodsy." Their steeply pitched roofs shed snow accumulations and are rigid enough to withstand tremendous weight. Second-story sleeping quarters are easy to incorporate, too.

Conventional frame construction is not difficult if you're moderately handy with carpenter's tools. Avoid shed roofs in snow country, however, or any roof with a pitch of less than 6' height to 10' width. Accumulated snow can overload a flat roof. Come spring you may find it in the living room!

And there's no reason, if the budget is limited, why you can't build a simple, inexpensive tar-paper shack, just big enough for a bunk, a stove, and a sugar-barrel rocker. A 10'×14' cabin of this type can be erected at little cost and, in the right location, will probably afford you as much pleasure as a ten-room log lodge!

Whatever you build, spend a little time drawing plans, well in advance. These need not be the meticulously detailed drawings of an architect. But it will make possible changes *before* you start

A-frame cabin.

to build. If you scale your drawing with reasonable accuracy, you can figure your lumber needs. Then shop around at various lumberyards, as close to the site as possible. Buying *all* of the materials at one time from one dealer will bring you a better price than buying small amounts only as you need them.

In building Camp Hell'n'gawn, we were amazed at the savings we effected by buying directly from a sawmill located about twenty-eight miles from the site. The mill owner delivered all of the lumber for the entire cabin in one load, to within 2½ miles of our lot, over a rough logging road, for slightly more than half the cost of the lumber at a retail yard. And he renewed my faith in mankind. Without even asking for our home address, he accepted a check in full payment.

Up to this point, we had been playing at cabin building; the planning, the shopping for materials, the purchase of new tools, all these had been fun. The task ahead of us proved formidable. Every stick of the lumber had to be relayed in a utility trailer and on a car-top rack on the jeep. Eleanor joined in lumber handling, our son Bill and his wife Lee spent their "vacation" with us, loading and unloading, as the jeep made twenty-two round trips over the two miles of boggy wheel tracks, most of the way in four-wheel drive!

But there was more. The lumber then had to be carried by hand about 500 feet over our swamp trail to the cabin site. We all toted lumber at first, enough so that I could then remain at

The author's son, Bill, carried much of the lumber used in building Camp Hell'n'gawn. Photo by Eleanor Riviere.

Before erecting the walls, make sure the sills are level—the author doing just this! Photo by Eleanor Riviere.

"The two Bills" lift the first side-wall frame into position. Photo by Eleanor Riviere.

the site and start assembling the main stringer and the sills. While I worked at this, the girls lugged the lighter boards; Bill, the heavy stock. Among the three of them, they delivered virtually every board, plank, and nail that went into 20′×24′ Camp Hell'n'-gawn! When they were finished, they took up tools. We had the cabin fully enclosed in ten days, only the inside finish and exterior painting remaining.

We wanted a fireplace, of course. What's a cabin without one? However, toting bricks that distance was out of the question and there were no fieldstones to be found. So we installed a Franklin fireplace, a cast-iron stove whose front can be opened for a fireplace effect, or closed for greater heat. Getting the Franklin stove across the swamp ended *my* chores for that day (and slowed them for several days afterwards). It weighed 285 pounds. Bill, who

Bricks for a chimney were too heavy to carry to such a remote site, so a galvanized metal "roof jack" was used. Photo by Eleanor Riviere.

lugged the other end of it (we made forty-two rest stops, I think!), took the canoe and caught himself a mess of trout.

Later we toted such furnishings as we could not build or make ourselves—bed frames, box springs, and mattresses. Our dining table, the kitchen unit (it drains into a sump hole), shelves, a desk, woodbox, we built from scrap lumber.

Friends have offered us the use of an electric-light plant and a gasoline water pump. We want neither. Our light comes from Aladdin lamps which burn kerosene and give a soft light, easy to

Eleanor was not happy on the staging, but she painted the entire camp singlehanded. Author's photo.

read by. We carry drinking water in a five-gallon plastic jug from a nearby spring; wash water we dip from the river. Life at Camp Hell'n'gawn is simple, uncomplicated, in keeping with the big woods that surround us.

Our only communication with the outside world is a small transistor radio. It gets only three stations, but that's enough. Since we spend much of the summer at the cabin, our one worry is possible illness or injury, or the jeep failing to start. We've considered installing a battery-operated Citizen's Band radio to communicate with friends who have a cabin some four miles from us, across the river. I suppose we should concede to good judgment and put in a wireless rig.

Outhouses are an uncouth topic in certain segments of society, but in the backwoods they're a vital institution. We could have

thrown together a ramshackle facility and let it go at that. Instead, we built a solid structure over a five-foot hole, well ventilated by screened openings and even including a full-size screen door in addition to the plank door. It's about as rodent- and insect-proof as a woodland building can be. And we located it more than 100 feet from the riverbank. We figure that a slightly longer walk at night eliminates the chance of polluting the water.

"Closing up camp" in the fall is a sad occasion. It tugs at one's innards. The long summer is over and it's time to go home. But what about the cabin?

It has to be made snug. First we hoist the canoes into specially prepared racks under the rafters. Bedding is hung on platforms suspended by wire from the crossties, so that mice won't claim squatter's rights for the winter. Our books are stored in a large metal suitcase. All food is removed—every crumb, every spot of grease is washed from the kitchen area. We want no enticements for bear to break in. The entire building is scoured for stray matches and these are sealed in a friction-top can. Mice, gnawing at matches, can light them! The Indian pump is drained, the roof jack is covered and wired tight so that snow can't blow in, nor birds fly into our chimney. The woodbox is filled, and topped with an armload of dry kindling; it may be a cold, rainy day when we arrive in the spring.

The roof must be propped, too. Four cedar poles are wedged upward against the crossties, their bottom ends supported by heavy planks laid on the floor, close to the main stringer. We don't want to worry all winter about the snowload on the roof. Finally—and this is a heart-wringing move—the padlock is snapped on the door, and the windows are sealed with plywood.

Then we scout the campyard, not that we expect to find anything. Preparations for closing have been underway for two days. But this last-minute scanning delays our departure a moment or two. The woodpile is covered, the outhouse door is locked, there's no litter overlooked. We start down the path. At the last moment each of us turns for a final, longing glance. We are silent all the way to the jeep.

Appendix

INFORMATION SOURCES

U. S. GOVERNMENT AGENCIES

Bureau of Indian Affairs
Department of the Interior
Washington, D.C. 20242

Bureau of Land Management
Department of the Interior
Washington, D.C. 20240

Regional offices

P. O. Box 1828
Cheyenne, Wyoming 82001

P. O. Box 11505
Salt Lake City, Utah 84111

P. O. Box 2965
Portland, Oregon 97208

P. O. Box 1449
Santa Fe, New Mexico 87501

Federal Building, Room 3008
300 Booth Street
Reno, Nevada 89502

Federal Building
316 North 26th Street
Billings, Montana 59101

Federal Building, Room 334
550 West Fort Street
Boise, Idaho 83702

Federal Building, Room 14023
1961 Stout Street
Denver, Colorado 80202

Federal Building, Room 4017
650 Capitol Mall
Sacramento, California 95814

Federal Building, Room 3022
Phoenix, Arizona 85025

555 Cordova Street
Anchorage, Alaska 99501

FISH AND WILDLIFE SERVICE

Bureau of Sport Fisheries and
  Wildlife
Department of the Interior
Washington, D.C. 20240

Regional offices

Post Office and Court House
  Building
Boston, Massachusetts 02109

809 Peachtree—Seventh Building
Atlanta, Georgia 30323

1006 West Lake Street
Minneapolis, Minnesota 55408

P. O. Box 1306
Albuquerque, New Mexico
  87103

P. O. Box 3737
Portland, Oregon 97208

FOREST SERVICE

Department of Agriculture
Washington, D.C. 20205

Regional Offices

Region I
Federal Building
Missoula, Montana 59801

Region II
Federal Center
Building 85
Denver, Colorado 80225

Region III
517 Gold Avenue S.W.
Albuquerque, New Mexico
  87101

Region IV
324 25th Street
Ogden, Utah 84401

Region V
630 Sansome Street
San Francisco, California 94111

Region VI
P. O. Box 3623
Portland, Oregon 97208

Region VII
50 Seventh Street N.E.
Atlanta, Georgia 30323

Region IX
633 West Wisconsin Avenue
Milwaukee, Wisconsin 53203

Region X
P. O. Box 1628
Juneau, Alaska 99801

GEOLOGICAL SURVEY

Department of the Interior
  GSA Building
  Washington, D.C. 20242

Geological Survey
Washington Distribution Center
1200 South Eads Street
Arlington, Virginia 22202

National Park Service
Department of the Interior
Washington, D.C. 20240

National Park Service
Western Regional Office
450 Golden Gate Avenue
San Francisco, California 94102

Superintendent of Documents
Government Printing Office
Washington, D.C. 20402

NATIONAL AND REGIONAL GROUPS

American Alpine Club
113 East 90th Street
New York, N.Y. 10028

American Forest Institute
1835 K Street N.W.
Washington, D.C. 20006

American Forestry Association
919 17th Street N.W.
Washington, D.C. 20006

American River Touring Association
1016 Jackson Street
Oakland, California 94607

Appalachian Mountain Club
5 Joy Street
Boston, Massachusetts 02108

Appalachian Trail Conference
1718 N Street N.W.
Washington, D.C. 20036

Colorado Mountain Club
1400 Josephine
Denver, Colorado

Green Mountain Club
108 Merchants Row
Rutland, Vermont

Izaak Walton League
1326 Waukegan Road
Glenview, Illinois 60025

Mazamas
909 N.W. 19th Avenue
Portland, Oregon 97209

The Mountaineers
Box 122
Seattle, Washington 98111

National Parks Association
1701 18th Street N.W.
Washington, D.C. 20009

National Wildlife Federation
1412 16th Street N.W.
Washington, D.C. 20036

Nature Conservancy
1522 K Street N.W.
Washington, D.C. 20005

New England Trail Conference
P. O. Box 153
Ashfield, Massachusetts 01330

Ozark Wilderness Waterways
Club
P. O. Box 8165
Kansas City, Missouri 64112

Pacific Crest Trail System Conference
Hotel Green
Pasadena, California

Sierra Club
1050 Mills Tower
San Francisco, California 94104

Trailfinders, Inc.
P. O. Box 716
Banning, California 92220

Wilderness Society
729 15th Street N.W.
Washington, D.C. 20005

CANADA

Canadian Government Travel
Bureau
150 Kent Street
Ottawa, Ontario

Map Distribution Office
Department of Mines and Technical Surveys
Ottawa, Ontario

Newfoundland Tourist Development Office
St. John's, Newfoundland

Prince Edward Island Travel
Bureau
Charlottetown, Prince Edward
Island

Nova Scotia Travel Bureau
Department of Trade and Industry
Halifax, Nova Scotia

New Brunswick Travel Bureau
Fredericton, New Brunswick

Department of Tourism, Fish
and Game
Quebec, Province of Quebec

Department of Tourism and Information
Toronto, Ontario

Tourist Development Branch
Department of Industry and
Commerce
Winnipeg, Manitoba

Tourist Development Branch
Department of Industry and
Commerce
Regina, Saskatchewan

Alberta Government Travel Bureau
Edmonton, Alberta

British Columbia Government
Travel Bureau
Victoria, British Columbia

Department of Travel and Publicity
Whitehorse, Yukon Territory

Northwest Territories Tourist Office
400 Laurier Avenue West
Ottawa, Ontario

Bruce Trail Association
33 Hardale Crescent
Hamilton, Ontario

Hudson's Bay Company
Northern Stores Department
Hudson's Bay House
Winnipeg, Manitoba

For information regarding the various states, write to the "Conservation Department," or to the "Department of Forests and Parks" at the appropriate state capital.